# HITLER'S MIRACLE WEAPONS VOLUME 3

*From the 'America Rocket' to an Orbital Station*

*Germany's Efforts to Develop Intercontinental Weapons and the First Space Programme*

**Friedrich Georg**

Translated by Geoffrey Brooks



Helion & Company Ltd

Helion & Company Limited
Unit 8 Amherst Business Centre
Budbrooke Road
Warwick
CV34 5WE
England
Tel. 01926 499619
Email: info@helion.co.uk
Website: www.helion.co.uk
X (formerly Twitter): @Helionbooks
Facebook: @HelionBooks
Visit our blog at https://helionbooks.wordpress.com/

Published by Helion & Company 2009. This new edition 2025
Originally published as *Hitlers Siegeswaffen Band 2: Star Wars 1947 – Die Geheimgeschichte der Raketen und Flugkörper des Dritten Reiches. Teilband B: Von der Amerikarakete zur Orbitalstation – Deutschlands Streben nach Interkontinentalwaffen und das erste Weltraumprogramm* by AMUNVerlag in co-operation with Heinrich-Jung-Verlagsgesellschaft mbH, Germany, 2004


Designed and typeset by Farr out Publications, Wokingham, Berkshire
Cover designed by Paul Hewitt, Battlefield Design (www.battlefield-design.co.uk)



ISBN 978-1-804519-38-7

British Library Cataloguing-in-Publication Data.
A catalogue record for this book is available from the British Library.

# *Contents*

# *Acknowledgements*

It is my pleasant duty to end this book by thanking those persons without whom it could never have been completed. In the front rank stand those contributors who provided me open-handedly with advice, facts and material: Antonio Chover, Pat Flannery, Phil Henshall, Kurt Grasser (IBA), Kristian Knaack, Jak P. Mallmann-Showell, Renaud Mangallon, Thomas Mehner, David Monaghan, Richard Lewis Mendes, Herminio Pimentel, Henry Stevens (GRP), Nigel Wylde and Daniel Velasco. My gratitude extends to all those who prefer to remain anonymous but made available important documentation for publication. Finally I would like to draw attention to the work of Igor Shestakov (illustrations) and my secretary Uschi whose assistance was indispensable. Above all I thank my family for the patience and support they gave me throughout this work.

INTRODUCTION

# *Hitler's Revolution in Space*

How would the world look today if Hitler had achieved his objective of raining down rockets on New York? The effects of such an offensive would have been far wider-reaching than the terrorist attack on the World Trade Centre of 11 September 2001 because Germany's 'America Rocket' would have been armed with an atomic weapon.[1]

The assertion appear fantastic. Was there ever such a danger? The automatic response today is that the 'America Rocket' was merely a drawing board project, and to the war's end Peenemünde was only ever involved in the development of the V-2 rocket. Yet despite the numerous published accounts about Peenemünde, one suspects that there might be a secret about which virtually nothing has become known: something overlooked? Newly released secret documents, and declarations by former Peenemünde workers who consider that the "oath of silence" which binds them has gone on long enough, support the years-long research by the author to gain some insight into what Hitler was ultimately aiming to achieve with his fabulously costly rocket and guided missile programme. To this may be added rumours of atomic warheads, intercontinental rockets and piloted aircraft designed to navigate beyond the Earth's atmosphere, either well-advanced or in the prototype stage, which went down with the Third Reich in its *Götterdämmerung*.

Immediately after the capitulation the victors moved in for the spoils, sharing between themselves Germany's trove of high technology. What they said at the time gives more substance to the theory of a secret. The true dimension of German technological advance in the Hitler age will probably never be known: contemporaries of the period die, material is destroyed and much of the documentation will remain in deep archives perhaps for ever.

Nevertheless, the author believes that sufficient evidence exists to enable him to find certain answers, and at least point the way forward for future research. The book takes a fresh look at Hitler's costly armaments programme in large rocketry. It may be that some people will not be able to accept the ideas put forward, since to do so will require them to cast into doubt the numerous legends and comforting assurances held up as sacred over the last six decades.

Friedrich Georg

1 Allied contemporary wartime sources were positive that an apocalyptic explosive was close to being operational in early 1945. This was not nuclear, however, but "built on the atomic principle". (Translator's footnote, hereafter referenced as Tr.)

PART I

# *Was the V-2 the End of the German Rocket Programme?*

*The Germans were preparing rocket surprises for England in particular and the whole world in general which would have, it is believed, changed the course of the war if the Invasion had been postponed for so short a time as half a year.*
Col D Leander Putt, Chief, Air Technical Services 10/1944-8/1945, Deputy Commanding-General USAAF Intelligence, Air Technical services Command[1]

## The mystery of the missing design files

Modern historians writing on the subject of German rocketry in the Second World War assert that sixty years after the war's end, everything worth knowing about the Peenemünde Development and Test Centre has been known for years. In this regard it is therefore all the more curious that the major part of the confiscated Peenemünde project and design documents seized at Dörnten by the Americans remain classified.

At the end of the war, 15 tonnes of paperwork was spirited away. By September 1988, only 462 kilos(!) had been returned to the Federal Republic of Germany.[1] Even if one accepts that these documents exist in triplicate, one wonders why the tonnes remaining have not been declassified after so long. The obvious answer can only be that the papers contain developments and secret designs which even today must on no account ever be disclosed.

## Peenemünde's "hibernation" after 1942

The published history of Peenmünde and its work had a notable parallel in the "official" explanations regarding the German atomic weapons project. What the historians insist is that the leading scientists of both projects slipped into a lasting inactivity from about the mid-point of the war, and so much so that one gains the impression of as little being accomplished in the last three years or so of the war as had previously been possible in a few months. At Peenemünde, the important elements of the A-4 (V-2 rocket) development phase were concluded in 1939. On 10 October 1942, Wernher von Braun ordered development work on the A-4 discontinued, for from this point on a start was to be made with mass production. Peenemünde was thus deprived of its primary technological task. The halt enabled Wernher von Braun to report to the *Kommission für Fernschiessen* (Commission for Long-Range Bombardment) on 9 September 1943 that to all intents and purposes the development of the A-4 rocket was terminated.

Shortly beforehand, on 26 August 1943, *SS-Gruppenführer und General der Waffen-SS* Dr (Ing) Hans Kammler had ordered the creation of the new underground factory at Nordhausen for the mass production of the V-2 rocket. Obviously a series of technical difficulties had to be resolved before the rocket would be operational (e.g. the problems of breaking up in the air and the fitting of the ready warhead in the rocket nose), but these were mere structural issues requiring the attentions of individual departments or engineers.

The logical question which ensues therefore enquires what the ever-expanding technological plant at Peenemünde did between September 1943 and May 1945 in its development works, test laboratories and wind tunnels once the A-4 project was finished. Apparently, the highly skilled scientific workforce of this gigantic modern organisation occupied the time from 1943 onwards exclusively in rectifying faults for the Nordhausen V-2 assembly plant, contributing a few minor improvements; built the *Wasserfall* flak rocket and the *Pfeilgeschoss* (the concrete-piercing arrow-shaped grenade) and worked on some drawing board projects.

All the more strange therefore that Peenemünde in hibernation should retain the highest category of priority for its endeavours (3 October 1943) and continue thus after the SS took it over in July 1944. A brief glance at the Peenemünde story reveals to the impartial observer that something is amiss with its history, and in view of the pall of silence which shrouds German rocket research during the last 18 months of the war, one is forced to conclude that rather than doing not very much, the scientists at Peenemünde must have been devoting their energies on a massive scale to the realization of other schemes with far greater dimensions than the V-2.

## Dr Wernher von Braun's hypersonic wind tunnel

In December 1943 at the Walchensee Hydro-Power Station (WVA), Kochel, work began to build a gigantic hypersonic wind tunnel. Of enormous diameter for the time, it was designed to provide speeds of Mach 7 (seven times the speed of sound), with a later increase to Mach 10. The energy required to drive such a structure was not available at Peenemünde and it was for this reason that WVA in Upper Bavaria had been selected. The plant's production capacity of 120 Megawatts was to be greatly increased for the desired windspeeds. Management of the new test facility was the responsibility of the Peenmünde Aerodynamic Institute, which was relocated in Upper Bavaria for the purpose.In the meantime scientist Siegfried Erdmann had achieved a windspeed of Mach 9 using an inexpensive invention at the old Peenemünde wind tunnel. Following the transfer of the Peenemünde Institute, the large wind tunnel at Kochel was in routine operation from the summer of 1944. A question never previously asked in this connection is why this enormously expensive project was necessary when at this stage the V-2 and *Wasserfall* rockets had reached the limits of their developments. Was this not an unnecessary waste of valuable personnel and materials which the Third Reich war economy could barely afford unless something crucial to the war effort was to be attempted?

On account of its great capacity for energy production, Kochel had been selected some years before, and to requisition it in 1944 can only have been linked to plans for long-range rockets such as the A9/10 and other such EMW projects which required these very high test speeds. The Peenemünde wind tunnel had been perfectly adequate for the Mach 4.4 needed to test the V-2 and all foreseeable jet aircraft designs. One wonders at the "coincidence" in May 1945 when Kochel wind tunnel scientists Hermann and Kurzweg knew so much about space satellites, space stations and the conditions for interplanetary flight that they were able to brief the Americans on the subject at their interrogations. An American expert present was the Chinese-American Dr Hsue-Shen Tsien, after the war a leading US aero-dynamicist and later founder of the Chinese rocketry and space programmes. [2, 3]

Supersonic section of the wind tunnel at Kochel. (Source: Simon)

The hypersonic wind tunnel is evidence that after completing the A-4 project, Peenemünde did not go into hibernation as is asserted by historians today. Former Peenemünde scientist and member of the US 'Paperclip' team Peter W Wegener, to whom the author is indebted for many of the details regarding Third Reich wind tunnel research, was at pains to point out however that he was "only" directly involved personally in the development of rocket control surfaces and rudders and therefore knew nothing about the "hot projects". Was Wegener being careful not to give away too much in order to preserve the Peenemünde myth? Without any evident necessity to do so, he was quick to state, as is their custom, and in much the same word order as other former Peenemünde staff, that during all the time he spent at Peenemünde and Kochel, nobody mentioned even once anything about an atomic bomb. Had he been coached at some time or was he plagued by conscience?

## The V-3

During the war all informed offices on both sides were aware that other V-Weapons were to follow the V-2. The term 'V-3' has long been current coinage in the literature. Nowadays it is generally considered to have been Dr Coender's multi-chamber high-pressure gun *Fleissiges Lieschen* (Busy Lizzie). The question is here, was this next or was it a mere front for other weapons developments? The designation 'V-3' is also applied to a multitude of weapons systems under development or suspected to be in the pipeline during the end phase of the Second World War. This goes as much for the A9/10 'America Rocket' as for the German atom bomb, the piloted V-1, the U-boat V-1, the Henschel Hs 117H air-to-air missile and the German isotope weapon.

In his table conference with Rumanian Minister-President Antonescu in August 1944, Hitler promised the operational introduction of the third and fourth V-Weapons without specifying what they were.[4] The radius of annihilation which he attributed to one of them suggests the plan to use a WMD.[1] One cannot be definite as to which weapons, if any, were officially designated 'V-3' and 'V-4' before the war's end. More intriguing still is what the 'V-Weapons of the second generation' were to be and what stage had been reached in their development. The path leads back to Peenemünde, the forge for the first generation of V-Weapons.

PART II

# *'Thor's Hammer' – Hitler's Intercontinental Rocket Projects*

*When I left the rocket airport at Berlin, I knew that these young enthusiasts were preparing those weapons in order to aim them across the Atlantic to hit us in America some day.*
Journalist Lady Drummond-Hay, after her visit to Berlin-Reinickendorf, Autumn 1930

## Section 1: The EMW A-10 'America Rocket' – only a myth?

### A. Development & technology

#### The A9/10 Intercontinental Rocket – Peenemünde's Great Secret?

Did anything similar to the Peenemünde 'hibernation' – the expansion of the centre and the setting up of hyper-modern research units – occur elsewhere in Germany? For decades it has been accepted as fact that the intention to build a two-stage intercontinental America-Rocket was one of the future projects at Peenemünde which had not left the drawing board by the end of the war. Nobody denies the existence of the project but the experts are unanimous that all preparatory work for the rocket was stopped in 1941 or 1942. Here is an interesting parallel with the German nuclear project which was also reportedly wound down in 1942.

It was not until the summer of 1944, so the official account reports, that more thought was given to the A9/10, although nothing came of it. In support of this line, Wernher von Braun's official biographer Ordway emphasizes that in the postwar period, though a few rumours did circulate regarding the existence of an America-Rocket, these were purely nonsensical.[5] Yet how is the advertisement placed by the US firm Convair, which appears on the following pages, to be explained? On closer examination it can be seen that it was prepared before the Japanese defeat. The two pages are so unequivocal that no further commentary is necessary. It is stated therein that the European war ended only a very short time before the Germans were due to strike with their miracle weapons.

Critics will naturally react by stressing the purpose of the advertisement as being merely to convince the US public of the need in the immediate postwar period for a strong domestic armaments industry and an advanced military technology to frighten off any potential enemy. The American armaments industry may of course have needed a new enemy to secure their future profits but it is improbable that they would invent fabulous achievements by the Nazis, so recently defeated, for this would amount to a glorification of Nazi military science, a policy which the US Government would have been most anxious to disavow unless they believed it was true.

Especially amusing in the advertisement is the Wehrmacht officer addressing the American readership with a clenched fist while he explains what would have happened had the war lasted only a few more months – massive attacks with ICBM America-Rockets and intercontinental jet bombers striking at targets on American soil from Europe.

Convair states that after capturing a German underground factory, US technicians discovered blueprints for a weapon called 'the V-Bomb' intended to fit into a rocket with a planned range of 3000 miles. An unnamed German rocket engineer had even informed the Americans that the destruction of New York and other East Coast cities was hoped for in November 1945.

Convair also states that in a salt mine converted to armaments production the American search parties found an assembly plant for long-range bombers. These aircraft were to have dropped high explosive payloads on East Coast cities of the United States before returning to Europe. Göring promised that these bombers had been test flown and would be operational within three months. Probably in order not to betray too much the sketch artist drew the exotic looking but harmless Dornier Do 335-A-11 fighter-trainer, but the Horten Ho XVIII and (Heinkel?) America-Bombers were probably what was meant.

The advertisement discloses the existence of other German weapons systems of which nothing was known publicly then (nor now). The release of such publicity by the Convair firm can probably be best explained as resulting from the euphoria of victory on the termination of hostilities in Europe, and also from that fact that the American military had promised domestic industry at least some share in captured German technologies, thus guaranteeing large scale savings in time and development costs.

Whether or not one accepts the Convair advertisement as evidence, there can be no denying the long list of witnesses which follows and who confirmed the America Rocket and/or the German intercontinental jet bomber: high and very senior Allied officers, officials and organizations (e.g. Chief of the US General Staff Marshall, US General Arnold, Major Bromley, the 21st Army group HQ, US Navy Secretary Forrestal,

Colonel Donald Leander Putt and FEA Leo Crowley; former Mittelbau-Dora prisoners Benjamin Jacobs and Alex Baum, German Armaments Minister Albert Speer in his book *Infiltration*; SS secret weapons specialist Otto Skorzeny and Bormann's stenographer at Hitler's table, Henry Picker, plus astronaut Gordon Cooper).

# ...by the Skin of our Teeth

SEVERAL TIMES **during the European phase of this war, victory was almost within Germany's grasp** . . . on land, on the sea, or in the air.

Above all, knowing the vital importance of air supremacy, the Nazis tried time and again to wrest it back from the Allies.

**And they almost succeeded.**

## Time ran out

Especially in the last months of the war, our margin of safety was slimmer than most of us suspected.

Just how slim it was is known best to certain American military experts **who have since inspected some of Germany's underground research laboratories and war plants.**

Here they saw secret weapons in various stages of development . . . **weapons which might conceivably have turned the trick for the Nazis if they could have used them boldly in a last desperate gamble.**

**Some of these things can now be revealed. Others cannot—yet.**

In one plant, the U. S. Army officers found partially assembled jet fighter planes of radical new design. There were planes potentially better than anything the Allies had in combat at that time.

If time hadn't run out on the Germans, **quantities of these jet planes might have changed the balance of air power in their favor.**

In a V rocket plant, burrowed 800 feet deep in limestone rock, our technicians found blueprints for a fearful V bomb with an estimated range of 3000 miles.

"We planned to destroy New York and other American cities starting in November," said a German rocket engineer.

## Target: U. S. A.

In a converted salt mine, our ordnance officers examined nearly completed jet-propelled heavy bombers . . . **bombers claimed by the Germans to be capable of crashing high explosives into the industrial cities of the eastern United States and flying back again across the Atlantic.**

Goering himself said the planes had been successfully test-flown and would have been in operation if Germany could have held out 3 months longer.

But those catastrophes, and others, never quite came to pass on the German timetable of war. **We managed, right to**

2

In the 27 August 1945 edition of *Life* magazine, US armaments firm Convair placed a two-page advertisement mentioning Hitler's advanced rocketry. The publicity argues that in the future the United States must do everything possible to avoid a recurrence of the threatening situation which existed shortly before the end of the Second World War. "The race we must win."

the end, to maintain the air supremacy we had achieved . . . sometimes *just by the skin of our teeth.*

# How about Japan?

What's happening in those war plants the Japs have built underground? We wish we knew! We, for one, are not selling *this* enemy short—**not on scientific ingenuity born of desperation.**

Every now and then—close on the heels of dispatches telling how our heroic flyers are knocking Japs out of the sky at a ratio of 10 to 1—comes a disturbing rumor of an entirely new Jap weapon.

**This is why it would be one of the costliest mistakes this country could possibly make, if we were to permit ourselves to be lulled into a sense of security because of our *present-day* air superiority.**

# The race we must win

We are woefully stupid if we assume that Japan isn't working desperately to develop new planes and air-borne weapons that will whittle down our air superiority.

Air supremacy, alone, of course, will not win this war or guarantee a lasting peace in the years to come.

**But if we maintain air supremacy in the Pacific, Japan *can't* win.**

And as long as we maintain our air superiority after victory, **no aggressor nation is apt to be foolhardy enough to dream of attacking us.**

**That is why *constant* and *continuing* research in the field of aeronautics is a MUST for America—today and always!**

But experimental research is only the first step in winning **the race that will insure America from attack in the future . . .**

The best planes periodically resulting from this research must be put in production in sufficient quantities to develop *manufacturing techniques and tools* and to keep the nucleus of a manufacturing organization which can be quickly expanded if ever needed.

**We must also have enough planes for our Armed Services to train the Flight and Ground Crews in their use. *One or two experimental planes are not enough* to keep our Air Force and manufacturing organizations ready for any emergency.**

Only when the design and production "bugs" always present in a new plane are revealed and eliminated by use—can our ever-improving aircraft be considered *proven* **military weapons.**

**LET'S KEEP AMERICA STRONG IN THE AIR!**

# CONSOLIDATED VULTEE AIRCRAFT CORPORATION

San Diego, Calif. · Vultee Field, Calif. · Fairfield, Calif. · Tucson, Ariz. · Fort Worth, Texas · New Orleans, La. · Nashville, Tenn. · Louisville, Ky. · Wayne, Mich. · Dearborn, Mich. · Allentown, Pa. · Elizabeth City, N. C. · Miami, Fla.

*Member, Aircraft War Production Council*

CONVAIR MODEL 37 *Pan American Clipper* · LIBERATOR *4-engine bomber* · LIBERATOR EXPRESS *transport* · CORONADO *patrol bomber* · PRIVATEER *search plane* · CATALINA *patrol bomber* · VALIANT *basic trainer* · SENTINEL *"Flying Jeep"*

## EMW Design 1936 – forerunner of the A-10

As early as 1936, the Wehrmacht rocket research group had begun planning the successor to the A-4.[6] The new rocket would have a 100-tonne liquid oxygen/alcohol engine and be able to carry a 4-tonne warhead over 500 kilometres. The warhead of the 1936 design rocket could carry approximately the same payload as the later Hiroshima atom bomb. The Peenemünde engine test beds, testing insatallations and halls were arranged in such a way that they could house the 1936 design. One can see from Peenemünde photos that the assembly and testing halls were of too grandiose a size to have been built only for the relatively small A-4, and it is probable that the dimensions of the installations were intentionally scaled up to build and test rockets of A9/10 proportions without the need for major conversions and modifications to buildings.

Hitler's order of 6 September 1939 reducing the priority of all Peenemünde projects, and the famous stop order for all subsequent weapons developments from 1940, forced Peenemünde to concentrate on the A-4. The work on the more efficient 1936 design was then rather thrust into the background. That was not the last word, however, for in 1941 the project was revived as a booster rocket for the A-9. Its planned thrust was increased to 180 tonnes which would have brought the United States into range from European bases.

## The A-10 comes into being

In 1939 General Walter Dornberger announced that Peenemünde was ready to build long-range rockets able to hit New York from Europe.[7] On 29 July 1940 engineer Graupe submitted the first design for a transatlantic two-stage rocket. In that early era of the technology, it was thought that such a range could only be achieved by a two-stage rocket with wings. As an alternative, high-energy fuels were considered, the production technology for which remained to be mastered at that time.

In 1941 the rocket pioneer Hermann Oberth became in the planning for the America-Rocket. His biographer Hans Hartl wrote: "One day Braun gave him a task to arouse his enthusiasm: he was to design the transatlantic rocket to reach New York." Von Braun was reported to have said: "We now have to press ahead with projects for long-range rockets. Please develop in theory a two or three stage America Rocket. How would it look? How much fuel would it need? What would it cost approximately?" By October 1941 Hermann Oberth had concluded his study[8], and on 18 December 1941 engine expert Dr Thiel proposed an aggregate of six 30-tonne engines for the A-10 primary stage. A second possibility was to fit the 1936 design with a super-engine of 180 tonnes thrust. In the meantime the United States had entered the war, giving the Germans a compelling reason to build the transatlantic rocket; but sadly for them, so we are told, General Dornberger allegedly suspended the project in October 1942 just when its forerunner, the A-4, was being signed off.[9]

## The apparent stopping of the America Rocket

The officials histories and the historians who cobble them together insist that the America Rocket was never more than a paper project. In 1941, or at the latest 1942, all preliminary studies had been completed and, as Michael Neufeld declares in his book *The Rocket and the Reich*, on page 283: " ... The A9/10 was never more than a drawing board concept and was shelved in 1942".[10]

How did this idea come about? Dornberger remarked in *V-2: Der Schuss ins Weltall* that until October 1942 a major part of the work at Peenemünde was dedicated to a study of the A9/10 concept. Countless flight trajectories of the America Rocket had been worked on by the outstanding ballistics scientist Dr Steuding, and all factors such as the curvature of the Earth and its spin had been carefully considered. Rocket guidance studies and equipment design had begun. Dornberger had then been forced to suspend all future work in favour of an urgent conclusion to the A-4 programme, and the project group alone was permitted to occupy its time with the America Rocket thereafter.

All this shows that up to this point a great deal of effort had been put into the America Rocket and a major section of the Peenemünde staff had been engaged on the project. Dornberger's book is silent as to what happened after the stop date. Certainly there would have been a temporary reduction in priorities unfavourable to the A9/10 until the A-4 project was concluded. The latter finished in the summer of 1943 and it is difficult to believe that the design teams at Peenemünde then took it easy for the rest of the war, since it can be inferred from a Kammler document that at the end of October 1943 the America-Rocket project had not been abandoned by any means.[11, 12, 17]

On 20 October 1942 Kammler had sent Dr Brandt, Himmler's scientific adviser, a telegram for the information of the *Reichsführer-SS* stating that an agreement had been made the same day "to construct an underground test base to develop the America Rocket with tenfold thrust." For this purpose caverns in the mountains close to Traunstein were to be enlarged. Kammler reported: "Once a bombproof testing site was found and accepted by telegram from *Generalmajor* Dornberger, the Waffen-SS received from OKH a contract to carry out the construction project. Pursuant to the meeting with *Generaloberst* Fromm on 20 October, we will complete the preliminary project by 10 November 1943. *Generaloberst* Fromm and *Reichsminister* Speer then agreed to take the necessary steps to proceed with construction work. The preparations have already begun today. I request that the *Reichsführer* be informed accordingly."

In their well-known meeting of 7 July 1943, Hitler ordered *Generalmajor* Dornberger and Wernher von Braun to produce the larger design together with the A-4. By the beginning of 1945 he wanted to have the A9/10 in series production, operational and able to hit the target. He was hoping that with this intercontinental rocket he would bombard the Americans into a frame of mind where they would be 'ready for peace', especially so after the rockets were each to be armed with several small 'uranium-bombs'.[13] From this it will be understood why to the present day the true history of the America Rocket is denied and papered over, for how could one admit the existence of a weapon which was designed to hit the United States with 'uranium-bombs', when everybody was supposed to know that Germany neither wanted to, nor was able to build atom bombs after 1942? To deny one weapon meant that the existence of the other also had to be concealed.[14, 15, 16, 17]

## The Factories for a 'Paper Project'

Although the A9/10 apparently remained a 'paper project' to the very end, there are budgets, plans to order materials and the assembling of a workforce to produce it. Even how the scientific team was distributed for the project is known.[18] The report on talks held between 2 and 5 May 1942 concerning the planned series production of the A-4 by the Zeppelin firm at Friedrichshafen promises: "With regard to the future completion of the A-10, it would be possible to enlarge the exit to be 8 metres broad and 9 metres high without great difficulty."

On 17 August 1943 the A9/10 programme withstood the heavy air raid on Peenemünde. Rocket pioneer Arthur Rudolph stated that at the last moment, Wernher von Braun managed to save the important plans for the A-4 and A9/10 from the strongbox in his burning house.[19] Even the 20,000 square-metre assembly hall with its nave 30 metres high and 60 metres wide 'built to take the A-10'(Rudolph) remained undamaged.[20]

A former inmate of Buchenwald described[21] with what energy Wernher von Braun devoted himself to the realization of the America Rocket project. Alex Baum had been imprisoned as a German-speaking member of the French Resistance, and after a period at the concentration camp was put to forced labour on rocket production at Peenemünde and later Nordhausen. Baum stated that he knew von Braun through his work at both centres but the SS had ordered him to have no direct contact with the scientist or other German engineers.

Alex Baum, a native of Alsace-Lorraine, understood German well and had heard von Braun speak of the 'ultimate weapon' which would destroy the United States and all others. Baum had the impression that von Braun was desperate to have the thing up and running, and he would have known precisely how matters were proceeding. From this it may be inferred that at Peenemünde, at least until the relocation of production to Nordhausen, work on the America Rocket was forging ahead.

Besides Peenemünde and Nordhausen, there was at least one other location where Wernher von Braun's 'ultimate weapon' was to be realized. By order of the OKH dated 20 October 1943, the SS was given the task of constructing a gigantic underground complex codenamed *Zement*. The date when the first plans were drawn up cannot be determined.[22, 23] *Zement* was near Gmunden/Traunstein in Austria. It was situated in a narrow valley through which the Traun flowed and was served by a single road. This enormous and most modern rocket development plant was to have been installed in a bombproof three-storey system of galleries with the Seeberg at the southern end of Ebensee. The test stands for the A9/10 engine unit and the bombproof rocket silos were sited on steep slopes in the surrounding mountains.

The gigantic construction of at least three-storey galleries (Modules A and B) would have made possible a planned transfer of the entire Peenemünde site to Gmunden. Two galleries of *Zement* A were clearly built in such a manner that A9/10 tests and trials could be carried out there. The gallery height of around 27 metres in some places indicates that the two-stage rocket could have stood vertically.

In the end the transfer from Peenemünde to Ebensee fell through. On 6 July 1944 Armaments Minister Speer suggested to Hitler that the *Zement* gallery systems should be used initially for the production of panzer engines and ball bearings because of delays in the conversion work. In galleries II to IV on Module B, from the beginning of 1945 ball bearings were turned out under the management of Daimler-Steyr-Puch AG, while in Module A from the autumn of 1944 eight distillation plants were installed which continued in operation long after the war was over.

Even the construction of additional test, injection and pump installations did not run to plan at Gmunden. A number of completed sections were awarded the general cover-name *Salamander*. This included the three planned rocket-testing launch ramps. Their target area was the lower Tatra mountains, around Arlberg and the Ortler Massif.

Was the Ebensee A9/10 facility abandoned because the entire installation, including the first production run, did not appear possible until the spring of 1946? As an interim solution, it was proposed at a conference in August 1944 to make available a gallery at Mittelwerk for the test assembly and leave everything else at Peenemünde, although better protected against air attack. Another suggestion was to expand the *Rebstock* project, an underground factory near Mittelwerk, housing the most important offices and laboratories in underground rooms.

Since it can be demonstrated that in December 1944 more designs for project *Salamander Z* at Ebensee were drawn up (see Volume 2), one asks why the plans for building the America Rocket in the Modules A and B were abandoned, particularly in view of the fact that a number of Peenemünde scientists were already at Gmunden (although what they were working on is mostly unknown). Was there a third gallery system or factory development on the surface additional to Modules A and B? A number of pointers support this hypothesis.

A solution to the mystery of the missing America Rocket production factory suggests itself when one looks at the events of the summer of 1944. The rapid collapse of the German fronts in the East and West, and the loss of the Channel coast and its launch facilities signalled to the leaders of the Third Reich that not much time remained. Simultaneous with the breakthrough in the development of weapons of mass destruction in the summer of 1944 the need for a

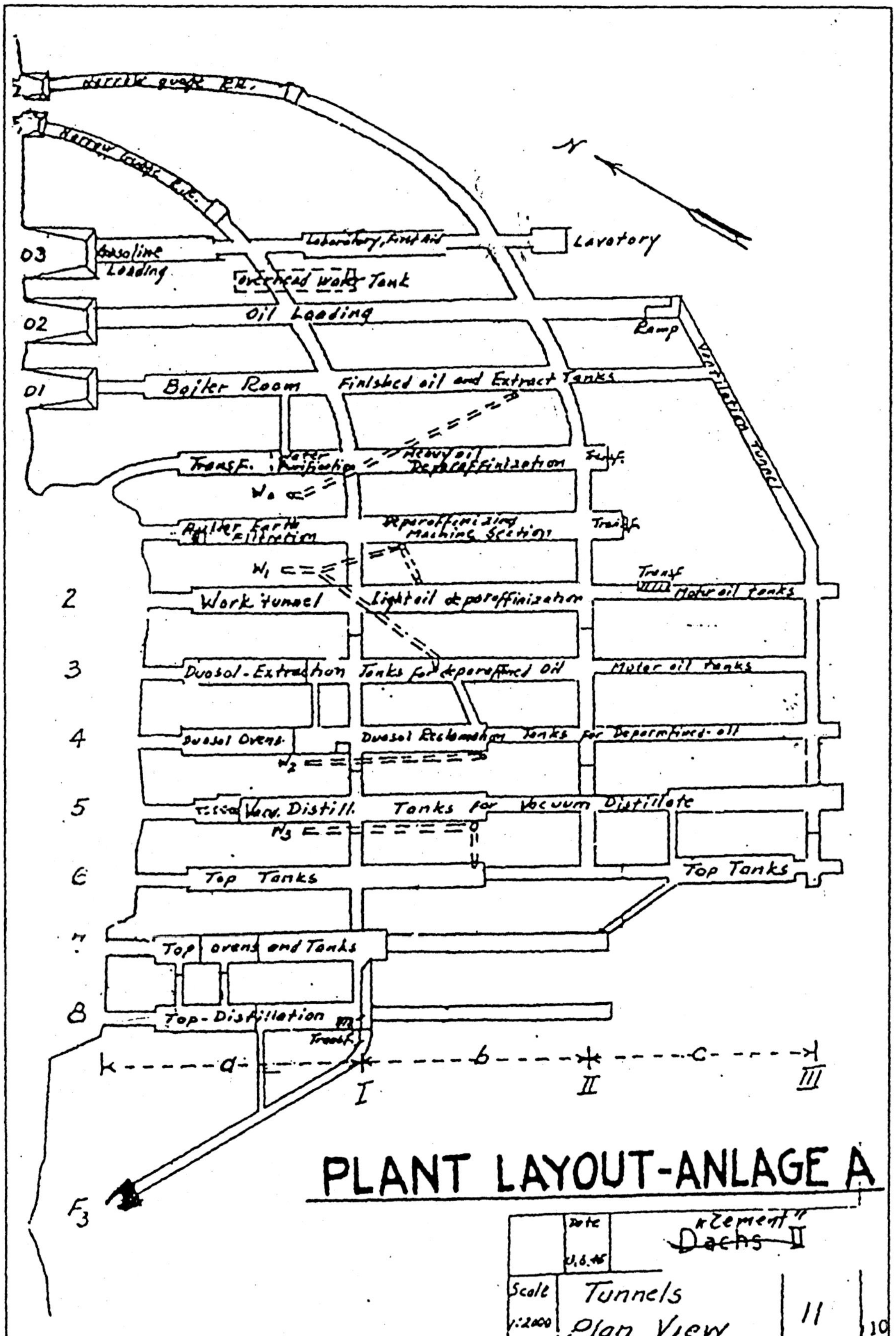


A-10 factory at Ebensee. Module A (‚Anlage A'), according to BIOS/CIOS was a distillery plant for rocket fuel, Module B (facing page) a production and accommodation area.

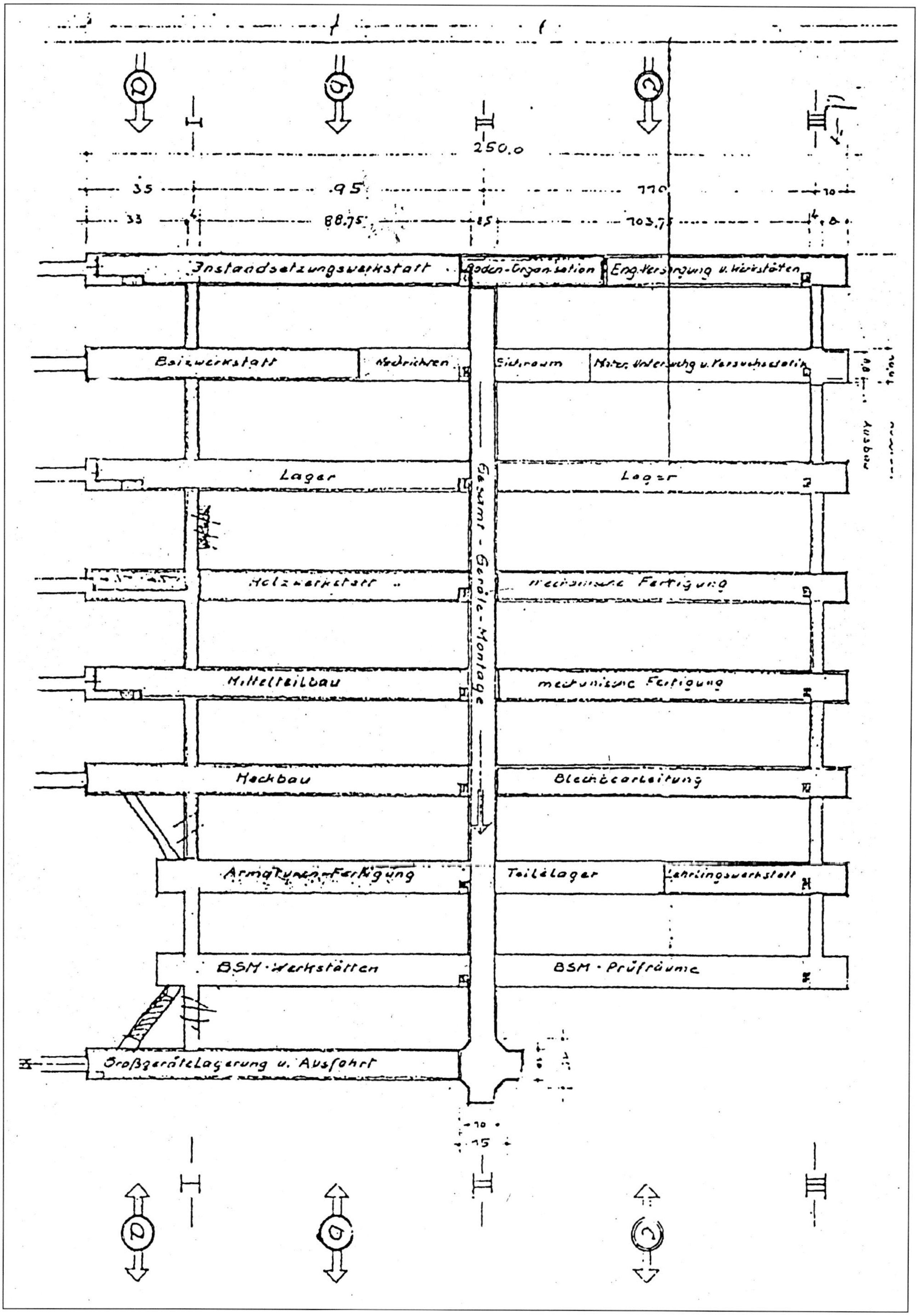
250.0
Lager
Lager
Holzwerkstatt
Mittelteilbau
Heckbau
Teilelager
BSM · Werkstätten
BSM · Prüfräume
Gesamt - Geräte - Montage
Großgerätelagerung u. Ausfahrt

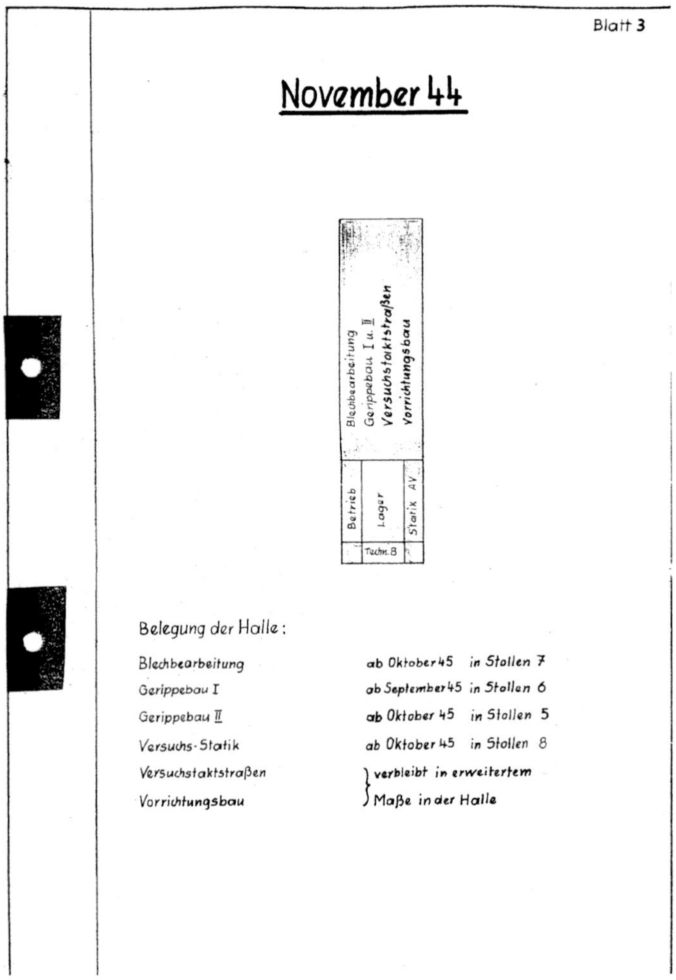
Blatt 3

November 44



Belegung der Halle:

| | |
|---|---|
| Blechbearbeitung | ab Oktober 45 in Stollen 7 |
| Gerippebau I | ab September 45 in Stollen 6 |
| Gerippebau II | ab Oktober 45 in Stollen 5 |
| Versuchs-Statik | ab Oktober 45 in Stollen 8 |
| Versuchstaktstraßen | verbleibt in erweitertem |
| Vorrichtungsbau | Maße in der Halle |

"Warehousing" at Pinsdorf/Gmunden – it is rumoured that twenty A-9 intercontinental rockets were built here. (Source: IBA/Kurt Grasser)

long-range and invulnerable carrier system became pressing. What could have been more reasonable than to abandon the costly expansion at *Zement*, and go instead for the quick 'interim solution'? This would allow major parts of the A9/10 to be manufactured by decentralized suppliers, and the final assembly plant could then be relatively small, with only a limited requirement for individual parts. This policy is suggested not only by rumours and claims, but exists also in published Allied documents, according to which the V-3 was being built at Überlingen, Leitmeritz, Nordhausen and near Ohrdruf troop training ground in Thuringia.[24, 25, 26] In this regard the entry of 4 April 1945 in the G-2 diary of US 4th Armoured Division is interesting: '... In a completely camouflaged factory, all access being sealed off, about two miles north of Gossel, V-1s were being built on 3 April and V-3s experimented on.'

Another source states that in the winter of 1944 one of Himmler's main projects was to bombard New York and Moscow with the A9/10 from launch platforms near Ohrdruf. This project was handled by *SS-Hauptsturmführer* Albert Schorz using a labour force from Buchenwald. Thomas Mehner, a co-author of *Das Geheimnis der deutschen Atombombe*, provided this author with a previously unpulished report by a person claiming to have been a member of Kammler's circle, in which it was alleged that the subterranean galleries and halls at Gossel were actually Kammler's own rocket research installation, assisted in some manner by the Skoda Works. At this locality A-9 mock-ups were experimented with. There was also a production line for the A9/10 ready for operations from 3 April 1945 so that production could have started at once. The witness did not state if individual test – or pre-series prototypes were completed.

Dr Kammler also wanted to produce intercontinental weapons above ground. It would appear that he was opposed to concentrating the A9/10 project in one place, thereby exposing it to the risk of total loss in a single Allied air raid. In 1944 at Pinsdorf near Gmunden a giant grain silo built five years previously was requisitioned, and in October 1944 a start was made there on rocket fuselages and rib framework. Pinsdorf had a road leading to a test site. In the south part of the hall was an upright V-2 (or A-9) and staging. How far the manufacture of the reported twenty A-9 intercontinental rockets had proceeded at Gmunden is unknown.In addition it is certain that the series production of parts for the *Taifun* flak rocket had commenced. In 1961/62 *Taifun* parts were found buried close to the hall. Digs for the A9/10 in the 1990s produced nothing. According to unconfirmed reports, at the beginning of 1990 an Austrian search team at Nordhausen found graphite jet vanes 'too large' for the A-4. Unfortunately it has not proved possible to inspect this alleged evidence.

The former important Peenemünde member to whom I refer frequently stated postwar that the America Rocket was assembled basically at two locations. Unfortunately he was not forthcoming as to where.[27]

Test stands for the A-4, A-9 and A-10 were to have been set up in a small, narrow mountain valley near Ebensee/Traunsee in the Salzkammergut region under the codename Salamander. The planned area is clearly visible from the available plans. Test stand for giant rocket motors of 200-t thrust (top); Test stands for A-4, A-9 and Wasserfall rockets (bottom). (Source: Deutsches Museum, Munich.)

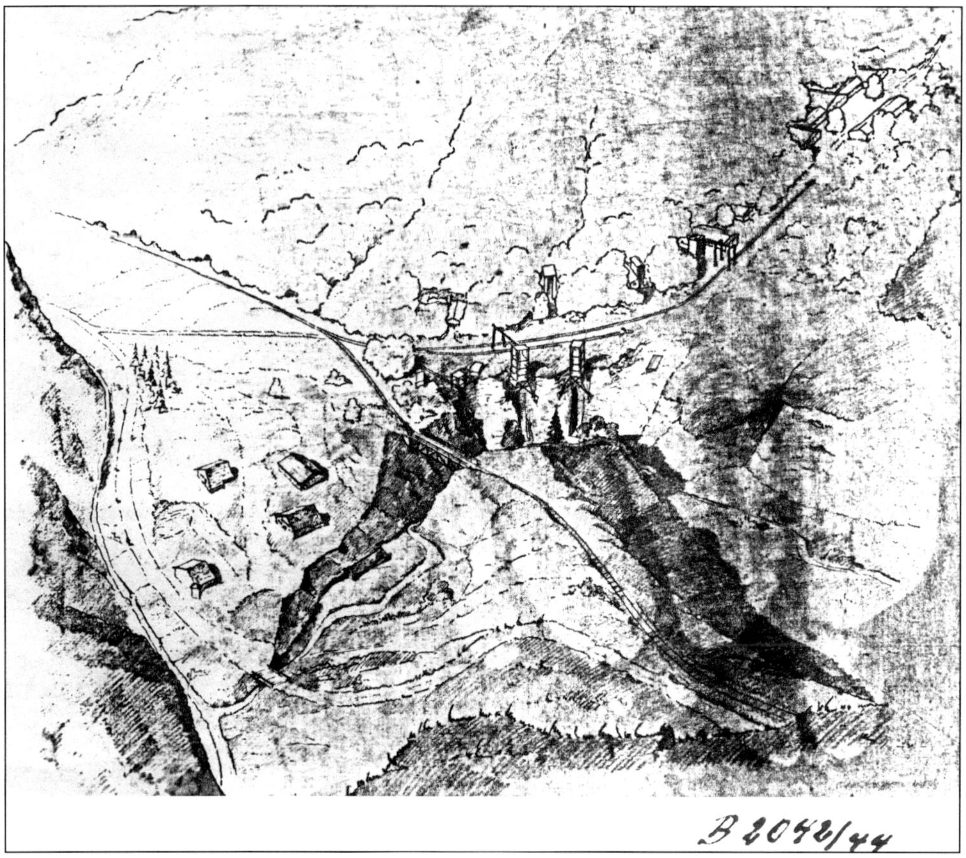

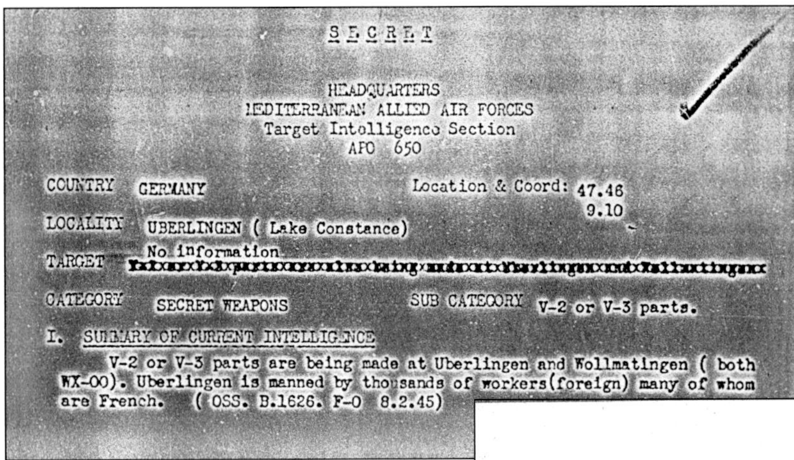

S E C R E T

HEADQUARTERS
MEDITERRANEAN ALLIED AIR FORCES
Target Intelligence Section
APO 650

COUNTRY GERMANY Location & Coord: 47.46 9.10

LOCALITY UBERLINGEN ( Lake Constance)

TARGET No information

CATEGORY SECRET WEAPONS SUB CATEGORY V-2 or V-3 parts.

I. SUMMARY OF CURRENT INTELLIGENCE

V-2 or V-3 parts are being made at Uberlingen and Wollmatingen ( both WX-00). Uberlingen is manned by thousands of workers(foreign) many of whom are French. ( OSS. B.1626. F-0 8.2.45)

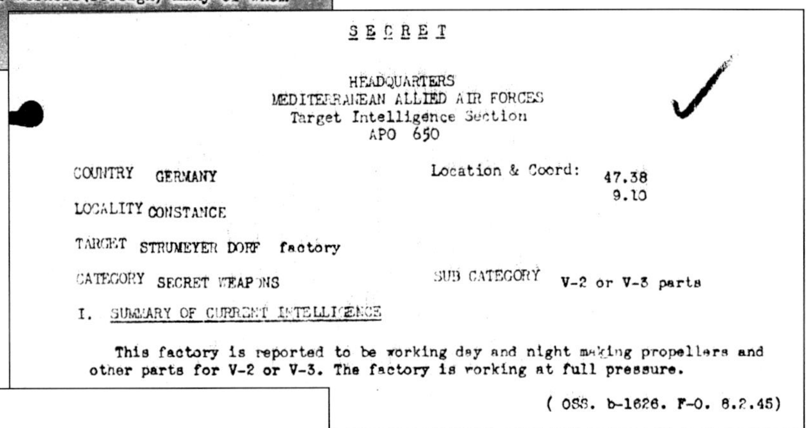

S E C R E T

HEADQUARTERS
MEDITERRANEAN ALLIED AIR FORCES
Target Intelligence Section
APO 650

COUNTRY GERMANY Location & Coord: 47.38 9.10

LOCALITY CONSTANCE

TARGET STRUMEYER DORF factory

CATEGORY SECRET WEAPONS SUB CATEGORY V-2 or V-3 parts

I. SUMMARY OF CURRENT INTELLIGENCE

This factory is reported to be working day and night making propellers and other parts for V-2 or V-3. The factory is working at full pressure.

( OSS. b-1626. F-0. 8.2.45)

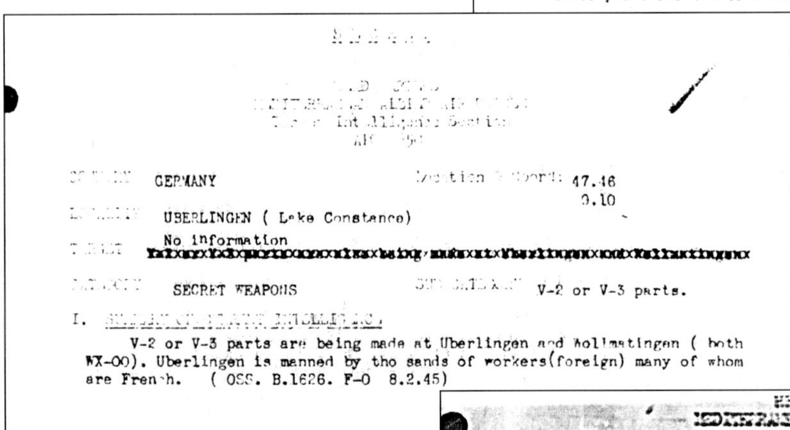

GERMANY Location & Coord: 47.46 9.10

UBERLINGEN ( Lake Constance)

No information

SECRET WEAPONS V-2 or V-3 parts.

I.

V-2 or V-3 parts are being made at Uberlingen and Wollmatingen ( both WX-00). Uberlingen is manned by thousands of workers(foreign) many of whom are French. ( OSS. B.1626. F-0 8.2.45)

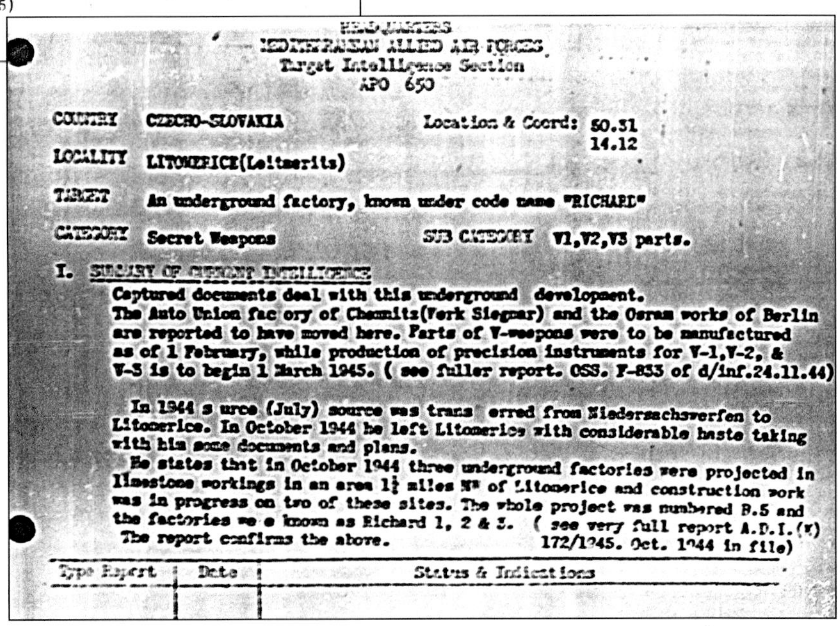

HEADQUARTERS
MEDITERRANEAN ALLIED AIR FORCES
Target Intelligence Section
APO 650

COUNTRY CZECHO-SLOVAKIA Location & Coord: 50.31 14.12

LOCALITY LITOMERICE(Leitmeritz)

TARGET An underground factory, known under code name "RICHARD"

CATEGORY Secret Weapons SUB CATEGORY V1,V2,V3 parts.

I. SUMMARY OF CURRENT INTELLIGENCE

Captured documents deal with this underground development.
The Auto Union fac ory of Chemnitz(Werk Siegmar) and the Osram works of Berlin are reported to have moved here. Parts of V-weapons were to be manufactured as of 1 February, while production of precision instruments for V-1,V-2, & V-3 is to begin 1 March 1945. ( see fuller report. OSS. F-833 of d/inf.24.11.44)

In 1944 s urce (July) source was trans erred from Niedersachswerfen to Litomerice. In October 1944 he left Litomerice with considerable haste taking with him some documents and plans.
He states that in October 1944 three underground factories were projected in limestone workings in an area 1½ miles N* of Litomerice and construction work was in progress on two of these sites. The whole project was numbered B.5 and the factories we e known as Richard 1, 2 & 3. ( see very full report A.D.I.(K) 172/1945. Oct. 1944 in file)
The report confirms the above.

| Type Report | Date | Status & Indications |
|---|---|---|

The Allies were aware that the Germans were busily engaged on some enormous military project. V-3 production sites at Überlingen, Wollmatingen, "Strumeyer Dorf"(?) and Leitmeritz (Czech Republic) are mentioned in recently declassified US microfilmed material.

## Virgin territory – the revolutionary technology of the America Rocket

The A9/10 was a two-stage rocket which may be seen as the forerunner of today's ICBM rocket, since its range with a winged second stage as calculated in 1940/41 was at least 4,000 kilometres. Later sources nearer 1945 speak of 6,000 kilometres. That would have been sufficient to hit various cities on the eastern seaboard of the United States with a one-tonne warhead. The finished A9/10 combination was designed to be approximately 26 metres high with a maximum diameter of 4.75 metres. The total all-up weight was about 100 tonnes.

The first-stage burn would take the combination to 24 kilometres and so greatly increase the range. The A-10 stage was a giant missile body 20 metres in length and 4.15 metres in diameter, of 87 tonnes overall weight, 62 tonnes of which was fuel. The burn lasted 50 seconds and provided a speed of 4,320 km/hr. At the end of the first stage, the A-9 second stage, jacketed in the neck of the A-10, was ignited by special batteries. The A-10 would then glide to Earth below a 2,500 square metre parachute canopy and ditch into the sea for recovery and re-use. After the war the same principle was used by the German Dr Theo Knacks when designing parachutes for the NASA moon capsule, and one might ponder the origins of his expertise.

The A-9 second stage, a variant of the A-4, was planned to accelerate to 11,000 kms/hr under its own power, rising to a ceiling of 350 kms. The project details show that the winged A-9 rocket would glide for 4,000 to 6,000 kilometres to the target with warhead. Without wings the range would be less, but the rocket could have reached the Urals from Germany.

Various propulsion units were considered for the A-10. The simplest would have had six EMW A-4 motors, each of 27.4 tonnes thrust led through a simple Venturi jet. With the help of an automatic thrust regulator and gyro-course system this would have provided differential guidance at lower speeds. Fuel was A – and M-. The Peenemünders hoped to develop a variant of the A-4 motor developing 30.5 tonnes of thrust using 'Visol' and 'Salbei'. The motor, also to be fitted to the A-9, would have been 20% more efficient than the standard A-4 motor. A single motor of 200 tonnes thrust using the same combustible was hoped for later. This would have required graphite jet rudders for steering purposes during the burn.

A further increase of power for a third A-10 engine version was to be expected from the J-4 fired afterburner. Thus was born a new three-phase motor (Visol, Salbei and J-4 diesel) with an enlarged combustion chamber. The improved output was to be achieved by injecting vaporized diesel oil into the chamber to increase temperature and so increase thrust.[28] The J-4 gas-oil method could be used for the 180-tonne '6-star' as well as the 200-tonne single furnace motor. After the loss of the French bases for the A-10, every kilometre of range gained was of vital importance once the intercontinental firing points were withdrawn eastwards into the Reich.

Together with the development of supersonic wings for the second stage, and setting up engine factories, stage separation was the third major problem confronting A9/10 designers. A difficulty was the manufacture of a suitable battery type for the separation and to ignite the second stage burn under the extreme conditions prevailing in the stratosphere. These batteries would not have to be too large, or they would increase take-off weight. The existence of

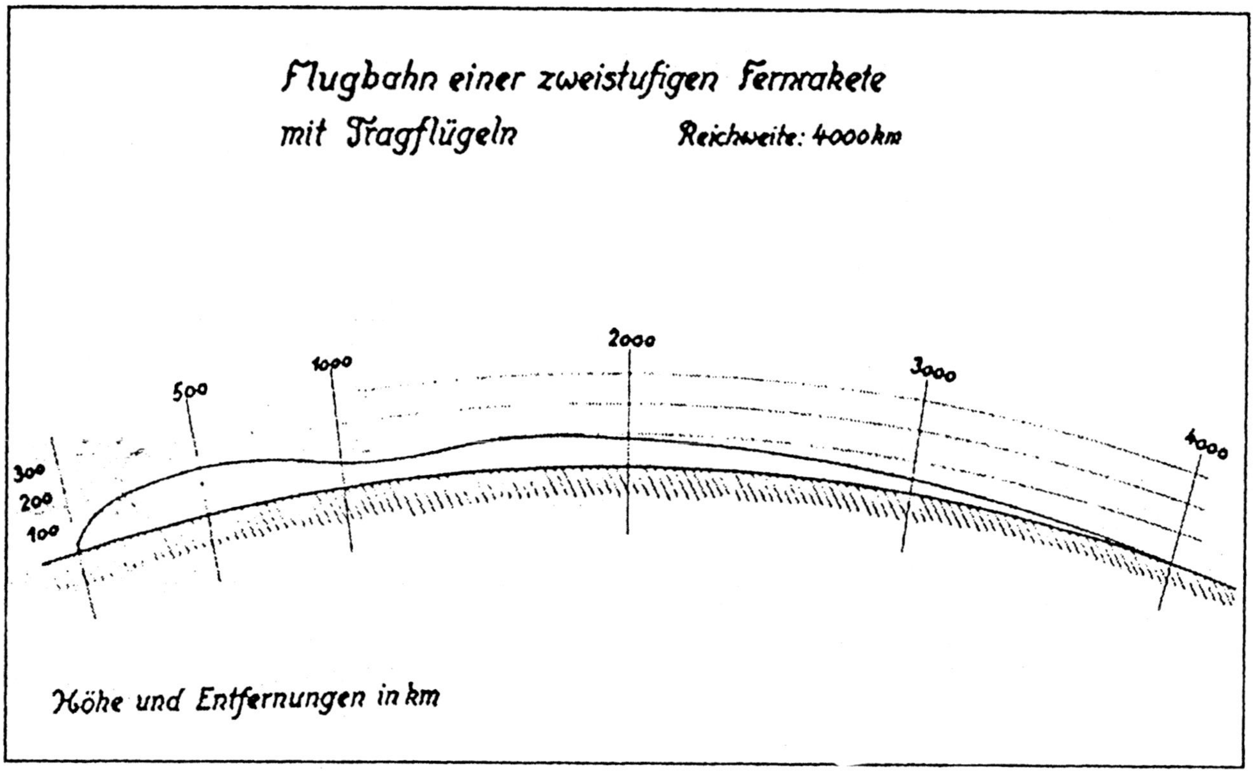


From the original 1940/41 idea for an A-10 with 4000 kms range ...

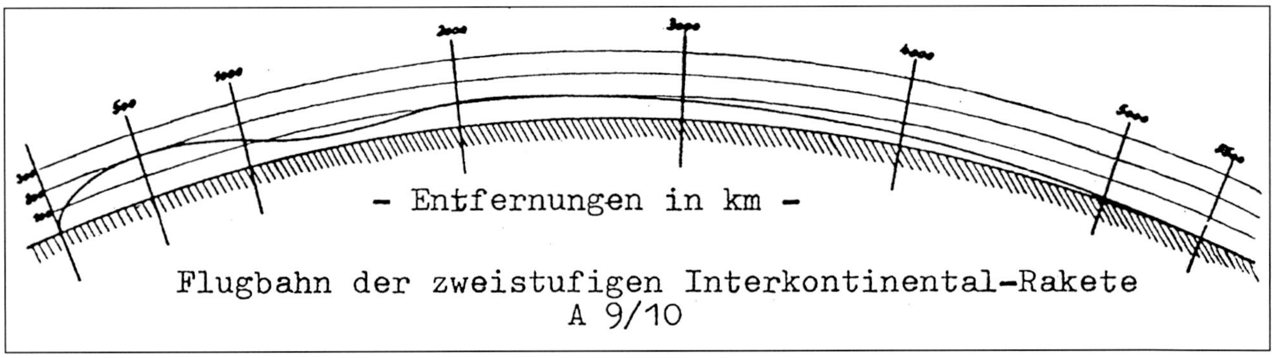


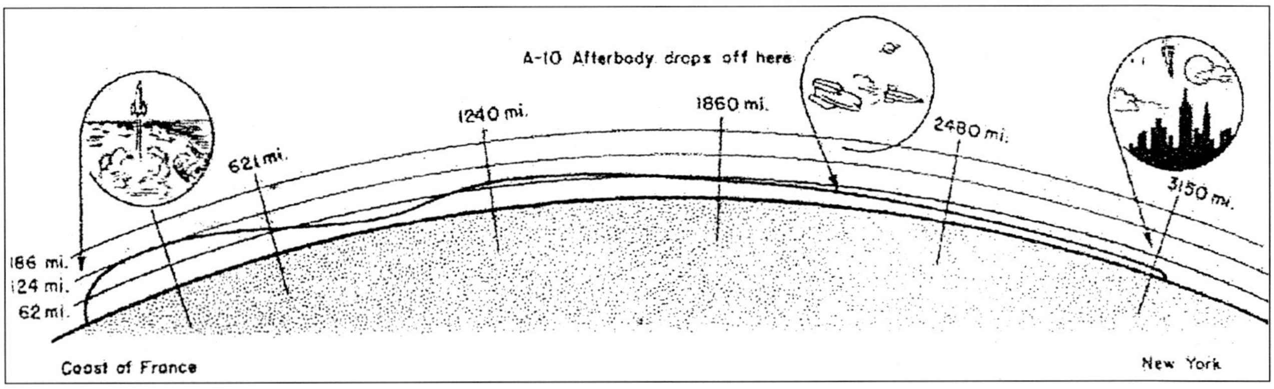


… to 5500 kms in 1944. By the war's end the Germans were expecting a further increase in range to 6000 kms. US postwar drawings limit the two latter estimates for unknown reasons to 3150 miles (5068 kms).

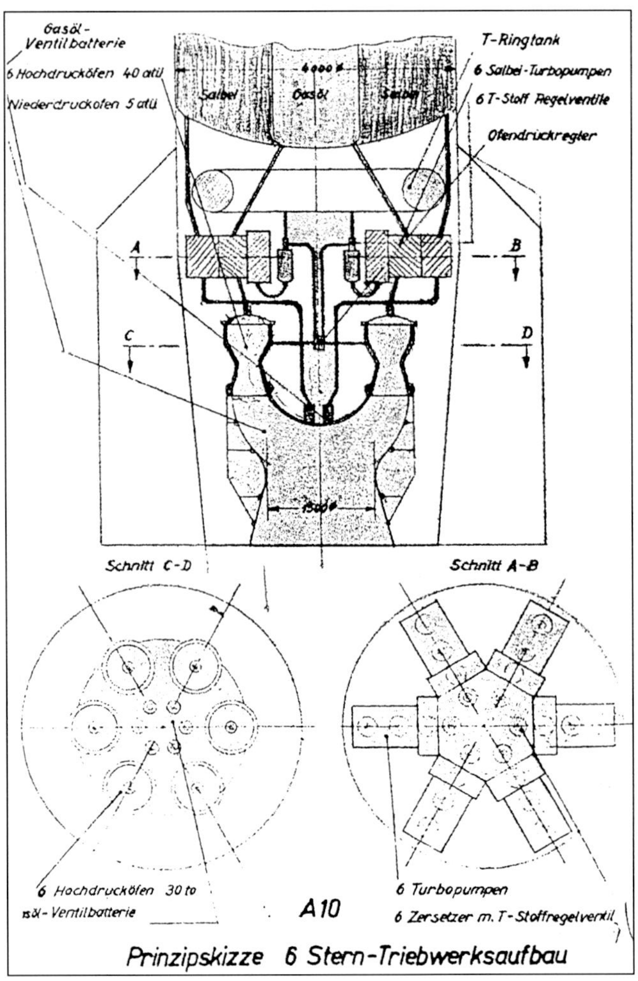


Peenemünde design for the 180-t-thrust A-10 motor mit J-4-, 'Gasoil' afterburner. Note the six 30-t high pressure chambers (40 atm) Visol/Salbei and the 5-atü low pressure chamber and Gasoil (Diesel) steam nozzle.

such batteries would constitute certain proof that work was undertaken on the successor to the A-4 project. No less an authority than Professor W.O. Schumann was engaged on the creation of a 'super battery' until at least 1943 at the Technical University, Munich. This was an independent project of the *Deutsche Forschungsgemeinschaft*, the forerunner of the *Reichsforschungsrat* (Reich Research Council). An experienced battery manufacturer was then awarded the contract to turn out the 'super battery'.[29, 30] Despite many years of experimentation, the successful separation of rocket stages, even in the 21st Century, has remained a problem, and many hopeful starts have come to nothing for this reason. How much greater must the problem have been in the war years in Germany?

### Versions of the America Rocket

Between 1940 and 1945 at least seven versions of the America Rocket were designed. Besides piloted and unmanned types, the fluidity of the frontlines from August 1944 resulted in greater ranges being required. The following versions were planned:

1) A-10/A-4A, six motors, (early): long range ballistic missile, warhead 980 kg (HE/nerve gas), fuel: alcohol/liquid oxygen.
2) A-10/A-9, six motors, (early), LRBM, winged second stage, warhead as above, fuel: Visol-Salbei, later J-4 diesel added.
3) A-10/A-9p six motors (early), piloted A-9, wings of various sizes, warhead as above or atomic type, fuel: as (2) above.
4) A-10/A-4A, single motor, intermediate version, A-10 Visol-Salbei fuel, second stage elongated A-4 with fine nose, warhead WMD.
5) A-10/A-9p, single motor, intermediate version, as (2) above but with Visol-Salbei 180 to 200 tonne motor: warhead WMD.
6) A10/A-9p (Lorin). piloted A-9 with additional Sänger ramjet to increase range to US inland cities. Design only, warhead unknown.
7) A-10/A-9 single motor (final version). The stern section of the A-10 fuselage was plumper than with previous versions as the motor had an afterburner added. Through a nozzle fitted in the ejection jet of the motor diesel fuel was expelled as steam to raise temperature

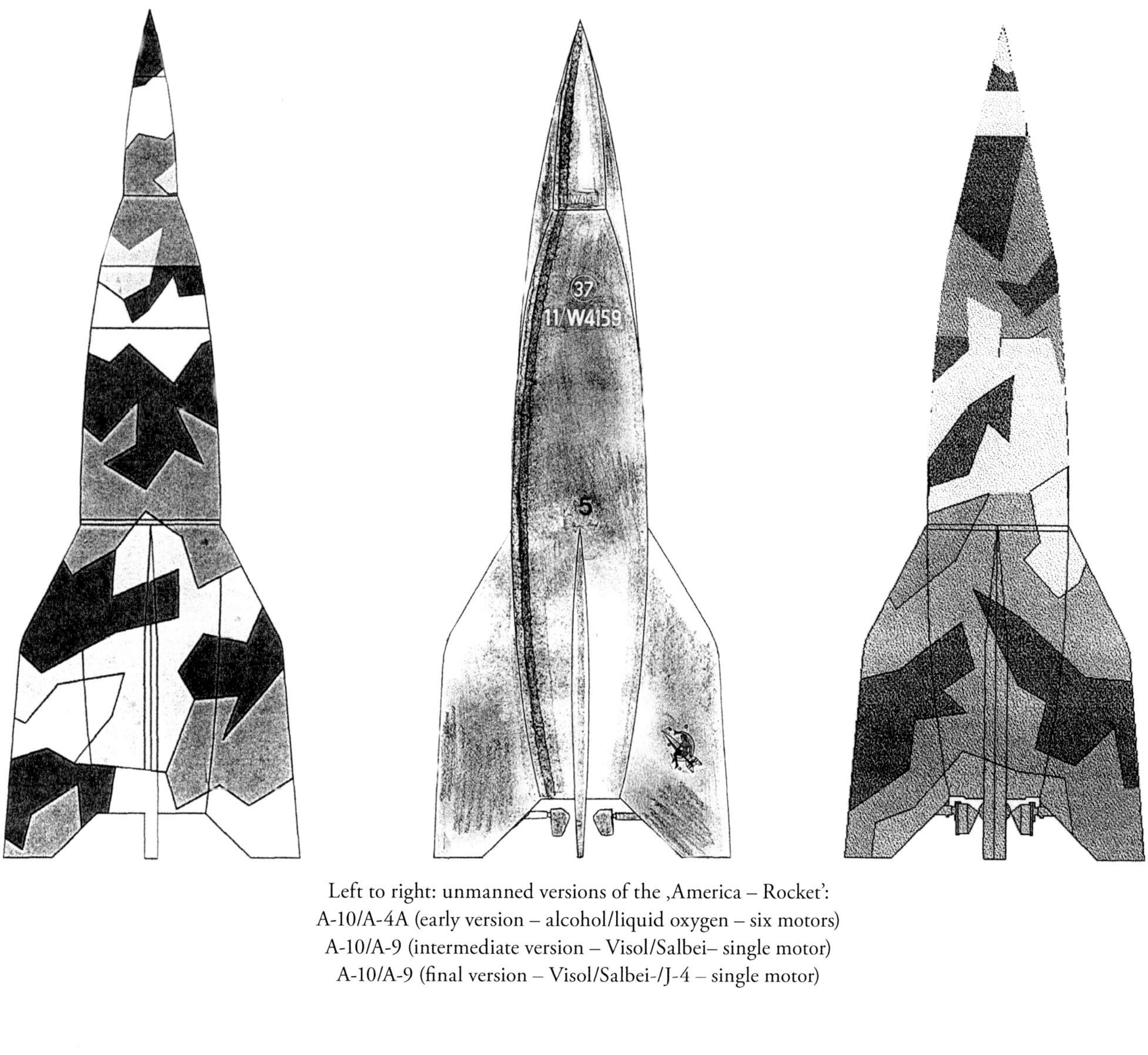


Left to right: unmanned versions of the ‚America – Rocket':
A-10/A-4A (early version – alcohol/liquid oxygen – six motors)
A-10/A-9 (intermediate version – Visol/Salbei– single motor)
A-10/A-9 (final version – Visol/Salbei-/J-4 – single motor)

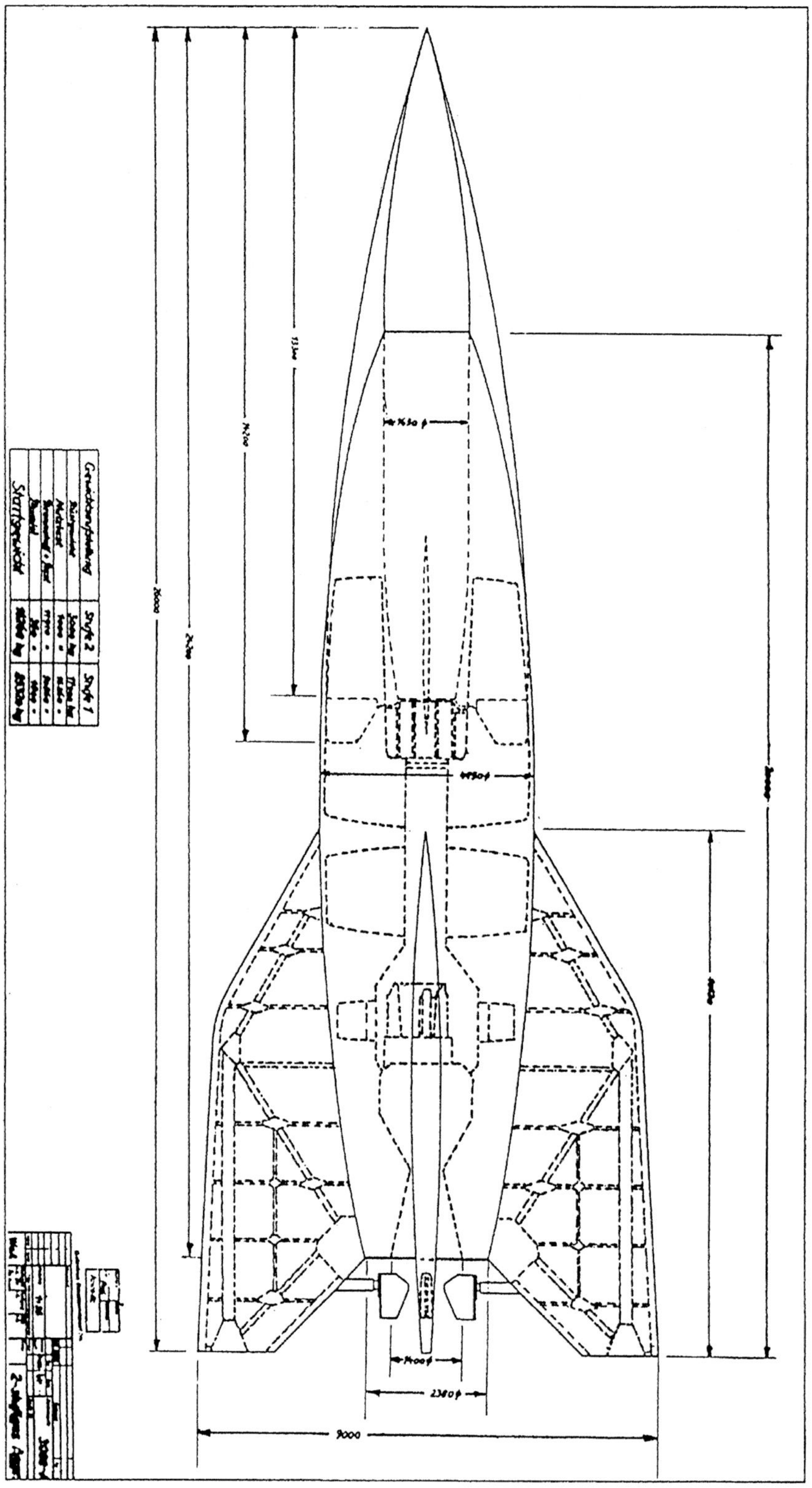

Profile of the A-9/A-10 (Source: Deutsches Museum, Munich)

and increase thrust. A J-4 afterburner was planned for later versions. Outwardly this variant differed from all the foregoing A-10s. The A-9 did not protrude so noticeably and was jacketed within four fuselage sections of the A-10, these opening like a flower at the separation stage to release the A-9. The four sections also acted as air brakes to guarantee that the A-10 parachute system deployed correctly. Warhead: WMD.

It is not known what version was finally selected although probably both piloted and unmanned rockets were tested before the war's end.

### A-10 Project *Ross und Reiter* (Horse and Rider)

The author has found traces of another advanced A-10 variant. On 11 July 1957, the Americans terminated their intercontinental XSM-64 *Navaho* missile programme once the basic concept had proved itself as the way forward. The programme laid the foundations for all later US intercontinental rocket management with regard to engines, cryogenic fuel technology, guidance systems, equipment and so forth.[31, 32, 33] Although considered a waste of money at the time, the Navaho possessed an aerodynamic shape so nearly perfect that even today the experts do not believe it can really be much improved.

The *Navaho* was an intercontinental rocket on the so-called Horse-and-Rider or 'piggy-back' principle. It differed from the classic two-stage rocket by having the first stage carry the smaller second stage rocket alongside. Upon reaching its final acceleration stage, the second rocket detached and headed independently to the target. Nowadays the *Navaho* (versions G-26 and G-28) is almost forgotten but nevertheless belongs amongst the most important cruise missiles of history. Not only did it contribute to raising the standard of technology of intercontinental missiles and rockets, but it appears to trace its ancestry back to Hitler's America Rocket.

A number of recent reference works consider the *Navaho* G-38 to have been the culmination and final development of the A9/10. It had been broadly assumed in the past that the 'piggy-back' concept was associated only with the V-2, but USAF General Arnold spoke later of German attempts to cover intercontinental distances by piggy-back techniques.[34] To the present day unfortunately no project sketches of the concept have come to light. The US designs of the early *Navaho* rockets which have become available subsequently, the NA 704 and XSSM/A-2 missiles, are on closer inspection simply duck-winged versions of the EMW A-9 with rocket and/or ramjet propulsion.

It is known that the Horse-and-Rider A9/10 was to have been built in a piloted version. The traces were retained into the postwar period. When the US firm developed its X-15 rocket aircraft further, which had much in common with the German EMW 'A-6' war project, it was suggested that a piggy-back version of the X-15 could be put into orbit around the Earth using one or three *Navaho* (alias A-10) rockets. This interesting proposition for manned space flight was similar to German ideas for orbiting the globe with manned rocket aircraft (See *EMW Space Rockets*). Nothing came of the *Navaho*-X-15-piggy back space aircraft idea, however, against competition from the *Mercury* space capsule and X-20 *Dynosoar* programme, and the concept awaits realization today. Based on information supplied by my former Peenemünde source Dr X., the A-11 and A-12 projects were also to have been Horse-and-Rider designs.

## B. Competition to the A-10

### The giant ramp at Artois

As an alternative to the A9/10, it was proposed to launch the A-9 alone by catapult start. According to Dr Walter Dornberger, a long, inclined catapult had been designed to impart to the A-9 a take-off speed of 350 m/sec which would have been sufficient for an unproblematic flight by a fuelled-up A-9 to New York.[35] Was this a serious project? A report dated 30 October 1944[36] states that during their reconquest of France the Allies came across a giant ramp for firing a rocket 3200 miles to the United States. In this article, from SHAEF HQ, the *Daily Mail* reporter described the discovery of immense concrete works on the peak of a hill at Artois near Saint Omer. These were the launch points for those 'flying bombs' which, according to German accounts, would have reduced New York to ashes and rubble. Thousands of workers had been involved in building the tunnels and the cupola, 250-feet in diameter, on the brow of the hill. Lorries and trains could travel directly into the heart of the hill. According to the report, German engineers had informed the local French population that after the installation of all the machinery, and reaching readiness to fire, the district would have to be evacuated for six miles around. Frequent RAF raids delayed the work until the Allied advance form Normandy forced the Germans to dismantle the installations and abandon the territory.

Was a gigantic concrete ramp erected at Artois for launching single-stage A-9 rockets against New York? The 'flying bombs' mentioned in the article may have been the winged A9 rocket. The British report seems to link in the silo at Wizernes, which was to have housed A-10 rockets. So

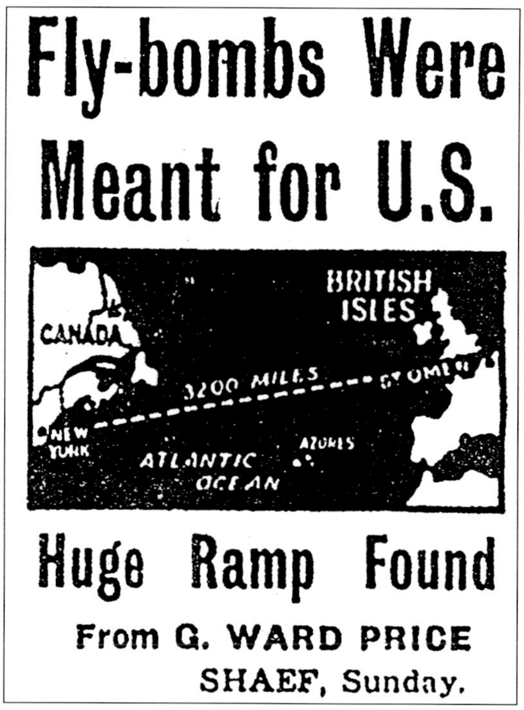


*Daily Mail* report of 30 October 1944 on the ‚giant ramp' to bombard the United States. At that time there was only talk of the V-1 flying bomb. Information as to the existence of more advanced weapons was withheld so as not to cause disquiet even though the V-2 had been operational since September 1944.

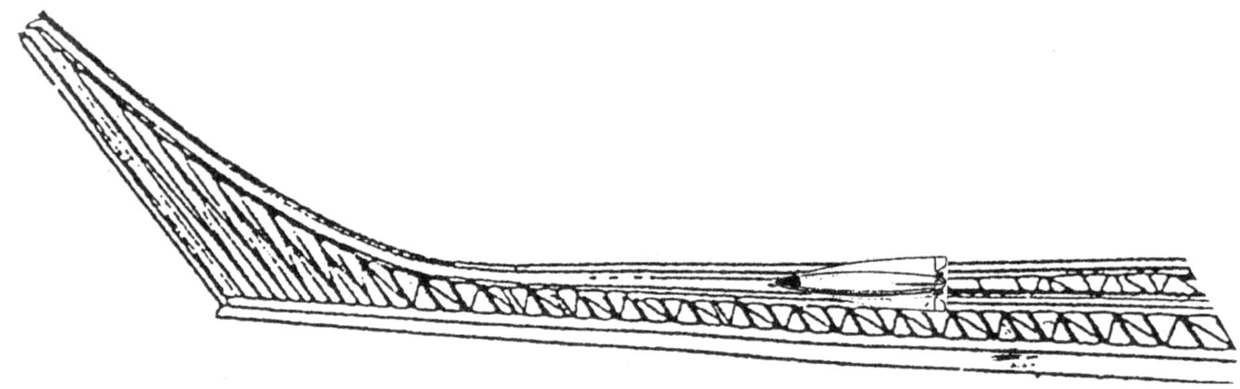

The A-9 'America-Rocket' on a large firing ramp as an alternative solution to the A-9/A-10 two stage rocket.

far as is known, Wizernes had no ramp to catapult winged rockets or missiles. It is also possible that Dr Dornberger's alternative idea for the A9/10 was to have been realized there. The sketch accompanying the *Daily Mail* article shows clearly that this ramp was meant to fire rockets to hit New York. Hardly surprisingly, however, the literature is devoid of plans or photographs showing the captured concrete ramp. The warning by the German engineer that the district would have to be evacuated for six miles around is a clear indication that WMDs were to be involved, and that the intention was to protect the local residents from risk in the event of premature detonation or an accident on the ramp.

In 1948 when the USAF awarded the North American firm contracts to produce rockets with 1,000, 3,000 and 5,000 miles range, Dr Dornberger's giant ramp was one of three launching procedures investigated, the others being vertical blast-off from a platform and the aircraft start.[37] The idea was not proceeded with however.

## Ramjet-propelled to America

### Lorin – The giant motor for an unknown ramjet project?

From 1940 onwards, Professor Eugen Sänger worked for the Reich Air ministry (RLM) on the development of ramjet engines. It was hoped to produce a ramjet engine for an interceptor able to climb to 12 kilometres altitude in two minutes and remain there operational for an hour. For this never-realized fighter (code-named *Feuerlilie*) Professor Sänger developed several experimental ideas tried out on Do 17Z and Do 217E-2 bombers between 1942 and 1944 at the DFS Ainring facility. At the end of August 1944 these test flights were suspended by the Reich Research Bureau because of fuel shortages. That is the official version. Nobody appears to have wondered why a 150-cm experimental ramjet with 20 tonnes of thrust should have been flight tested between March and the end of August 1944. The giant engine upset the trim of the Dornier carriers to the extent that it was not capable to test it fully, from which it is obvious that a ramjet so powerful can never have been intended for a small fighter, contrary to what has been asserted.

At the war's end the Luftwaffe had a string of ramjet-fighter projects; for example the Skoda-Kauba SK P-14, Messerschmitt P.1101L and Heinkel P.1080, all of which had only small ramjet engines. It would be another matter entirely if the 20-tonne thrust rocket was tried out on the back of a bomber to see how it might work on a missile or rocket. The power was relatively similar to that required for the Peenemünde A-4. A coincidence? A very large carrier must have been involved if a Do 217 medium bomber was too small for a full test of the mammoth engine. It comes as a surprise that neither Sänger nor anybody else who participated in the development ever said subsequently what the 150-cm ramjet was intended for.

According to the American author D. Myrha, Professor Sänger was informed by DFS Ainring that the ultimate purpose of his high-speed Lorin research was to perfect an engine to be used as an auxiliary for Wernher von Braun's manned A9/10 rocket.[38] Moreover the engine could be a useful auxiliary for a previously unknown intercontinetal glider. Although used for flight tests from December 1942, the ultimate aim of the giant 1500mm-diameter ramjet remains unknown. In the summer of 1944 a smaller engine of 1000mm diameter was selected for use as the main or auxiliary propulsion unit for rockets and aircraft, and was tested on a Do 217 E2. All test flights with Dr Sänger's ramjets were suspended from 30 August 1944, the setback proving to be permanent. Nevertheless supersonic speeds to 1.5 Mach and the efficiency of the Sänger engines at altitudes of 18,400 metres were simulated in wind tunnels and smoke chambers until the war's end. What might have been possible with this technology had a proper programme been set out for it from 1942?

### Lorin's giant motor for the America Bomber – a stopgap solution?

The halting of Dr Sänger's great Lorin ramjet project may be connected to incidents at that time in France. After their successful landings in Normandy, the Allies embarked on Operation Dragoon from 15 August 1944 in which a strong combined US-British force landed on the French Mediterranean coast between Cannes and Toulon under the protection of five battlerships, nine escort carriers, 28 cruisers and numerous smaller warships. Do 217K bombers of the remains of KG 100 operating from airfields in southern France flew their last desperate missions against the landings. The now swiftly deteriorating war situation in southern France forced KG 100 to evacuate all its aerodromes as from 20 August 1944, among them Istres. They withdrew to Giebelstadt in Germany and suffered serious losses in personnel and materials while doing so. Aircraft which the Germans had not been able to fly out were disabled by the simple expedient of retracting the undercarriage. There are many wartime photographs in existence showing the results of this interesting procedure.

At Istres aerodrome, two special Do 217K aircraft were 'ruined' thus. An aeronautical engineer writing for the British magazine *Aeroplane* (5/2000 edition) recalled that during a training flight with three Vickers Varsity aircraft in February 1952 he landed at Istres to refuel. He noticed on the edge of the runway two large aircraft which appeared to be Dornier bombers. The undercarriage of each had been retracted but apparently not in the course of making a belly landing. On the upper side of the fuselage above the wings a ramjet was mounted. On the flight out of Istres, the writer continued, he saw a French SE-Languedoc experimental aircraft with a Lorin on the back of the fuselage.

In a later edition of *Aeroplane* magazine (7/2000) another reader confirmed seeing the two Dornier Do 217s at Istres in February 1953 or later, but by then the Lorin engines had been dismounted, although the fixtures could still be seen on the fuselage. He had force-landed at Istres with a technical defect while flying to the UK from Cologne in an RAD Valetta transport aircraft. The crew was informed that the ramjet Dorniers 'had been intended to bomb New York during the war'!

Here one may consider if Professor Sänger's ramjets were also to be used as an emergency solution for an improvised attack on New York. Apart from the 150-cm experimental tube too large for a Dornier bomber, there was a smaller 100-cm experimental engine which rather looked as if it had been designed for a Dornier bomber.[39, 40, 41] Unfortunately no photographs showing the Do 217K fitted with such a Lorin engine have come to light. On the basis of statements made by the two former British aviators alone, there was at least one other Do 217K converted in the same way but all photographic evidence has disappeared. Here are grounds to suspect that an effort has been made to kick over the traces.

The only known photograph to survive showing the Sänger ramjet mounted is that of the obsolete Do 217E at Ainring. From a purely technical point of view the Do 217K, even after removal of all non-essential equipment, would not have had the range to reach New York with or without the ramjet mounted, not even for a one-way mission from France. Nevertheless the account of the British witnesses is not without interest.

In August 1944 Istres was the last major aerodrome in France left to the German bomber arm. A night operation against the United States could only have started from there. Besides Do 217s there were four-engined He 177 bombers attached to the same squadron at Istres. As already described in Volume 1 of this series, the Germans considered attacking New York from France using the 'towed aircraft' concept in which a He 177 would have towed a ramjet-propelled Do 217 to some point in mid-Atlantic from where the Do 217 could have reached New York under its own power. This would make sense. The Lorin ramjet would probably have provided the Dornier with enough speed to outpace all pursuers near the target. The bomber would have dropped a WMD on New York before ditching in the sea or putting down somewhere on the American mainland. Was this one of the reasons for Dr Sänger's Lorin project?

Like KG 200, KG 100 was a special squadron for such operations early on. The question is why two Dornier ramjet machines at Istres were abandoned. Was the loss of Bordeaux as the advanced starting point for a New York attack significant from the range aspect, making the risk too great, or were the aircraft ready and the WMDs not? Perhaps the Do 217s were not yet sufficiently operational, or in the end did other causes intervene to prevent the aircraft being flown back to the Reich? It seems unlikely that the French would mislead the RAF fliers at Istres, and it is interesting that the final abandonment of Professor Sänger's major Lorin ramjet project coincided with the evacuation of Istres.

## A-9p: Ramjet propulsion

As explained previously in the section on Eugen Sänger's ramjet system, the Germans were hoping for a major increase in range by using a ramjet for the A-9. Conventional rocket motors first provided the necessary thrust to reach hypersonic flight speed after which the 'air-breathing' ramjet would take over in the upper atmosphere where it functioned best. A considerable gain in range was expected over a pure rocket engine.

Wernher von Braun believed that the manned single-stage A-9 could achieve a range of 3,000 miles using the combination of propellant systems. This distance would have brought New York into range using a single-stage rocket from Western Europe. German scientists were aiming beyond that, however, for with a further increase in fuel efficiency they hoped for a range of 13,500 kilometres (liquid oxygen/alcohol) and 23,500 kilometres (tetra-nitromethane/Visol).[42] Scarcely a point on the Earth's surface would then have been safe against the sub-orbital manned rocket. What was the technical basis for such estimates? Postwar, the German expectations of range from this sytem were condemned as completely over-optimistic and unrealistic. The available ramjet technology could not achieve such distances. Had the German planners conceived a method forgotten or concealed today? German plans dating from the last months of the war which alone can answer that question have never surfaced. Nevertheless, on the basis of postwar sketches by 'Paperclip' scientists, and similar-looking 'coincidental' designs by German scientists of the Hitler period later in forced Soviet employment, it is possible to establish how the war project appeared. The combination was a duck-winged A-9 second stage with a more elongated and supersonic first stage, a ramjet being an additional propulsion system.

Recently the US revealed that the Germans had been planning for an A-10 rocket carrying a ramjet A-9 along its side. This would be an intercontinental version of the 'Horse and Rider' principle (see Volume 2). Later in the postwar period the Americans and Soviets attempted to build similar missiles with their *Navaho* and *Burya* projects respectively. The swift development of ballistic intercontinetal rockets led to the shelving of the idea for decades, but the rocket/ramjet concept is enjoying something of a revival in the opening years of the 21st century. Perhaps Peenemünde had the same idea in 1944/45.

## The long-distance Glider D6000 – a rival to the A-10?

In 1944 a call went out for the immediate production of 'America Weaponry'. This breathed life into an alternative project to the A-10. The new idea was the D-6000, an intercontinental guided missile with a propellant on the Trommsdorff principle. In 1935 Professor Trommsdorff had developed ramjets in which the necessary oxygen was fed into the combustion chamber during flight. The preferred fuel was hydrocarbons. Further experiments were made with propane, hydrogen sulphide, ether liquids, acetone, tetraline, decaline and diesel. These fuels were forced into the combustion chamber by centrifugal force and gas-pressure injection jets. From there the exhaust gases were expelled through pressure jets to provide the thrust.Professor Trommsdorff developed a long series of ramjet-propelled projectiles as shells, an engine for the V-2 rocket (see Volume 2) and missiles of various sizes and designs.[43, 44] His D-series included a number of studies for intercontinental glider ramjet missiles of which the D-6000 project was the furthest advanced. Initially it would be transported by a large carrier aircraft in Mistel fashion to an altitude of 8000 metres for release. The aircraft-shaped missile was 10.24 metres in length, 1.12 metres in diameter and weighed 9 tonnes. Operationally the D-6000 needed to be carried to 14,000 metres before release and required a launch speed of 720 kms/hr (Mach 0.67). These conditions would make enormous demands of potential carrier aircraft so that few would come under consideration for the task. Once released, the D-6000 would enter a dive and reach a speed of Mach 2.8, aided by two auxiliary rockets at the wingtips. The final plan was to fit a ramjet to take the D-6000 to its final planned operational altitude of 24,000 metres.

A later idea was the catapult start. Two auxiliary rockets would provide the projectile with a starting velocity of 850 metres/sec. The ramjet would then cut in and build up speed to 4,248 km/hr. From an altitude of 24,000 metres the D-6000 would have a range of 5,300 kilometres (including the 300 kilometre descent path), which brought the cities on the US East Coast within its ambit. As with the A-9, the warhead payload was 1 tonne. In the nose a search-receiver under special glass(!) was to be included, the guidance system being located behind it. This plan was allegedly only a study. The first sketch came to light in 2002. The report attached to it speaks of a planned D-6000 test scheduled for the end of 1944 but which fell by the wayside for lack of fuel for the carrier aircraft. From the description the D-6000 bore numerous similarities to the 'VU' and Junkers rocket gliders: whether these were competitive designs or were all part of a single complex weapons system is not known. It remains to be seen whether Lusar's report on "other glider-bombers which were ready for operations at the war's end" and to which reference was made in Volume 2 of this series is identical with the Trommsdorff D-6000 intercontinental missile. There may be a surprise in store for us here. In the spring of 1946 in the former Reich capital the Soviets founded *Institut Berlin* whose primary purpose was the reconstruction of flak rockets, but which also duplicated the anti-tank rockets *Rotkäppchen* and *Panzerfaust*, and the long-range *Rheinbote*. Most secret was the independent Special Section No 4 under N.A.Sudakov which carried out "work for the reconstruction of the Trommsdorff missile".[45] This means that at least prototypes of the Trommsdorff glider must have existed during the war.

In 1955 Pierre Sartre proposed for the 'monostato' project SE X-223 of the firm Sud-Est a missile virtually identical to the D-6000. This was turned down in favour of the more conventional piloted Mirage IV as the future French supersonic atom bomber.[46]

## A secret behind the Sputnik rocket SS-6?

After 1945 the two Super-Powers, the USA and USSR, both had the means and motivation for the earliest possible start in building the respective intercontinental rockets. The Soviets took the lead and in 1957 had their R-7 (NATO designation SS-6 *Sapwood*) operational. At that time it was the biggest rocket ever built. Whilst the Americans in the period 1947 to 1954 laid more emphasis on winged cruise missiles, the Russians followed the other path and with the R-7 made a major contribution to solving the problem of transporting a first-generation hydrogen bomb warhead over intercontinental distances.

Lacking large rocket-motors the Soviets resolved this problem by aggregating several single motors. Although the R-7 was one of the best Soviet missiles, it received little mention in the literature.[47] This is all the more surprising since it was with an R-7 variant, *Sputnik I*, that the first artificial satellite orbited the globe on 4 October 1957. This carrier system remained in service. Even when long surpassed, the first Soviet cosmonaut Yuri Gagarin was fired into space orbit aboard one on 12 April 1961. When the opportunity arose to present this great technological achievement to the world, a deliberate effort was made to keep the precise details secret. It almost seems as if it was more important to keep something secret than to reap the prestige and propaganda benefits by disclosing the details.

The R-7 was based on an idea of the forced-labour German Groettrup team[48] and in this regard the report of Luigi Romersa comes to mind respecting the discovery by the Russians at OKH HQ Zossen in 1945 of the design for a large rocket of which the *Sputnik* carrier rocket later turned out to

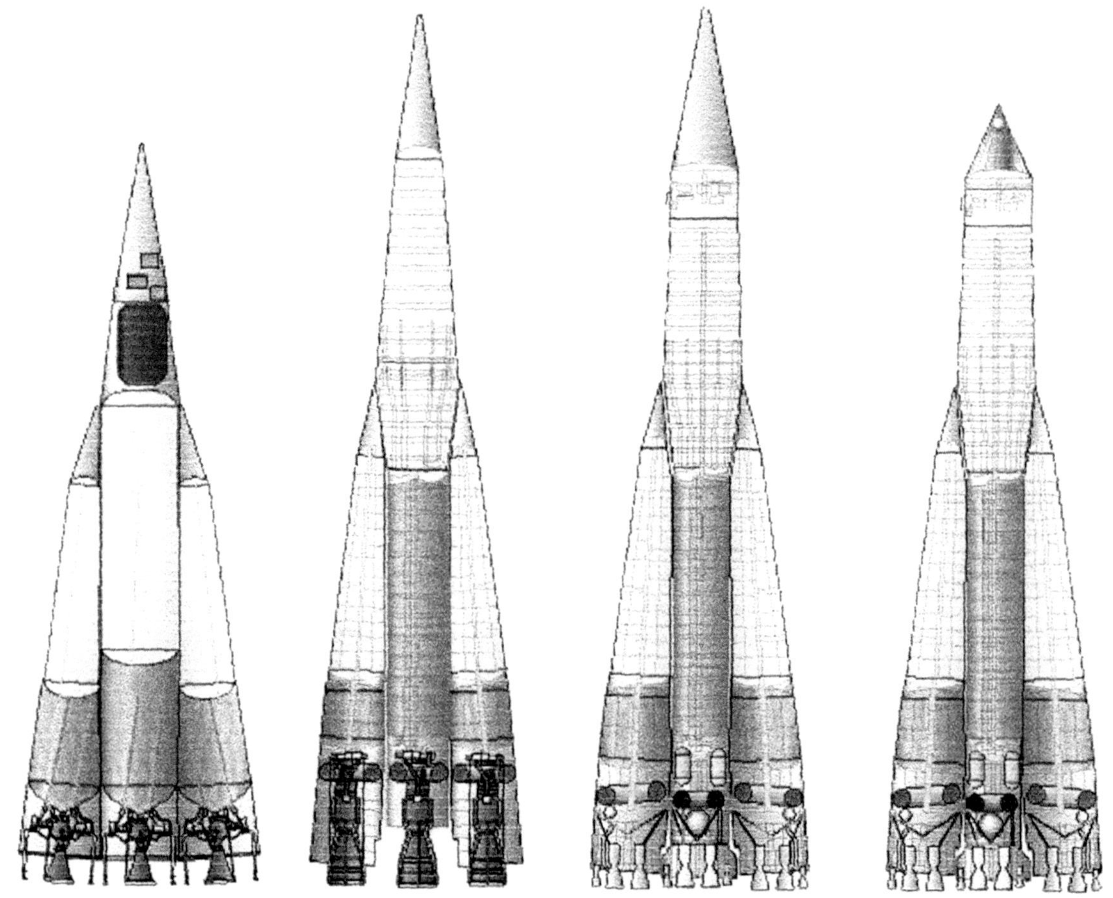


From Groettrup's G-5- aggregate rocket to the SS-6 (R-7) (Source: Astronautix.com).

Captured wind-tunnel model of a V-2 ‚aggregate rocket' tested originally at Kochel. (Source: Simon)

be the twin sister. The 1952 Groettrup design bore the Soviet designation G5/R-15 and was propelled by an aggregate of five rockets of the V-2 improved G-4 type. It could carry a 3-tonne nuclear warhead. A comparison of the G-5 and R-7 shows that these were two very closely related designs, even if everybody was too polite to say so.The question which interests us here is how far this development for Soviet space travel by engineer Groettrup – the 'Russian Wernher von Braun' – rested on World War Two aggregate rocket projects? The Soviets never tired of pointing out that though German scientists in the postwar Soviet Union knew all about German wartime developments in their own field, it was deliberate policy that they should not participate in the technical progress of the postwar period. Was it the reason for the Soviet reluctance to allow the world to explore the history of the R-7 that the amazing Sputnik rocket was an aggregate rocket design which originated in Hitler's Germany, and was the Zossen project the basis for the G5/R-15?

In this connection an American report from August 1945 is worth considering.[49] That month the naval rocket specialist Robert P. Havilland proposed either aggregating several V-2 rockets, or having a stage aggregate of carrier rocket and manned satellite. His suggestion had been preceded in June 1945 however by a paper to the US Navy Bureau of Aeronautics containing ideas and projects for missiles and satellites. The author was no less than Wernher von Braun, at that time in American captivity …

### Was 'Thor's Hammer' a crossbreed with hybrid propulsion?

Besides the manned and unmanned A9/10, was another giant rocket flown? Allied reports respecting the last months of the European war make repeated reference to rockets 'bigger than the V-2' or to so-called V-2s with a range of thousands of kilometres instead of the 300 kilometres of the standard V-2. Here one wonders if there was a rocket crossbred between the A-4B and the A9/10, or an A9/10 with hybrid propulsion, perhaps 'reinforced' by combining motors with liquid and solid propellants. Though appearing unlikely many German weapons developments in the final phase of the war received this kind of interim improvisation in a bid to gain time. In the second half of 1944 when great efforts were being devoted to building long-range versions of the Peenemünde designs, besides the stage separation problem (still existing today) there were three other setbacks to fast completion: (1) the A-9 proved difficult to build (2) its supersonic swept wings needed testing to see how they would behave on re-entering the Earth's atmosphere and (3) a major difficulty to overcome in the A-10 was the decision between a rocket motor composed of a combination of several liquid propellant burners or the single 180 to 200 tonne liquid propellant motor.

According to *Encyclopaedia Astronautica*, it was decided as an interim solution to develop an A-4B booster rocket. Unlike the A-10 this did not use a liquid propellant but solid combustible in powder form. Although the place of production remains unknown, on 9 December 1944 "10 large solid propellant rockets were delivered by the *Wehrmacht* to Peenemünde for Test Site (*Prüfstand*) XII".[50] It was planned that the work at Peenemünde would be sufficiently advanced by the end of March 1945 that flight testing with the long-range A-4B solid fuel crossbreed rocket could proceed. Apparently Peenemünde was to be evacuated before this test took place.

As will be explained later it was possibly the planned firing of such long-range rockets that was the real hidden reason for the 'premature' abandonment of Peenemünde in February 1945. *Prüfstand XII* is always linked with the America Rocket. It may therefore be asked if the test firing of the large *Thor's Hammer* rockets in the spring of 1945 described in the literature were not A9/10 but the A-4B hybrid with solid propellant booster. Rocket test attacks in March 1945 on the Urals may have been of this variant. The range of the A-4B hybrid is unknown. At Skoda Pibrams Works solid propellant motors had been developed for the V-101 rocket the basic stage of which had a thrust of 100 tonnes. It is not known if more powerful solid propellant motors were delivered for the boostered A-4B or whether it was to have the V-101 motor. Allied CIOS reports conclude a connection between Peenemünde and 'unofficial' work on the V-101.

The V-101 had a range of 1800 kilometres, too short for New York but sufficient to reach parts of the Urals. The first stage was propelled by an aggregate of several small solid-fuel motors, and it may therefore have been possible that the V-101, through a combination of solid fuel engines originally envisaged for the second stage, could have achieved the 180 to 200 tonnes thrust planned for the A-10. Possibly the hybrid was intended to accelerate the development of the A-10 as its test vehicle, but the pressure of war events resulted in it being pressed into operational testing at the front.

By fitting an additional group of large, solid-propellant rockets to the sides of the A-10, the thrust of the America Rocket could have been increased so substantially that it would have been able to transport a payload into orbit. This possibility merits consideration and will be looked at again later.

## C. How far was the project advanced at the war's end?

### Was the A-10 ready?

Despite all denials in the established technical literature, it continues to be claimed that a start was made on building an A-10. Hitler's original planning scheduled the A-10 to be ready by 1945. Peenemünde was more optimistic. In 1941, Dr Thiel estimated three years to develop the A-10 as the first stage of the America Rocket, which means that construction work could have begun in 1944.[51] At the end of 1944, Armament Minister Albert Speer advised a conference of the Armaments Council for German Industry that: "the V-3 which was under preparation to bombard New York is so far advanced that one may expect the first test flight before the end of this month, therefore in December 1944".[52]

Did this mean that Hitler's projected completion date had been reached early? Working round the clock, Wernher von Braun and his team had succeeded in placing the complete plans and files for the A9/10 rocket before the German leader by the beginning of 1944.[53] Hitler, whom this project had long fascinated, ordered the rocket built immediately, the testing period shortened and industrial production undertaken at once. The same reference source states that between February 1944 and April 1945, in a series of written instructions, Hitler kept up the pressure on von Braun to turn out the America Rocket as soon as possible, and promised von Braun " … all the money in the world, inflicted on his workforce a 15 – or 16-hour working day without a break, calling them heroes when he was happy with progress and vilified them as the worst traitors in history when it seemed to him that the pace had fallen off somewhat … " Who can seriously talk of Peenemünde 'going into hibernation' after it concluded the V-2 development in 1942/43! On 24 January 1945 after a test start, Wernher von Braun even went so far as to announce that technical problems in the upper rocket stage had been resolved.

The former DDR author Julius Mader wrote that the advance of the Red Army ensured the America Rocket did not become operational and so saved the United States from a planned 'Fascist rocket strike'. Mader also mentioned that about half a dozen rockets were test fired from the woods south of Wolgast. These Wolgast rocket starts are very interesting. In his book *V-2 – Der Schuss ins Weltall*, General Walter Dornberger wrote that after the *Fernraketen Lehr-und-Versuchsabteilung* firing detachment was transferred from Heidekraut testing ground to Wolgast, there were no more tests.[54] Why Mader should assert the contrary with his half dozen rocket starts suggests their importance.[60]

SS secret weapons specialist Otto Skorzeny declared after the war that the America Rocket was "practically ready by the end of March 1945 and could have been in series production from June."[55] The expressions 'practically ready' and 'only a month from series production when the war ended' indicate the existence of completed prototypes or pre-series examples at the end of the war. Wernher von Braun told his friend Luigi Romersa that the A-10 was being built[52] – a statement at variance with those established writings which remain in print!

A leading former Peenemünder calculated from statements by Skorzeny and von Braun that at least seven A-10 prototypes and four pre-series rockets were ready by May 1945[56] while Buechner and Bernhart mentioned in their book that four rockets known as *Thor's Hammer* or America Rocket had been flight tested.[57] Even if one prefers to ignore such assertions, it must be accepted that Allied information services, military authorities and prestigious newspapers such the *Washington Post, Los Angeles Times* and the London *Times* all admitted after the war the existence of German intercontinental weapons, and spoke of a piloted rocket with a possible range of 3000 miles.

On 14 June 1945 the British *Daily Mail* published an interview with US Major William Bromley. This officer was assistant to the Chief of 'Special Mission V-2' (James Harmill) and was familiar with all details and operations of the unit. He was also the man who controlled the removal of 100 V-2 rockets from Nordhausen to the United States between 15 and 20 May 1945, and it was there that the interview with the *Daily Mail* took place shortly before the unit was wound down. Bromley, who is recognized by 'established' historians, told reporters in a rather unguarded moment that the mass-production of a "V-2 with a range of 3000 miles" (therefore the same as the A-10) "would have been possible within six months of VE-Day" (8 May 1945). He added that the rocket in question could have been in mass production before VE-Day had it not been for the RAF air raid on Peenemünde in August 1943. Since it is normal practice before mass-production that prototypes, test specimens and 'hand-finished' pre-series examples of the expected mass-produced version are completed first, Major Bromley must have deliberately withheld information so as not to shock the readership.[58]It cannot be denied that leading German and Allied authorities, independently of each other but in unison, have confirmed that the America Rocket was under construction and on the threshold of mass production when the war in Europe ended. All the more surprising is it therefore that to the present day neither photographs nor parts of these allegedly complete rockets have come to light. The only question which remains to be determined is whether no proper search was conducted, or the traces have been kicked over.

## The America Rocket and/or Atomic Research at Traunstein

On 9 August 1945 the *Daily Mail* and *New York Times* reported that the Germans had had experimental atomic research stations at Peenemünde, Ryukan (Norway) and on the Chiemsee in Bavaria.[59] Near Chiemsee in the mountains between Traunstein and Traurent was to be found a series of subterranean galleries. According to local residents, in the Second World War it was a test centre for explosives. Most recently the electrical giant Siemens had had an interest in the installation (why?)[62] If these sources suggest some kind of atomic research, a telegram from Dr Kammler to Himmler's scientific adviser Dr Brandt dated 20 October 1943 *proves* that the great caverns in the mountains near Traunstein were scheduled for the setting up of a subterranean test station for the America Rocket.[61]

Where was Traunstein mountain? The author's Spanish colleague Antonio Chover discovered old land maps have a mountain near Traunsee (*Salamander*) identified as 'Traunstein B.G.'. This would mean that there was a rocket test plant in a cavern in the Traunstein range and not too far removed from the Ebersee A and B underground modules where the A-10 production plant was to have been. If it exists, the test cavern has not yet been found. There is also no document giving information as to what became of the Traunstein plant – there was sufficient time available before May 1945 for considerable progress to have been made.

D. V-2 GLIDER BOMBS

The V-2 flying bombs are assembled in the EAST Works (see Appendix A) which has about 3,000 engineers and workers. Two types of V-2 have been built: Type A 1, which is about 23 m long and 4.5 m in diameter, and Type A 4, which is about 18 m long and 2.5-3 m in diameter. Only the latter is in mass production. The experimental launching of V-2 used to take place every Saturday afternoon from Mar 43 to Mar 44. At the latter time it was rumored that HITLER had visited the center and had demonstrated his anger at the slow progress of the experiments. From this time on the frequency of the bomb launchings was increased to every other day. When PW left the center in July 44 there were still some launchings which were not successful due to the fact that the bombs were not able to be radio-guided, although they were launched successfully.

All experiments conducted with V-2 were done without explosive charges, except once, in HITLER's presence. It is rumored that on that occasion the bomb was guided to HELA Island, near DANZIG. Invariably a small explosive charge with a fuze is placed in all bombs lest a bomb drop intact into some foreign country - Sweden, for example.

When a V-2 bomb is launched all the workers of all four factories listen to the noise of the bomb as it climbs to the stratosphere. When it becomes apparent that control is lost over the bomb, everybody makes a mad rush for a shelter, since sometimes the bomb returns and hits a factory.

PW once had an opportunity to observe the launching of one of these bombs from a distance of 200 m. The bomb stands on a concrete platform, inclined about five degrees in the direction of fire. It is

4

~~S E C R E T~~

DECLASSIFIED
Authority NND-[illegible]
By [illegible] NARA, Date [illegible]

Extract from the American document in which a German deserter described details of the production of larger kinds of V-2 rocket.

## Rocket parts manufactured at Peenemünde until July 1944

In the autumn of 1944 a 24-year old chemist from Danzig defected to the Allies. From May to July 1944 he had been engaged at Peenemünde, and supplied his interrogators with a finely detailed report about HVA Peenemünde. The Allied secret report on the interrogation dated 14 December 1944 was not declassified until 1993. An important part reads: " … two types of V-2 were built – Type A-1, approximately 23 metres long and 4.5 metres in diameter, and Type A-4, approximately 18 metres long and 2.5 to 3 metres in diameter. Only the latter is in mass production". He also stated that rocket parts were manufactured at Peenemünde until July 1944. The A-10 was 25.9 metres overall and so the description of the first rocket is almost correct, probably 'A-10' lost the '0' due to an error in transcription (source: MU 500, CSD 16 West, 7th Army, Ref. No. 579, 14 Dec 1944, via Grp).

## Were There Tests?
## 'VZBV': the Sudden Evacuation of Peenemünde

On 31 January 1945 an order arrived from Dr Kammler for the immediate evacuation of the test institute and its removal to the vicinity of Mittelwerk in the Harz. On 3 February 1945 Wernher von Braun consolidated the order so that 'the whole organization' would go, thus retaining the complete structure so that work at the new location could be resumed straight away.[62, 63] It is reported that the same day and in great haste all test and control installations and the most important office equipment were packed in chests and prepared for the transfer. Many 'superfluous' drawings and documents were destroyed, but there was no time to demolish the buildings or test sites. This panic is interesting in view of the fact that the Russians were still three months away.

After the last A-4 was test fired from Peenemünde on 17 February 1945, the first 4,325 scientists, engineers, technicians and their families left the peninsula in lorries, railway trucks and even by sea. When the road transports were held by military police it was noted that all vehicles bore a placard with the letters 'VZBV' (*Vorhaben zur besonderen Verwendung* – Project for Special Purposes) which gave them priority even over the huge numbers of military vehicles blocking the highways on their journey to Bad Sachsa, Lehesten and Nordhausen. By March 1945, Peenemünde was a ghost town. At least, that is the official version even though the Red Army, allegedly the reason for the hasty abandonment of HVA Peenemünde by Dr Kammler, was so far away that it did not take possession of the territory until 4 May 1945, three months later. After Kammler gave the order, military commanders at the front and the *Gauleiters* of Pomerania were up in arms against what they considered the 'premature and over-early evacuation'. Wernher von Braun joked about it years later: "I had ten orders on my desk. Five threatened me with the firing squad if we left, and the other five said I would be shot if we didn't".[64] Kammler had the last say, however, and the evacuation proceeded despite all the objections.

Was Peenemünde a ghost town in March 1945? It is known that of the staff involved there on problem solving for the V-2 and other rocket projects about half remained. This makes no sense unless there was important research to keep them there. It would not have been possible for people to have stayed behind without official permission, and 'no time' was left to destroy the buildings and test sites at the February 1945 evacuation. Yet in a period of acute energy shortage in Germany, Peenemünde was still up and running when the Russians arrived.[65] It can be shown that important activities were proceeding there after 17 February 1945, and it is also evident that the Germans were straining every nerve to keep RAF reconnaissance aircraft away from the 'abandoned island' as if there were something worth seeing there.

Thus on 9 March 1945 the pilot of a photo-reconnaissance Mosquito (MM 283) reported having been chased away from Peenemünde by three Me 262 jets and had a narrow escape through cloud.[66] This would indicate that the Germans were prepared to commit Me 262 jet aircraft – desperately needed for anti-bomber work – against single RAF reconnaissance aircraft photographing an allegedly abandoned test range. Although the interception may have been coincidental, the question may be asked whether the jets were expressly on station to prevent Peenemünde being filmed? Certainly until now no Allied aerial photo of Peenemünde taken in March 1945 has been found in the archives. Is there something on these photographs that remains classified secret over 60 years later? What we do know is that when the evacuation of Peenemünde was ordered, the order did not extend to the rocket-firing teams on the test sites ...

## The Evacuation of Peenemünde: Dr Kammler 's ruse or was Allied espionage responsible?

The attempts with SS and Gestapo help to hermetically seal off Peenemünde from the world after the great air raid of August 1943 were not very successful. The Americans state that they were being updated daily as to events at Hitler's secret rocket test station, besides which they could read ULTRA coded messages and had aerial photographs. Even so, their intimate knowledge of the details can only be explained by espionage involving the foreign workforce engaged there or treason by German military and civilian personnel.

In 1944 Allied air attacks were founded on knowledge gleaned from these sources. Allied espionage could no longer hinder the operational use of the V-1 and V-2, and production of the V-Weapons had been transferred to underground factories and was thus no longer vulnerable to Allied aerial attacks. In consequence Operation *Hydra* pinpointed not the test sites but the scientists' and workers' residences.

If Dr Kammler's staff wanted to test or make operational certain rockets which required the special installations at Peenemünde, the German planners had to expect that the Allies would probably know this beforehand and react. It should not be overlooked that Allied air mastery had become many times more powerful than in August 1943 while the retreat for German plans, *Zement* at Ebensee with its underground production and test firing facility, had not been completed to schedule. What better alternative therefore than to provide the Allies with a piece of theatre in which it appeared that Peenemünde had been evacuated 'in panic and disorder'? This would have been notified at once to the Allies by their usual agents who, so the Germans were probably hoping, would find themselves amongst the thousands of evacuees, or if not would be left with an espionage network so chaotic that the Allies would lack information about Peenemünde at least for a while.

In the apparently abandoned base those activities could now proceed for which the personnel at the rocket test firing positions had been held back and the great Peenemünde power station had been kept running. Its output capacity was so enormous that it kept all research installations, the oxygen production unit, workshops, centres of accommodation and the wind tunnel supplied with energy. To raise steam for the generators four anti-rust boilers had been installed, each able to consume 64 tonnes of coal hourly.[67]

It is not known if the ruse to deceive the Allies worked, or if they continued to be informed of events on the Usedom peninsula as before, but the lack of any Allied aerial photos after the February evacuation indicates that they knew the secret of Peenemünde in the last three months of the war. It is odd that the Western Allies made no direct attack on Peenemünde in that period while the Soviets, who could count on making the German base their own sooner or later, launched massive air strikes by IL-2 bombers against V-2 firing ramps on the Wollin peninsula. Put another way, why would the Soviets, who supposedly believed Peenemünde to be closed down and defunct, attack their future prize while the Western Allies watched events at Peenemünde and Miesdroy as mere observers?

### Incredible or true: tests and operational firings of the A-10?

Although Armaments Minister Speer had scheduled the first America Rocket tests for December 1944, there is no evidence that he kept to the timetable. For the period between March and April (or early May) 1945, however, there are reports that tests of several-stage giant rockets were made at two locations, these rockets being called *Thor's Hammer* or America Rocket, and in this connection Peenemünde and Rudisleben north of Arnstadt in the Harz have been identified as the firing centres. Reports speak of four tests at Peenemünde.[68, 69] Three *Thor's Hammer* rockets were test fired into the Atlantic, the fourth into orbit or outer space. The purpose of these tests and whether they were considered to have been successful is unknown. Possibly the test firing of an America Rocket was even observed in its final phase by the Allies. In the DDR period, independent witnesses swore depositions as to the firing of a two-stage winged rocket about 30 metres in length at Rudisleben near Ohrdruf on the night of 16 March 1945.[1] The rocket flew north (Baltic/North Sea?). Whilst no files are available regarding the success or failure of the large rockets tested at Peenemünde, the Rudisleben witnesses agree that the launch on 16 March 1945 was fully satisfactory. Thus at least five major rockets were test fired before Germany's collapse.

Two aerial reconnaissance photos were taken of Rudisleben in the daylight hours prior to the alleged firing of a giant rocket on the night of 16 March 1945. The photos were examined by Nigel Wylde, a former British Army ammunition and guided weapons specialist and Technical Intelligence Officer of the German Military Mission to Germany. He knew the area in the period 1982-1984 when there was no remnant of the facility visible. There is no record of this Third Reich site in the database of military facilities in Germany.

Rudisleben is a small village on the highway from Erfurt to Arnstadt in Thuringia. Mr Wylde found that the wartime facility there consisted of at least 150 barely camouflaged buildings ranging from accommodation barracks to bunkers and would have taken thousands of forced labourers over two years to construct. The area covered was roughly 2500 metres (west to east) and 1500 metres (north to south). At the western edge of the facility was a large concrete circle with a black area of ground to the east. This black area was scorch damage probably resulting from a very high temperature conflagration on the concrete circle, the most likely cause being an accident involving rocket propellant possibly while mixing fuels prior to launch. Mr Wylde considered that the concrete circle was the base for the support mechanism for a vertically launched guided missile or free-flight rocket, and was similar to the launch pad at Peenemünde.

He regarded Building 12 in the main photograph as the most significant on the site, this being the missile fuelling building. He based this assessment on the static water tank nearby, the only one in the whole facility, it being the German custom to locate such tanks close to significant fire risks. The main building was 65 x 15 metres in area and would allow for up to four giant rockets to be under construction there at the same time. Prior to fuelling the rockets would have been assembled in buildings 15 and 15A where the electrics and hydraulics would have been tested before fuelling. From building 12 the partially fuelled-up rocket would have been taken to the launch pad where the second fuel would be mixed with the first if the combustible was a mixed-fuel propellant. Building 13 was the launch control building. The aerial reconnaissance must have been attracted by the previous accident and fire: by coincidence the giant rocket was fired that night, but no aerial photograph was taken of the site subsequently, or has not been declassified.[2]

Despite the extreme pressure of time in the last months of the war, it seems very possible that rather more tests were carried out. A Mexican researcher noted in a Spanish language edition of the Soviet magazine *Sputnik* an article in which the Russian author described several explosions which occurred in March 1945 against weapons factories near the Tobol river on the far side of the Urals. These 'terror attacks' by the 'perfidious Fascists' were compared to later American B-52 bomber raids on the Vietnamese port of Hai-Phong. The witnesses amongst the Russians workers reported having heard a great explosion followed several seconds later by a high-pitched whistle. This scenario can only be explained by a rocket. The workers confirmed that no German aircraft had been seen or heard.[70] Although the Luftwaffe had planned Operation *Eisenhammer* for March 1945, in which long-distance Mistel bombers were to attack Soviet power and hydro-electric plants in the Moscow and Gorki areas, they had no aircraft capable of making a round flight with a bombload to the Tobol river.

It is known that in connection with *Eisenhammer*, later cancelled, that numerous German agents were carried behind the Urals by aircraft and subsequently continued to send their reports to the Third Reich long after it had ceased to exist. It would certainly have been possible for them to set homing beacons at the target for the guidance of long range incoming rockets, and this was the procedure which was to have been used at New York.

The former leading Peenemünder who prefers anonymity did not deny the operational use of these rockets but condemned their use against the Russians instead of firing them at the United States as originally conceived. In our conversation he mentioned 'a couple' of A-10s launched against the Urals industrial region near the Ural and Tobol rivers. This confirms the details in the *Sputnik* magazine.[71] We discussed whether the operational use of these long-range rockets against the Soviets was a strategic mistake, since it was the policy of a strictly controlled Press and Information service to suppress any details about advanced rocketry during the war. This would not have been the case in the event of their use against the United States of course. As to the question of motivation, one wonders whether it was still hoped to achieve some military success against the Soviet Union by the use of a few intercontinental rockets, or perhaps it was expected that the Russians would notify the Americans immediately that targets in the Urals had been hit by giant rockets. In the latter case the Americans would have had received knowledge of the weaponry becoming available to the Third Reich to threaten New York or other US cities. If on the other hand the real reason for these militarily senseless long range attacks was to give the peace negotiators more pull with the Allies at the last moment it failed, for no evidence exists that the Russians told the Americans during the war.

Not until the Vietnam War decades later was any mention ever made of these assumed rocket attacks, and now the Soviet Union used them for political purposes in the Cold War, comparing the German A-10s to the American B-52s. The comparison was not taken up by other organs of the Soviet press: probably they were quietly reminded of the international agreement that German long-range rockets had not existed, and that section of the article was accordingly deleted from the German language edition of *Sputnik* magazine. My perusal of the German language version could find no 'Haiphong/Tobol article'. The idea was that sleeping dogs should be let lie: too many of the surviving witnesses might no longer have considered themselves bound by their oath of silence and might have launched into print regarding certain events at Peenemünde and Rudisleben 'which never were'. This may be a fruitful area for future research! At the end of the war it became the common practice to try out the prototypes of new weapons at the front, even if they were technically unproven or were purely test models. To that extent the front line testing of A-10 rockets followed the procedure of the time.

## Section 2: The 'Japan Rocket' EMWA-11. How far was Hitler from the world's first orbital rocket?

The rocket scientists at Peenemünde did not stop at the A9/10 America Rocket and had designed the A-11 with 1600 tonnes starting thrust. The A-11 belonged with the US *Saturn* family of the 1960s in which Wernher von Braun's *Saturn I-W* had a thrust of 785 tonnes, and the later moon rocket *Saturn V* 3,500 tonnes.[72]

If completed the A-11 would have been a pure ICBM with which the Third Reich could have struck at anywhere in the world with a payload between 1 tonne and 1.7 tonnes. It is ludicrous to think that so much effort and expense would have been put into a carrier rocket with a 1-tonne *conventional* warhead, and as with the A-10, this rocket must have been intended to carry a weapon of mass destruction. In his postwar utterances, Wernher von Braun naturally emphasized that Hitler's A-11 was only planned for the peaceful exploration of space, probably by putting up an astronaut into Earth-orbit.

Three EMW A-11 variants are known, each having little in common with the other two other than payload and the three-stage principle. While the first design resembles outwardly the American and Russians rockets of the 1960s, the second has the revolutionary flared shape of most modern American rockets. In the absence of official designations, these two designs are given Roman numerals in this book.[73]

EMW A-11/I – This design of conventional appearance was presented by Wernher von Braun to American officers at Garmisch as the A-11 and is known from a US Army drawing from 1946. It was an A9/10 rocket on the stacking box principle with a large additional start stage. The design would have been quickest to realize because of the initial start stage needed to be built and tested. Further development possibilities of the design were probably exhausted.

EMW A-11/II – This was a far-reaching new development for which two new stages had to be built but was a suitable foundation for future enlargements (V-12). Type II could carry a 1-tonne payload at 50° in an elliptical orbit at 180 kilometres altitude. All-up weight was 85.73 tonnes, overall length 66 metres. Fortunately there are details available of this revolutionary design. The A-11/II basic stage weighed 77 tonnes fuelled (70 tonnes empty). Length was 20.7 metres, diameter 13.5 meters and the wingspan (four wings) 13.5 metres. Thirty-four Visol-fuelled rocket motors provided a lift-off thrust of 1600 tonnes. The second stage was a modified EMW A-10, weight 69 tonnes, starting thrust 235 tonnes, set into the start stage with a flared base. The third stage was an A-9 winged rocket, manned or unmanned, total weight 16.259 tonnes, carried within the second stage.

EMW A-11 'Horse and Rider' – This is known only as a project for which no details are available. With the A-11 a pilot could have been fired into a low-energy orbit of the Earth after which he would have put the craft down in the conventional manner.[74] There are conflicting reports as to the extent of the project at the war's end. An important statement in this regard emanated from an unexpected source which, by obvious reason of the speaker's standing, offers a certain degree of proof. On 1 July 1945, the Stockholm newspaper *Dagens Nyheter*[75] reported on the grand parade in Olso for 'Allies Day' held the previous morning and attended by the King of Norway and various high-ranking Allied generals. At midday there was a press conference at which Air Chief Marshal Sir Arthur Harris and US General Bradley were introduced. Harris spoke on the subject of the air war and in response to a question asking whether the Germans could have built bomber aircraft to reach America, he replied, "If the Germans had held out long enough, they would have circled the Earth with a flying bomb to land in Germany at their backs." This mention of a bomb capable of flying round the globe amounts to an admission by Sir Arthur Harris that the Germans had an orbital rocket in preparation, although he avoided saying how far it was advanced at the war's end.

In the postwar period, the flames of the Peenemünde myth were fanned to replace Usedom's true history in the final phase of the Third Reich. Wernher von Braun informed Bergaust, author of *The Next 50 Years in Space* that the A-11 had existed only in his imagination. Against that, it is known

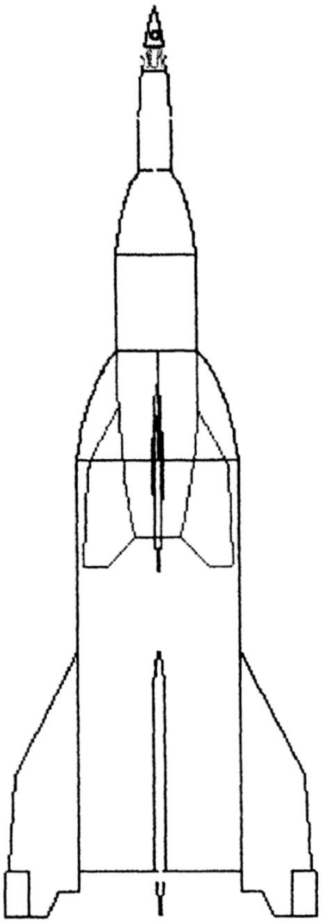

EMW A-11/I (Lowther). Notice the payload in the nose.

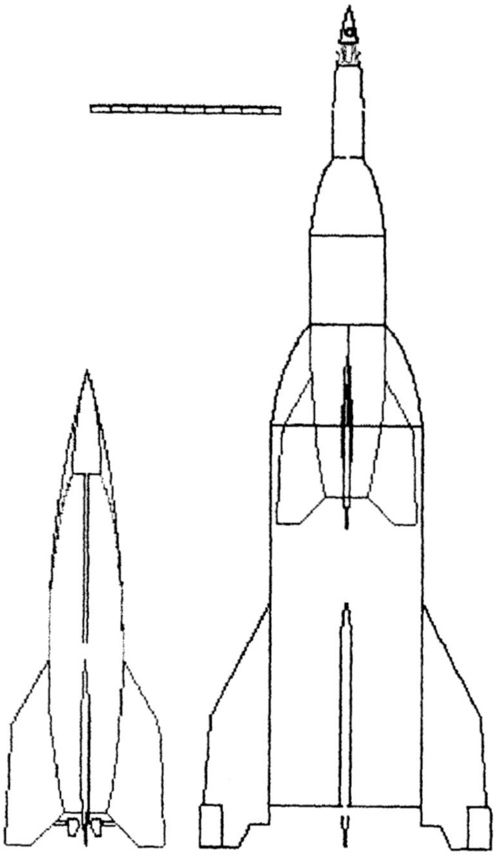

Size comparison between the A-10 ‚America- Rocket' and the A-11/1 ‚Japan-Rocket' (Lowther).

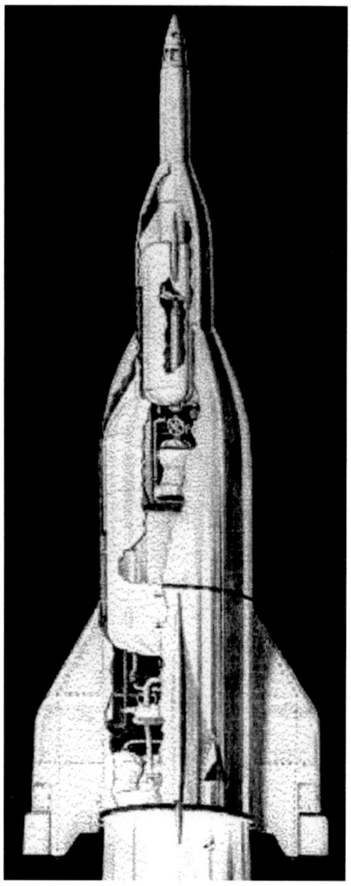

EMW A-11/I in a US Army illustration, 1946 (www. astronautix.com).

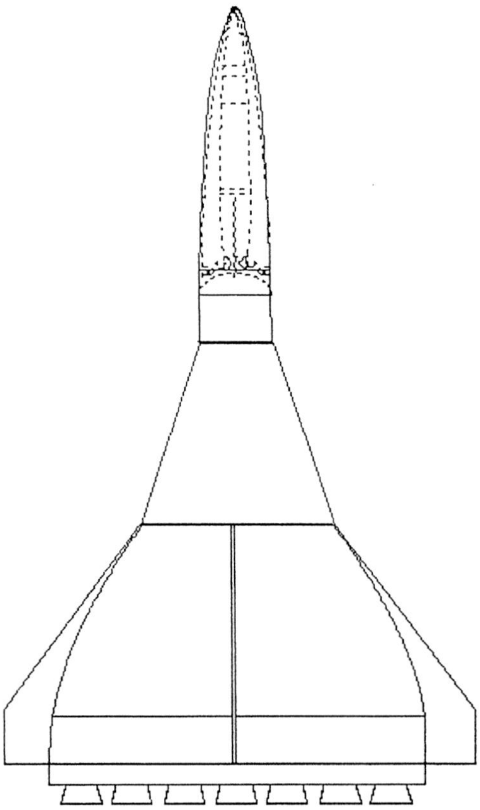

EMW A-11/II (Mark Wade, www.astronautix.com, 1999).

# Flaggalléer i Oslo på de allierades dag

*FRÅN DAGENS NYHETERS OSLOKORRESPONDENT.*

OSLO, lördag.

Norge tackade på lördagen sina stora allierade, Storbritannien, Amerika och Sovjetunionen, vilkas vapen gjorde det möjligt för landet att intaga sin plats bland de fria nationerna. Överallt var det stora festligheter till ära för de allierade, och staden var smyckad med alléer av allierade flaggor. Vid middagstiden paraderade stora styrkor med engelska, amerikanska och ryska trupper, som hyllades livligt i ett blomsterregn som varade under hela marschen genom staden upp till slottet, där kung Haakon talade till trupperna.

Kungens gäster vid de allierades dag, amerikanske generalen Omar Bradley, brittiske flygmarskalken Sir Arthur Harris och ryske generalmajoren Ratov samt den speciella ryska delegationen, som anlände från Moskva på fredagen och vars chef är flygmarskalk Falalejev, har under Oslobesöket varit föremål för stor uppmärksamhet. Vid en pressmottagning som hölls på middagen presenterades medlemmarna i det allierade överkommandot, flygmarskalk Harris och general Bradley. Harris berörde luftvapnens insats i kriget, och på en fråga om tyskarna skulle ha kunnat bygga bomber som kunnat nå Amerika svarade han: — Om tyskarna fått hålla på länge nog, skulle de kunnat tillverka en bomb som kunde gå jorden runt och slå ned i ryggen på dem i Tyskland! Bradley talade om kampen till lands.

## Barngrupp till Sverige på torsdag.

Det är stor glädje i många norska hem över att så många Oslobarn i sommar skall få fritt uppehålle i Sverige. På torsdag reser den första kontingenten på 180 barn från Oslo. En del av dem skall till Göteborg och resten till Stockholm.

De är inbjudna av Svenska Norgehjälpen och skall bo på större sommarpensionat, som tidigare har härbärgerat flyktingbarn. Företrädesvis rör det sig om barn från barnrika familjer i åldern från fyra till sju år.

## Quisling försvarar sig på 75 sidor.

Målet mot Quisling kommer troligen att behandlas i slutet av juli, och i målet mot honom står advokat Annæus-Schjödt, som har anklagelseakten klar om ett par dagar. Quisling har nu sitt försvar klart, och i dagarna har han översänt en dokumentsamling på 75 maskinskrivna sidor till rätten. Advokat Schjödt kommer också att föra talan mot Quislings ministrar, vilka mål kommer upp i lagmansrätten i Oslo efter Quislingmålet.

*Danens Nyheter* report of 1.July 1945 on the Allied victory parade in Oslo at which Air Chief Marshall stated that if the Germans had had more time they would have produced a bomb to circle the Earth. The orbital rocket!

# V2s with range of 3,000 miles

***Would have been ready by VE-Day***

By Daily Mail Reporter

**MASS production of V2 rockets with a range of 3,000 miles would have been possible within six months after VE-Day, according to American experts who have spent a month studying a huge underground rocket assembly plant near Nordhausen, in Germany.**

German scientists give the impression that they could then have turned out rocket bombs in large enough numbers to "neutralise any advantage which air superiority had given to the Allies."

But for the Royal Air Force attacks on the experimental plant at Peenemunde, mass production of the V2's might have been ready just at the time of VE-Day.

**"That raid was a life-saver for us," said Major William Bromley, who has directed the task of assembling 100 of the rocket bombs.**

"It set the German scientists back just about six months in their experiments. They admitted that it caused great damage to installations and killed 800 of their best experts."

The experts based their report on a survey of a huge rocket-assembly plant 800ft. under the Kohnstein Mountains, near Nordhausen, Germany.

One hundred ordinary V2 projectiles are ready to be sent to the United States.

German scientists believed that in two years' time they could have developed a rocket that could be fired from Britain to Japan. But they admitted that this belief was only theoretical.

The plant under the Kohnstein Mountains is said to be the largest underground factory in the world. The factory is housed in two huge tunnels, connected by a network of small tunnels through which runs a railway 25 miles long.

The plant was capable of turning out 900 V2's a month, in addition to other V-weapons and plane engines.

Sabotage by 12,000 slave workers in the plant and a shortage of materials kept actual production well below that level.

In the *Daily Mail* of 14 June 1945, US Major William Bromley confirmed that mass production of the A-10 ("V-2 with a range of 3000 miles") would have begun within six months of the war's end and that the rocket itself was ready on VE Day. Wernher von Braun's colleagues believed that the design stage of the even bigger "Japan–Rocket" (A-11) would have been completed within two years.

that the interned Peenemünde scientists at Garmisch showed finished plans for the A-11 to their American interrogators, this being confirmed by Major William Bromley in the 14 June 1945 edition of the *Daily Mail*.[76] By then Bromley had just completed his examination of a giant underground rocket factory near Nordhausen, probably Dora, as he told reporters. He added that German scientists had needed two more years to complete a rocket to hit England from Japan. This was the A-11!

There are more disquieting statements by others with special knowledge.[77] The former *Mercury* and *Gemini* astronaut Gordon Cooper (1927-2004) was a man with insider knowledge of the early manned space programme. As a professional he was informed as to all important facts of these systems and had had the closest contact to the former Peenemünder who participated in the design of all American rockets and capsules. Obviously Cooper knew the difference between gliding flight (A9/10) and the orbital flight of which the A9/10 was not capable. According to his statement, in April 1945 at Peenemünde a 'manned V-2' was almost ready for firing. Only one week more had been needed for the planned low-energy orbital flight to New York.

## Section 3: "From a blind start to the remote-controlled robot". The struggle for accuracy

### A. Had the necessary requirements been met by 1944/1945 for rocket and aircraft miracle weapons?

There is no doubt that the German leaders planned their rockets and missiles to be the weapons of victory. Had the necessary requirements been met or were the dreams of Hitler, Göring, Himmler and Kammler simply fantastic? To answer this question one must investigate the past to see if suitable warheads existed, how suitable the carriers were and the extent to which their development had advanced or was complete. The question regarding the availability of both systems must, in the author's opinion, be answered in the affirmative (see Volumes 1 and 2), but there was another important requirement, for even if one had such warheads and carrier systems, accuracy was essential. New demands thus arose for precision, guidance and control of the carriers, and without such technological breakthroughs their use would have served little purpose.

### B. German steel valves and radio control

Many authors maintain not only that the Germans never worked seriously on the A9/10, but also that even had it existed, it could never have been accurate enough, and for two reasons: (1) the electronics of the time were too primitive. Only glass radio valves existed, these were too large, too sensitive and too fragile besides needing too much current, and additionally it would have been impossible to build a functional electronic search receiver. (2) The inertial (electro-mechanical) guidance systems were too imprecise for targets 3000 miles away.

This argument overlooks the fact that steel valves had been developed in Germany in 1940. They were small and robust, worked at low tension and needed an incredibly small quantity of current. Of especial interest here was the 'DL 11' model from 1940 which needed only 1.2 volts for

**DL 11, seit 1940**

Niederfrequenz-Endverstärkerpentode für Rundfunkempfänger.

Heizung: 1,2 V und 50 mA direkte Batterieheizung

Anodenspannung: 120 V
Schirmgitterspannung: 120 V
Anodenstrom: max. 4,7 mA
Schirmgitterstrom: 0,85 mA
Steuergitterspannung: -6 V (4 V~)
Steilheit: 1,1 mA/V
Innenwiderstand: 500 Ω
Außenwiderstand: 22 kΩ
Ausgangsleistung: 0,35 W

Telefunken

Telefunken's steel valve DL 11 manufactured in 1940 was suitable for use in a rocket guidance system. How much further had the technology progressed by 1945? (Source: H.-T. Schmidt, www.hts-homepage.de/Dstahl/DSDL11.html)

60 milliwatts, and so one thousand 'DL 11' needed the same current as a light bulb. Any normal battery supplied 1.2 volts. Small portable radio sets could be made easily with these valves, and were indeed produced to the designs appearing in Volume 9 of *Fortschritte der Funktechnik* (Advances in Radio Technology) published in Germany in September 1941. The result was no larger than the transistor radios of the 1950s and was battery operated.[79] Using these steel valves it would have been perfectly possible to build relatively complicated electronic guidance systems. Since the valves were small and robust, and needled little voltage and output, they could have easily been put into rockets and cruise missiles.

The foregoing relates only to equipment at the 1940 state of development. It seems unlikely that in subsequent years modifications and new developments would not have been introduced which raised the output of the steel valves. Therefore even without transistors, whose roots are German, it would have been possible to meet the demands of electronic guidance to equip the 'weapons of victory'. It is certainly true that the first electro-mechanical guidance systems available to the Germans, such as the gyro devices of the *Vertikant* type, were not sufficiently accurate for long-range rockets. But it is forgotten (perhaps deliberately) that:

(a) work was proceeding on the improved models (Sg66 and Sg70)
(b) the gyro equipment could be assisted by radio or radar signals so that variables in inertial steering could be adjusted by suitable radio impulses and so an adequate technology of flight tracking and rocket/missile calibration already existed.

## C. "View Over the Horizon" – Eyes and Ears for Hitler's Miracle Weapons

### "Where is the Thing Headed?" Flight calibration and tracking – was it possible by the war's end?

In order to judge the chances of success of Hitler's rockets and missiles, one must determine the extent to which individual flight phases to the target could be exactly measured, tracked and if possible remote-controlled. In the spring of 1944 the situation at the beginning of the V-1 campaign was that remote control was still unavailable. Initially reliance was placed on the report of agents in London as to where flying bombs dropped and what effect they caused. In principle there were two ways to obtain more precise measurements: from aerial observation and ground radar.

*Aerial Observation*

Once Ar 234B jet reconnaissance machines became operational from August 1944, almost routine flights over England became possible once more, since these aircraft could outfly any Allied fighter. Two units, *Hecht* and *Sperrling*, operated regularly over the Western Front mostly at altitudes in excess of 10,000 metres and besides the usual strategic reconnaissance flew a number of V-2 calibration flights. The Ar 234 clocks were synchronized with the rocket battery and five minutes before every salvo the pilot circling over the target area received a radio warning and prepared to photograph the impact site. The pilots were probably not very impressed by V-2 accuracy: one of them reported a miss of 12 kilometres.[80] This kind of calibration flight was also tried out over Antwerp. V-2 reconnaissance flights by Ar 234 jets over London continued into 1945. An examination of the damage inflicted was the main purpose of these missions.

*Noise Measurement*

A ground control procedure employed in the attempt to obtain results was sound measurement. Acoustic methods were used by the Luftwaffe, Kriegsmarine and SS. The technique developed by the SS was based on the earthing of indirect sound waves (the other side of the dead area) which yielded measurements over a range of 300 kilometres. For this purpose *SS-Hauptsturmführer* Richter was transferred to France with his specially equipped sound monitoring team. The disadvantage of the procedure was that it required the setting up of a comprehensive support network. To what extent it was used operationally is not known, although the rocket silos at Watten and Wizernes had a special rocket observation station at Prédefin which beside radar equipment (see below) also had sound measuring installations.[81] Furthermore a chain of seismic underwater microphones was laid along the Channel coast for the sound measurement of V-1 and V-2 explosions.[82]

***Locating Devices***

In the summer of 1944 the first plotting devices were introduced when models of the FuG 23 set manufactured by the firm TKD were fitted into ten Fi 103 flying bombs. The equipment, which operated on the 345-500 KHz frequency, switched itself on 55 kilometres from the target and transmitted signals. The idea was to plot the impact location and so calculate adjustments for subsequent V-1 firings. The results achieved were poor because the cut-off point plotted by the ground stations differed from the actual point of impact. The reason here was that the V-1 was an unpiloted aircraft and did not possess a ballistic trajectory like a shell. Once it began to lose altitude it tended to follow a kilometre-wide descent path. Moreover the British discovered how to jam the FuG 23 signal relatively quickly. The anti-jamming ultra short wave transmitters requested by the firing batteries in December 1943 were not developed in time. By the war's end equipment for the remote control of the V-1 and other missiles invulnerable to jamming had been developed and was manufactured in a small series run (see appropriate chapter). While such precision devices were not available for the V-1 until 1945, the V-2 received them in 1944.

***Radar Control***

A further stage was so-called distant-search units. The development of these devices began when the Germans discovered that signals from the British 'Home Chain' radar early warning system could occasionally be detected over great distances, e.g. the Black Sea. The researchers established that these great ranges were obtained over the optical horizon by reflection from the ionosphere. By a coincidence, the Research Institute of the German *Reichspost* (investigating nuclear-type explosives, motors and new kinds of U-boat, see Volume 1) was involved in the development of long-range radar. From the documentation it would appear that a *Reichspost* team led by Dr Scholtz produced an improved model, based on the British 12-metre 'Home Chain' radar designated *Heidelberg* and which worked in the 23 MHz band with a regular range of up to 400 kilometres.

The experimental unit was set up 50 metres behind the sea wall at Nes on the Dutch coast in the spring of 1942. A later conversion worked on the 20-metre frequency. No information is available other than that *Heidelberg* was used to observe V-2 flights. All documents, drawings and maps have disappeared mysteriously, and only a single hand-drawn sketch of the system survives.[83, 84]

It is known that the *Reichspost* manufactured two other models, *Elefant* and *See-Elefant*. The *Elefant* transmitter used a fixed 90-metre mast with antenna. For receiving and maximum search a revolvable Wassermann-M-IV mast was erected with six horizontal dipole lines. Until now very few *Elefant* installations are known, one being at location *Max und Moritz* on the Dutch coast. From the end of August 1944 in typical weather conditions for long range search, a convoy could be plotted near Jan Mayen island 2200 kilometres away. *Elefant* was thus the world's first supra-horizon radar although obtaining maximum range depended on temperature and other factors.

One month later the deteriorating war situation compelled the dismantling and removal of the equipment, the opportunity being taken to implement modifications before re-erection on the island of Röm, western Denmark. The system was now called *See Elefant* and worked on the 23 and 28 MHz range with broad band aerials. The sets worked in the 25-29 MHz, 24-30 NHz and 30-38 MHz bands. The transmitter aerial was stretched between two 100-metre tall fixed masts, the transmitter itself being located in the equipment room of an independent *Mammut* radar station below. Revolvable 70-metre high *Wassermann* masts with eight horizontal dipole lines one above the other performed the beam and receptor function independently of each other. These masts were sited a kilometre distant north-west and south-east of the home station. The initial range for measurements was 400 kilometres increased tenfold, the distance between England and America, two months later.

This and other supra-horizon radars were used primarily to register V-1 and V-2 hits on London at 800 kilometres range. Rockets in the final phase of their trajectory were easy to spot at this distance and could be accurately tracked. Following the loss of the launch sites on the Channel coast, they were also used to track the aircraft of 3/KG 53 and 1/KG3 which approached the English coast at low level, ascended at a pre-determined point and released the V-1s they carried. A second *See-Elefant* unit at Norddeich was destroyed by flooding before completion. A descriptive paper gives the range of the *See-Elefant* system as being accurate to plus or minus one to two kilometres, the lateral accuracy plus/minus 5°, later reduced to 1°. Tracking at altitude and identity tagging were not planned but might have been possible as additions. This is important in that with such additional measurements not only was precise position fixing possible but also actual guidance over long distances. It would therefore be interesting to ascertain if the installations were so equipped later or if other *See-Elefant* systems had them. The mysterious absence of paperwork from the files is a serious hindrance here. Another of the locations for See-Elefant may have been *V-Waffen Gaustad* in Norway. It can be shown that identity-tagging was planned for another new long-range rocket radar, the so-called *Freya-Lang-Latte* based on an earlier Gema-research model, *Leibniz*, a smaller version of the *Mammut* system with a very promising degree of accuracy. This revolutionary system was fully mobile and used a Lange-Latte aerial consisting of a 3.6 x 1.8 metre frame and horizontal polarized broad-band dipoles. The *Frega LZ* radar which worked on the *Vollwismar 2* band was used as transmitter and platform. Fast tracking and course determination was to follow with the new *Blaustrumpf* system, this being the pre-condition for remote control of rockets after launch.

*Freya-Lang-Latte* was a mobile system which could be set up near the launch site. It required three aerials (transmitting aerials I and II and a receiving aerial), a generator lorry and the *Freya* transmitter and receiver. The various aerials were erected 30 metres apart. The difficult war situation allowed the production of few *Lang-Latte* installations. It is known that procedures of this kind were to be used for control in the start phase of the A-4B. The rocket would be identity-tagged with the aid of a shipboard *Erstling* set which released an answering impulse upon receipt of the appropriate signal. The two aerials mentioned served as an interferometer or locating installation for the accurate measurement of change in angles, either by the difference in time taken for a signal to reach the aerial or by phase differences. The latter was more precise. The data was then used for course corrections. For after-control a version of the *Egon* procedure was used for the A-4B. By October 1943 so great an accuracy had been achieved by this method that bombs remote-released from an aircraft at a range of 105 kilometres would fall within 600 metres of the target. It is not known to what extent this had been improved by 1945 and how close to the target a rocket would fall, although for the use of a WMD the October 1943 standard of accuracy would have been sufficient.

The advantage of the *Freya-Erstling* method was that all components were ready for use and needed only to be fitted, but the supply of the sets lagged because the radio industry could not turn out the numbers demanded: particularly in the last year of the war, during the retreat from Russia, nearly all German Army radio equipment was lost and had to be replaced; the assembly plants had to be relocated towards the heart of the Reich from the East, where they had once seemed safe, and this led naturally to reductions in manufacturing output. Emergency programmes were begun which were limited in effect because the transport system had become paralyzed.

In 1944 the *Hawai-II* system was introduced for post-launch measurements and guidance of the A-4 in the start phase. This was a mobile system using a modified *Würzburg-Riese* type radar installatrion (53-cm frequency) and used a similar principle to *Lang-Latte* except that in the rocket a *Messina* transponder was linked up to a *Capri* ranging radar and a *Palermo* command transmitter. These had been developed by the Dresden Technical University in collaboration with several radio and telephone manufacturers and were in series production. It was hoped to achieve accuracy within 500

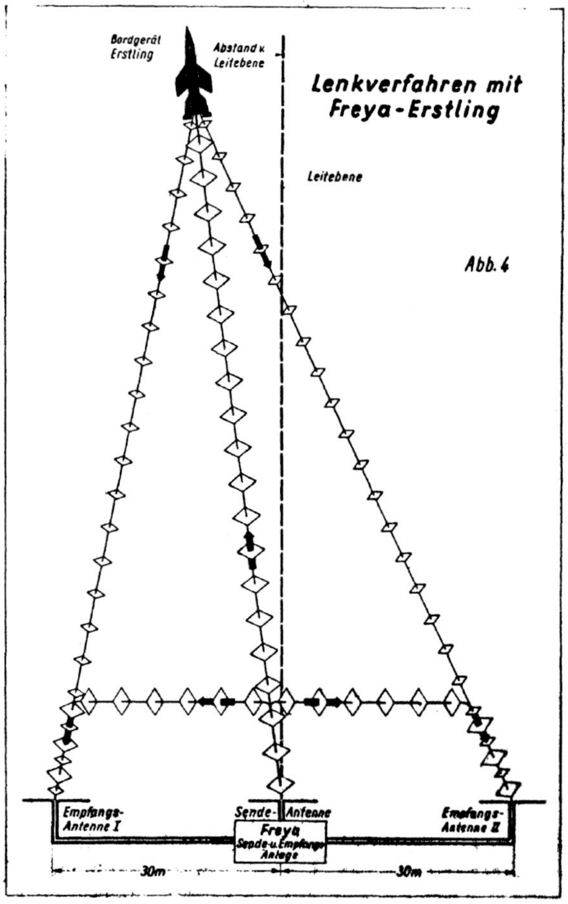


The proof that the A-4/A-9 had radar-guidance. The "Freya-Langlatte/Erstling" guidance system. (Source: Deutsches Museum, Munich)

B 29/45

The "Freya" installation at the launch point. (Source: Deutsches Museum, Munich)

B 30/45

metres of a target at 250 kilometres range. The *Messina* system was envisaged amongst others for the FK-railway batteries (See Volume 2).

It may be inferred accordingly that by the war's end rocket flights over distances up to 4,000 kilometres could be measured and plotted, and promising radar-guidance procedures had been developed for the A-4, A-4B, A9/10 and A-11(?). Technology at that stage would have enabled rockets and missiles to have been tracked over the greater part of their flights in favourable atmospheric conditions, and it follows that such launches and flights only took place in the right weather. Reliable weather reporting along the planned flight route and in the target area was therefore essential.

As in 1944 in its beginnings, early warning radars were sued to detect incoming rockets and missiles. To the end of the Cold War, the USSR had the most efficient system against any such attack, incorporating principally supra-horizon radars(!) and numerous phase-modulated 'Hen House' radar sites along the then Soviet borders.[85] These very modern radar systems are in a certain sense the offspring of the German systems of 1944/1945.

## "Hit?" The problem of guidance in early rockets and missiles

Nowadays guided weapons can be homed in to hit an individual chimney or an airshaft hundreds of miles distant. In the 1940s, in the birth phase of rockets and missiles, it was of course rather different. A V-1 or V-2 lacking a guidance system plummeted to earth up to 15 kilometres from the intended impact point at the end of its flight. In the case of the notoriously inaccurate Fi 103, a strong wind was enough to blow the flying bomb off course. Naturally although the dispersal of the V-1 and V-2 was much less over shorter distances, it was not accurate enough even for a WMD warhead.

Special problems attend the guidance of rockets. Simply put, without a properly functioning guidance mechanism a rocket is much the same as an artillery shell which can only be 'guided' by the angle of the gun barrel upon firing. There are two rocket types: aerodynamic and ballistic. Aerodynamic rockets fly in the atmosphere, behave similarly to unpiloted aircraft and are steered by a mechanism similar in principle to an auto-pilot. Ballistic rockets spend only a fairly brief period of their flight in the atmosphere. These will normally be giant rockets reaching enormous altitudes. Contrary to aerodynamic rockets which can be and need to be corrected during flight, ballistic rockets require controlling only during the initial phase. Once outside the Earth's atmosphere they are immune to disturbance by wind and air layers so that only immediately after launch is a control system necessary to maintain the rocket on its precise course to the target: by the latest at 40-50 kilometres altitude the aerodynamic rudders have no effect and the jet vanes are long burnt away. The only possibility to influence the ballistics of the remaining part of the flight is additional separate rocket motors for guidance. Whether such attempts were ever tried by the Germans is not known.

The A-4B, A-9 and A9/10 were hybrids between aerodynamic and ballistic rockets to which supersonic wings were fitted so that before re-entry into the Earth's atmosphere the rocket would skip rather like a flat stone hurled in a low trajectory over the surface of a lake. This had the advantage of so interfering with teh rocket's ballistic curve that an adjustment was also necessary during the relatively long descent, and in 1944/1945 attempts were made to resolve this apparently almost insoluble problem.

### *Remote Control*

In the case of the V-2, *SS-Werferabteilung* 500 fired rockets of ever-increasing accuracy with the help of radar-supported remotes in the 50 MHz band from the beginning of October 1944. For the last attacks the V-2s were fitted with the Victoria Remote Control device using two overlapping transmitters whose beams were received by two dipoles either side of the exhaust jet. 'Remote controlled' rockets are distinguished from standard rockets for this reason. A disadvantage of the system was that the two Opel Blitz radio vans fitted with the transmitters had to be located well away from the launch platform and set up in a very involved procedure at the same height above sea level as the firing point. In the unfavourable military situation the necessity for ever more frequent changes of firing point meant that the remote control procedure was not often used.[86] In 1945 in Holland fixed transmitters were used hidden in innocuous civilian buildings. When the Rhine bridge at Remagen fell undamaged into American hands, *SS-Werferabt.500* was ordered to demolish it with V-2 rockets. Previously the German frontline around the bridgehead had been pulled back a few kilometres which might suggest the intended use of a dangerous warhead for the Remagen V-2s, although finally only HE was used. It was a remarkable achievement for March 1945 that remote-controlled V-2s launched from a mobile platform 130 miles away should land within 300 metres of the bridge, and the results were not surpassed for many years subsequently.

The bombardment of the bridge at Remagen using eleven remote-controlled V-2s was a great success. On 17 March 1945 two earth-shattering near misses at 0930 and 1220 resulted in the weakened structure collapsing into the Rhine at 1500. Next day Hitler sent a message to *SS-Werferabt.500* congratulating them on their destruction of the Ludendorff bridge at Remagen.[88]

If the rocket silos at Watten, Wizernes (V-2) and Siracourt (V-1) had fired, they would have been directed from the Prédefin radar bunker. The mysterious silo at Wizernes had its own extra control centre at Roquetoire.[87]

Possibly during operations in 1944 an attempt was made to correct the flight of a few V-1s from the air. Allied sources reported that the nightly salvoes on Antwerp were supported by specially equipped He 111 bombers which appeared over the city at the same time as the V-1s. It was said that the aircraft steered the V-1 to the target by means of a strong radio beam and when over the city instructed the engine to shut down and so activate the descent mechanism at the right moment.[89] No German documents or photographs have been discovered to date, but it is known that in November 1943 at Peenemünde attempts were made to guide the V-1 with improved director

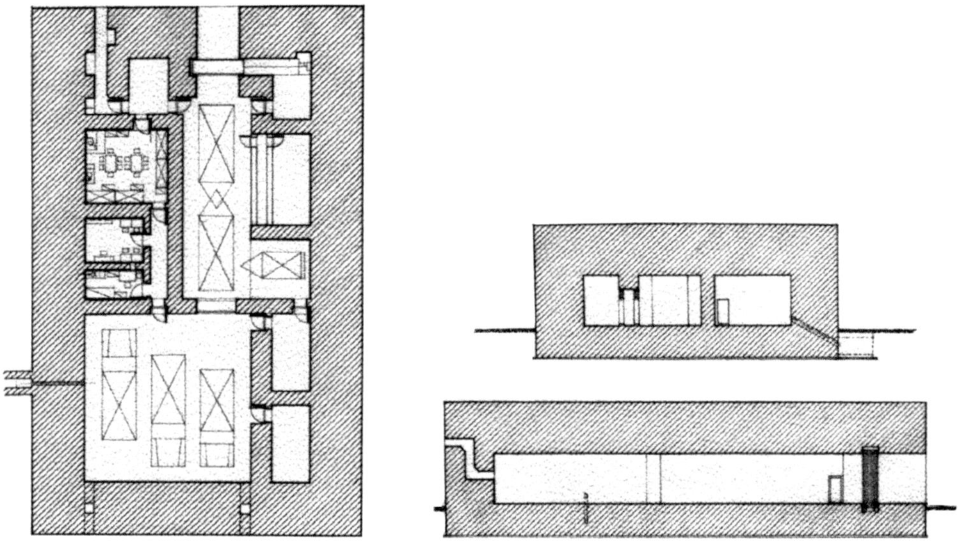

Director-beam bunker at Roquetoire (Source: IBA)

equipment aboard an He 111 H-6.[90] Possibly this method or a modification was used later on operations.

The French scientist and journalist Albert Ducrocq wrote in his book *Les armes secretès allemandes* (p.123) that Ju 388 reconnaissance aircraft cruising at 13,000 metres were there to guide the V-1 and V-2 to their targets under radar control. The Ju 388 was not used on regular Luftwaffe operations.

***Supra-horizon radio beam installations***

In the autumn of 1941, Telefunken converted the *Knickebein* radio beam installation at Bredstedt (Holstein) into the experimental *Knickebein J* (J=ionosphere) and obtained echoes from up to about 3,000 kilometres or, depending on the season and time of day, up to 10,000 kilometres, while the influence of Milky Way radiations was also noted.[73a] Unfortunately all other measurement results of *Knickebein J* have 'gone missing' together with the reports providing information on the extent to which supra-horizon radio beam installations were developed successfully. A major part of the success of German radar research is known to have been achieved in the last months of the war.

***Target-finders and radio beacons***

Another very promising solution was the development of target-finding apparatus and radio beacons. These methods were suitable for both missiles and rockets (for discussion on developments see Volume 1). The main problem was locating the beacon at the target previously by high speed aircraft or other means (agents, in ports by U-boats, etc). When the beacon was to be dropped from the air, a low level air raid in daylight and good weather would be made on the target, the beacon being concealed in a non-exploding bomb. V-1s or V-2s launched subsequently would home in on the beacon. These devices were codenamed *Steinbock*. It is known that various suitable beacons, even a watertight floating version, were tested at the front form March 1945 onwards, but then used in another connection.

***Radio direction for the V-1***

In the autumn of 1944, OKL issued a contract to DFS to develop a land-based method of improving V-1 accuracy.

Director-beam installation, Knickebein J (J=ionosphere), 1941. (Source: Trenckle)

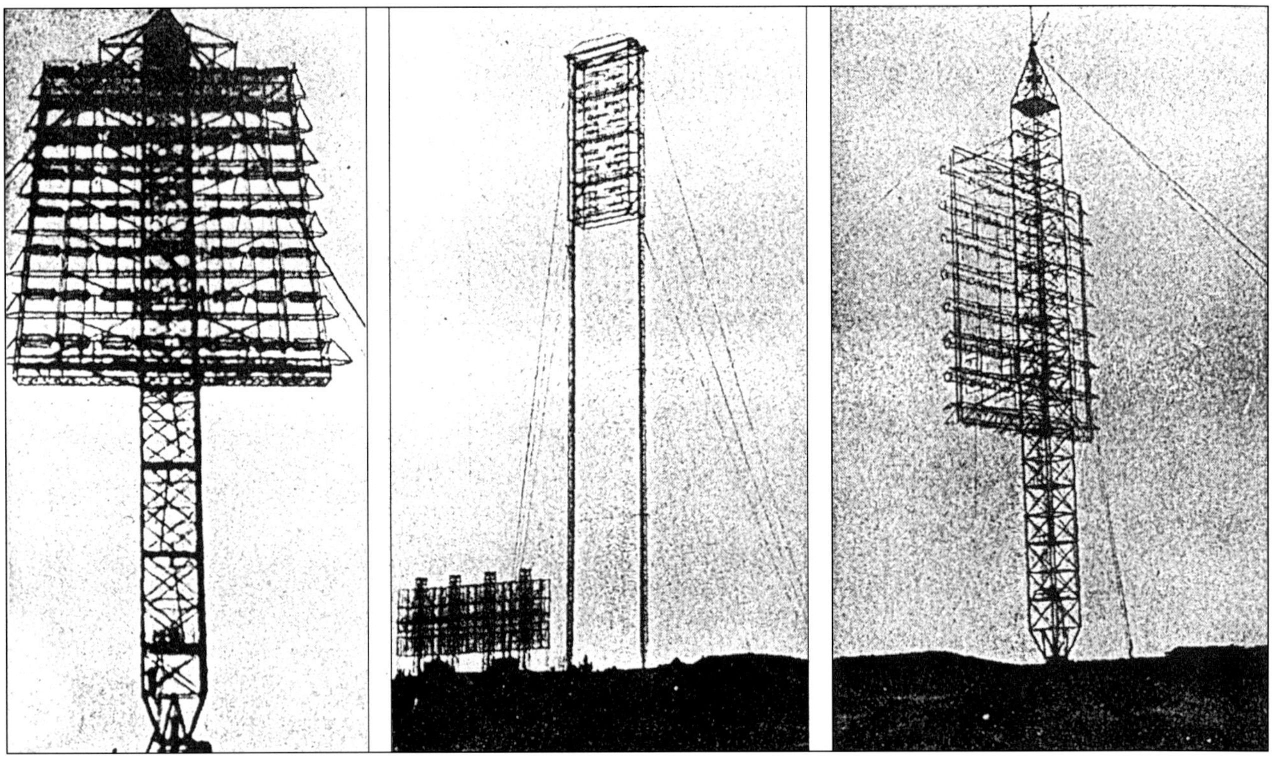

Left locating tower < - > (1 km distant) < - > free-standing transmitting aerial < - > (1 km distant) right locating tower. Supra-horizon radar *See-Elefant* at site 'Robbe' on the Danish island of Röm for tracking and range estimation of rocket and guided missile hits. (Source: Trenckle)

This resulted in the tracking procedure *Ewald II* and the radio direction unit *Sauerkirsch II.* One central and two other tracking stations were planned to send correcting signals to Fi 103 radio and command receivers. Using this method, every V-1 needed to be tracked only once and received a single correcting signal. The first experimental sets and subsequently a series were built by the Institute of Professor Eduard Fischel. The guidance method was tried out first with an aircraft. Additional tracking station were built near Ainring in 1945 and were ready for operations, but flight trials were not possible so close to the termination of hostilities.[91]

Ultimately guidance systems were built by which the missile could be directed by radio from a safe distance: an auto-pilot guidance or automatic target approach was also tried. In order not to overwhelm German radio equipment manufacturers, 200 such transmitters were ordered in 1942 from the Paris firm SADIR-Carpentier to be completed under German supervision in the Les Puteaux factory, but these were never ready in time for operations. Even today that type of radio signal is not absolutely reliable since over long distances it may wander and guidance orders will not be transmitted correctly. All director methods using radio signals run the risk of enemy disruption.TV cameras

Direct guidance using small TV cameras was also tried. Telefunken, Blaupunkt, Siemens, BHF, IFPF and Fernseh Berlin GmbH worked on systems with a range of 200 miles. A 10 kg TV camera codenamed *Sprotte* was developed, run by a dynamo-propellor at the nose of the missile. By the capitulation the range of the equipment had been increased to 60 miles (over water) but six months were still needed before mass production.[92] Quartz clocks were used to sychronize between transmitter and receiver to prevent enemy interference with signals.

### *I-Equipment*

From December 1944 onwards a new system , the Buchhold electrolite I-Equipment (intergration-acceleration radar) was introduced of which Siemens rushed out 5,000 units. Dr Dornberger estimated that from December 1944 onwards about 60% of all A-4s fired were fitted with this distance control.[93] (The Rex film theatre was said to have been hit by a V-2 equipped with the 'I-Gerät').

### *Inertial navigation*

Before the end of the war the Germans had introduced inertial navigation systems for rockets and missiles.[94, 95] These completely independent guidance systems are ideal for intercontinental rockets and missiles and are in use today. At a meeting of the SEP (*Societé Européenne de Propulsion)* in Vernon in 1992, former Peenemünde engineers disclosed that in the last months of the war an inertial navigation system known as *Trägheitszentrale* (Inertial Centre) had been fitted aboard V-2s. It consisted of a stabilized platform with three gyroscopes, one or two longitudinal and one transversal accelerometer, the structure being isolated from other fitments in the rocket. Known as Type Sg 70, the unit could be combined with the so-called *Bordnetz 4* I-Equipment to provide extremely high accuracy without ground radio assistance. These rockets were recognizable outwardly by having selector plugs below the rudders instead of alongside. Rockets so equipped were flight tested at the end of 1944.

### *Astro-navigation*

A further development of inertial navigation also independent of ground control, astro-navigation made possible post-launch course corrections which were of special importance for long-range rocketry. Since accuracy decreased the longer the flight time, this system checked and corrected the course by measuring the azimuth and altitude angle of certain stars.[96] According to the American researcher William R Lyne an astronavigation system would have been fitted to V-2 type rockets carrying a WMD.[97]

In the spring of 1945 General Patton came across 200 completed V-2 stored in a cavern at a salt mine. Upon informing his superiors, contrary to his expectation to ship the important find to the United States, he was astonished to receive orders to destroy them all and preserve nothing. It remains a mystery to this day what motive lay behind this 'crazy' decision.

It is not known how far the Germans had advanced in the fitting and testing of astronavigation equipment to rockets and missiles. In the autumn of 1944 a similar unit built by Dr Raumbuske at the Bayreuth Institute for Physcis Research was tested successfully when a motor launch sailed a complicated course on the Madu-See in Pomeria using the device. One of the final aims for the unit was to use it aboard the V-1.[98] William Lyne has an early example of a German astronavigation-inertial guidance box in his possession bearing the manufacturer's date 1943. This appear to have been a manually operated version of an automated system for rockets and missiles.[99]

On 10 April 1945 the Allied USFET Command at Franfurt was surprised to receive news of the arrival from Washington of a team from the Bulova watch company headed by its managing director Arde Bulova.[100] This civilian gentleman had been briefed previously by General Carl A Spaatz and other USAF generals. In Germany Bulova recruited an unknown number of specialists to be brought to the United States under military supervision for the '*Paperclip*' project. It is known that at least one of these specialists "worked on material later used by Bulova for research in long-range celestial navigation."

The first American long-distance flight by day using inertial navigation took place on 14 November 1956 when a long-range intercontinental missile of the Northrup *Snark* type was successfully tested with such a unit aboard. With the exception of inertial navigation, the best method for the guidance of 'miracle weapons' was probably a combination of flight direction and target seeking in which the flight was controlled by beam or radio commands. The target-seeking equipment then operated in the vicinity of the target.

### *Manual Operation*

There was one other method, primitive in comparison with the progressive electronic, mechanical and electrical developments to improve the accuracy of German rockets and missiles: the use of volunteer airmen to take manual control during the end phase of flight and steer the projectile precisely to the target. Hand-steered kamikaze versions of the V-1, A-4B and A9/10 are known. The advantage over having the complicated technical equipment was that a long development period could be dispensed with, the only necessity being to train the pilot. The disadvantage was a certain dependency on the weather, good meteorological visibility being required to guarantee success.

Would the pilot survive the start phase long enough to take control of the projectile over the target area? Besides gigantic acceleration forces and the heat on re-entry a multitude of space-medical factors worked on the volunteer in his narrow cabin behind the warhead. There is a photograph dating from the last months of the war showing a pilot wearing a pressure suit in the cockpit of a delta-winged aircraft with plexiglass hood. These 'aircrew combinations' are very similar to the space-suits of the postwar era.

On 20 October 1945, USAF chief General Arnold told the *Washington Post* that the V-2, perfected with wings and electronic equipment, could fly over 3,000 miles, and at 2,000 miles would hit the target 'on the button'.[101] From that it may be assumed that as regards the problems of inaccuracy and lack of tracking ability in flight, the Germans had either been on the verge of solving them or they appeared to have practically solved them in some systems so that despite the desperate war situation, tests of an operational nature could be ventured.[102]

## D. "Everything ready?" How far were the practical preparations advanced for the rocket attack on New York? V-Stelle Gaustad

In May 1945 on the peak of the 5,000-feet high Gaustad mountain very difficult of access, technicians of the British 21st Army Corps in southern Norway found a gigantic German 'weather station' equipped with comprehensive radar systems and radio transmitters of the greatest efficiency. This was the notorious *V-Stelle Gaustad*, rumours of which had filtered through to London in 1944. According to a 1946 publication this construction was the greatest and most expensive radio installation abandoned by the Germans. Its purpose, according to Allied specialists, was the transmission of transatlantic radio signals and the telecontrol of flying bombs on long-range flights.[103] Thus the telecontrol of transatlantic weapons systems was ready at the war's end. The exact details of Gaustad remain classified.[104]

## Controlled rocket flight over the Atlantic

In order to avoid risking blind shots to America, the A9/10 was equipped with radio guidance linked in flight by position checks with U-boats[105], the equipment being waterproof and pressure-proof remote control units (*Hawaii, Zirkel*, etc) installed on the U-boat after casing.[106] The signals would regulate the LS *Victoria* receivers on baord the A-9. It is probable that the Russians either captured or copied parts of this sea guidance system (and guidance ships) postwar. It is known that the firms GEMA and Siemens completed work on the newest long-rage rocket guidance systems after the war for the occupying forces. The Soviets then used them to remote guide their copied versions of EMW rockets over the Baltic. This shows that the system functioned operationally.

The original goal of the development was to track the rocket to impact. As tests did not provide optimism that adequate tracking accuracy was to be expected from the longest frequencies possible technically, tracking was limited to the horizon (200-250 kms). This would have made it necessary to station U-boats at stages at prepared waiting positions in the North Atlantic in order to carry out the guidance function.

Could this system have worked having regard to the failure of the U-boat War? Keeping to snorkel depth between base and taking up the waiting position, U-boats would have had to surface at the appropriate time after receiving the command to do so through the *Kondor* underwater receiver. This would have been hazardous because of the numerous Allied U-boat hunter-killer groups. If the A-10 bombardment of New York had occurred by night – which is probable – the problem would have been of lesser importance.

Information given by German PoWs to the Americans during interrogation included reference to statements between Hitler, Himmler and the No 1 General Staff Officer XIII SS-Corps in October 1944 regarding the necessity of a 24-hour period of air supremacy over the Atlantic before the operation of the miracle weapon. Beforehand U-boats operating the remote-control facility would not have been at liberty to wander off the spot.

In this connection, on 23 March 1945 Hitler ordered the completion and testing of the 4-motor all-weather long-range reconnaissance Do 335Z with all urgency. From Germany this aircraft could fly at 725 km/hr and had a range of 7,400 kilometres for cooperation with U-boats. Historians consider Hitler's request for the fast Atlantic reconnaissance aircraft with 'America range' so shortly before the war's end as a symptom of his madness, but with high probability the whole thing was perfectly reasonable …

German mastery of the air over the Atlantic in 1945, even for 24 hours, was no more likely than over the continent, and the fuelled-up rocket was extremely vulnerable to air attack during 'countdown'. In view of the desperate war situation were they prepared to risk the possible destruction of the rocket? Here one must investigate whether German U-boats were in waiting positions and awaiting orders along the route to the American coast. It is interesting to note postwar that in 1946 two converted radar-monitor submarines, USS *Spinax* and USS *Requin*, similar conversions to the German idea, could direct the V-1 copy *Loon*.

For the last phase of the flight, three possibilities existed depending on the version of the A-9 used: either a U-boat would have been stationed at the enemy coast to beam the unmanned rocket to its target or a beacon would have been installed there beforehand to home in the rocket or the third alternative was the use of a manned A-9p in which the pilot would disconnect the automatic steering unit and take over the manual controls once he sighted the target. For this flight the A-9 'astronaut' would have had aids in the form of a cartographic radar system and a course gyro installation. Provided he had survived all the perils of rocket flight, he would now have been in a position to steer the rocket precisely to the target. At 4,000 kilometres altitude at the earliest he could have ejected. At this point however the A-9 would have been in so precipitous a descent that he would have had little chance of coming through.

## The hidden influence of German guidance methods postwar

By the war's end the last German rockets and cruise missiles were capable of hitting with great accuracy and it is not very surprising that radio and radar masts had been erected in Norway and perhaps Greenland to guide these weapons over the Atlantic to America. This was described earlier. Until today moreover nobody has made the point that the Americans and Russians in the 1940s and 1950s had the same guidance systems for their own long-range weapons. Was this parallel development or did the victors appropriate the technology?

The deported German scientist Tellmann, a person whom much mystery surrounds and who, as a scientist in the postwar USSR reported on Russian attempts in 1947 and 1948 in which rockets were fired from the Leningrad/Kronstadt area and were directed during flight by radio and radar signals from control ship sin the Baltic. Over the target the flight would be intercepted by a radar centre and terminated by pushing a button. The rocket would then descent vertically and hit almost precisely on the determined spot. Tellmann's account corresponds to the procedures planned for the A-4B and A-9. Later he learned in conversation with German colleagues that an acceptable degree of accuracy was possible over a range of 2500 kilometres. For these tests the rockets were fired from Leningrad to the huge rocket testing grounds at Omsk.[107] Thus the Russians were working on radar and radio guidance for rockets and missiles, and everything they tried out in 1947/48 was most certainly based on German designs which must have been complete or nearly so at the war's end. All of which confirms that Germany's last developments of the war, whether rockets or missiles, had great accuracy.

In the West it was the same story: official USAF spokesmen confirm that the first *Atlas* intercontinental rockets of the A-C (and early D) versions, and the *Titan-I* were equipped with 'radio inertial guidance' or 'radio guidance' control systems. The Americans and the Soviets thus shared a common technology which is unlikely to have been coincidental. The

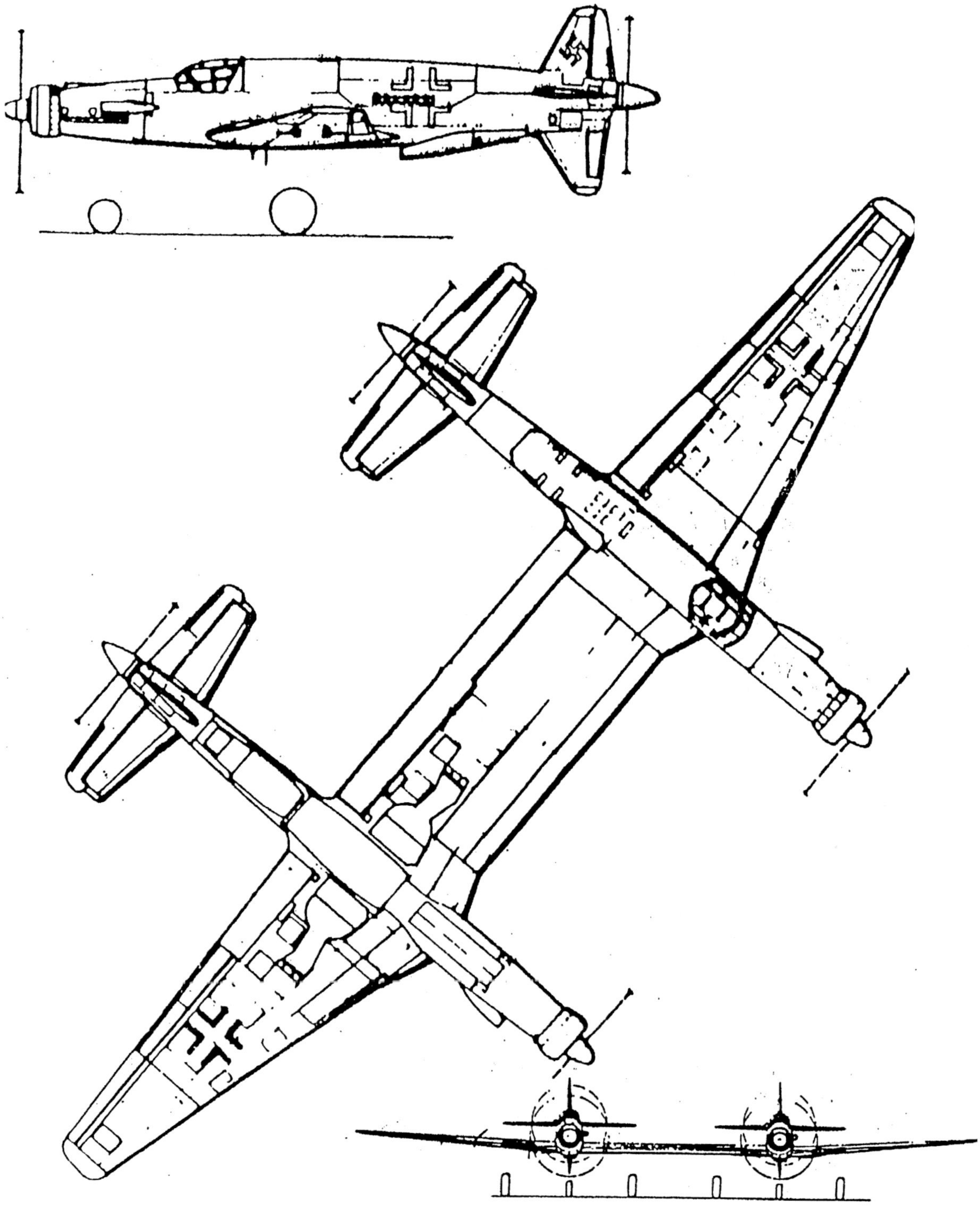

Dornier Do–335 Z long range fast reconnaissance aircraft. (Toad).

At a time when the Western Allies had already crossed the Rhine and the Soviets were preparing to launch their final offensive towards Berlin from the Oder, Hitler ordered the immediate production of a small series of Do–335–Z high performance long-range reconnaissance aircraft to work together with U-boats. Within a month fifteen Do 335 night fighters were to be converted to the new version. In April 1945, FAGr 5 was to begin long range missions over the Atlantic as far as the US coast from Lechberg or Neubiberg. It is clear that there was by then no intention to pursue the aims of the U-boat War, but the Do 335-Z could have been important in supporting miracle weapon attacks against the USA by V-1, V-2 and U-boats fitted with Ursel rocket batteries as well as those with radio-beam and guidance equipment. The plan was abandoned on 24 April 1945 for the shortage of available Do–335s. Whereas some of the machines might have been lost to war causes, it is surprising that none of the machines made available by Dornier for conversion could ever be found.

S E C R E T

PW INTELLIGENCE BULLETIN No 2/32

13. Fantasia, German Secret Weapons

Preamble. The following stories are from sources of doubtful reliability and may well be pure products of the imagination. However, in view of the striking similarity between them, they are printed for what they are worth.

First Story

Around 15 Sept 44, CP of 1127 Gren Regt 559 Inf Div was in REINANGE at GSGS 4416/U1/912797. It was a warm, sunny day, with a few scattered clouds and no wind. At about 1600 PW was standing near the church in REINANGE and observed a formation of Allied aircraft pass, flying from SW to NE, low enough to be recognized as four-motored planes. He counted up to 30 planes. They were flying in close formation.

While PW watched them pass by, he saw what he believed to be a small fighter plane (grey color, no identification marks) climb and approach the Allied formation from an easterly direction. PW states that the "fighter plane" was flying at an abnormally high speed and that it penetrated into the midst of the formation apparently without being fired at. Suddenly there appeared, where the "fighter plane" had been before, a red ball of fire, somewhat larger than the plane itself. A split second later, the ball of fire turned into a rapidly expanding red circle (parallel to the ground). This circle was bluish-red at its edge, and as its diameter increased, the interior of the circle became an empty space. As the circle enveloped the planes, they seemed to just disappear. In a matter of seconds the entire formation of Allied planes had disappeared, and the sky was just as it had been before.

PW discussed the incident with several others who had witnessed it, including a Hptm of 1559 Arty Regt. This officer (who was subsequently killed) told him that the "fighter plane" in question was a wooden miniature plane with a speed of over 1000 km per hour and which was operated by remote control. The name of the plane is KOMET. The Hptm told him that he had lived near an airfield where such planes were tested and that he had recognized it at once.

(Source: Werner LUTMER, Uffz. HQ 1127 Gren Regt)

HITLER's Plans. About 10 Oct 44, the CP of 1127 Gren Regt was visited by the 1st general staff officer (I-a?) of XIII SS Corps (an Oberstlt, name unknown). PW talked for about 10 to 15 minutes to this officer's driver, a Rottenfuehrer, who told him the following:

He, the Rottenfuehrer, had overheard a conversation between the general staff officer and HITLER and HIMMLER, who had visited the XIII SS Corps HQ a few days before. During the conversation he had overheard HITLER say that "the new secret weapon" would not be employed until a 24 hour mastery of the air and sea could be guaranteed. HIMMLER is supposed to have added that another prerequisite was a temperature of 10 degrees below 0.

(Source: ibid)

Extract from a US secret document declassified in 1998. According to a German PoW, Hitler and Himmler conversed with a third party about the necessity for a 24-hour sea and air supremacy as a precondition for the deployment of the miracle weapon. The author of the document labelled the account as a „fantasy" since it stretched his imagination a little too far …

accuracy of the early American rockets was not poor: they had a CEP (Circular Error Probability) of only two kilometres.

The radio/radar guidance systems tested by the Russians in 1947/48 for their rockets and missiles were undoubtedly based on German technology and the same goes for the American *Atlas* and *Titan* rockets. In 1944/45 the Germans had the technology with which to guide a rocket to its target up to 5,500 kilometres distant with a reasonable certainty of hitting it. The radio/radar control had serious drawbacks, being a system which would have been operational over a longish period of time, the signals of which an enemy would have been bound to discover how to jam eventually. If the weapon could have compelled the enemy to sue for peace within a month, the risk would not have been so great.

The first *Atlas* and *Titan* rockets had guidance systems but a number of important ideas were copied directly from the German files, although these are explained away today as 'further developments'. Two examples here are the American Convair MX-774 rocket, often identified today as 'the first true American rocket'. In 1947/48 the Americans came up with certain new ideas which had occurred to them allegedly independent of German technicians and files such as swivel-jets and unique high-pressure fuel tanks with extremely thin leak-proof walls. These were the so-called 'Steel Balloon Tanks' which stabilized the rocket by the fuel pressure. This saved weight without recourse to changing structural elements of the fuselage. Jan Karel Bossart is credited as the inventor of these inflatable fuel tanks today and the whole story can be viewed on numerous websites. It is therefore interesting that the German forced-labour scientist Groettrup in Russian had the same idea, but the Soviets did not have the necessary alloys and metals to realize the concept.

The inflatable fuel tanks, rocket re-entry systems (blunt/pointed rocket noses, cooling or heat-shield) were all almost certainly based on German wartime designs.[108]

## Section 4. Were the long-range rockets ready to fire?

### A. The incredible German plans, tests and preparations for the bombardment of New York with intercontinental rockets in the spring of 1945

#### How would the rockets have been made operational?

The A9/10, 25.8 metres long, 4.3 metres in girth and of 100 tonnes starting weight was far too large and heavy to be erected on a mobile trailer, much less so the A-11. The only possibility for a mobile transport for these giant rockets would have been a specially constructed railway low loader for short distances between the assembly and launch points. At Ebensee the rockets would actually have had to have been brought by rail from the assembly hall to the firing point in the nearby mountains. This idea was not fulfilled by the war's end. The same method was used postwar by the Soviets for their SS-6 rockets.A fixed location was needed for firing off batches of rockets. Mounting and firing these large rockets could be achieved in three ways. The first was simple: the rocket was stood upright underground and transported upright into the firing tower. This was feasible technically. The problems began at the burn stage. The rocket developed 180 tonnes of thrust and the exhaust gases had to be led off. This was a major technical problem but could have been solved with experimental results from the engine test stands. The danger here was that if something went wrong at launch (which happened often enough with the V-2) there might be a calamitous underground reaction involving 9.7 tonnes nitric acid with 2.5 tonnes gas oil and a one tonne warhead – or worse, a WMD.

The second possibility was to move the rocket out of the assembly plant on its side for elevation upright on the start platform. Because of its dimensions it would have been very visible, however, and according to witnesses at the ramp itself a period of two days was required to fuel up the A9/10.

The third possibility was a combination of both methods. The A9/10 would be stored horizontal under moderate protection. Before the start a concrete ceiling would open up and the rocket would be stood upright for fuelling. This method of moderately protected silos was used by the Americans postwar for their intercontinental missiles.

The following methods were employed by the Germans:

*Surface camouflaged positions*

These 'soft' positions were provided at best with moderate protection and relied on perfect camouflage measures. Examples of this can be found at Peenemünde, Rudisleben and Ebensee. Because of Allied air supremacy, it seems likely that the procedure was forced for the presumed A-10 starts in the spring of 1945 at Peenemünde and Rudisleben. Certain deceptions were found suitable: at Peenemünde the launch site looked abandoned, Rudisleben was perfectly camouflaged. Dr Kammler was very fond of rudimentary but effective tricks. The 'New Yorker' orbital rocket stood above ground at Peenemünde in April 1945 if we accept the allegation of US astronaut Gordon Cooper. Ebensee was never ready.

*Concrete rocket silos*

Examples of such underground systems were Watten and Wizernes in France and the 'water-cooled' silo design of the *Salamander Zement* project at Ebensee which also included the firing ramp for the smaller A-4B winged rocket (see Volume 2). Another possibility was the fully bunkered underground silo known for its modern application. According to British scientist Philip Henshall's research, silos for the small *Rheinbote* rockets were under construction along the French Channel coast. The expense of a similar installation for the A9/10 would have been enormous and in some respects technological virgin territory. Kammler was therefore ordered by Hitler to build a firing base for a smaller multi-stage rocket as a model for the later major bunker-silo. The location and state of progress of the project remain unknown. Dr Fiebinger, an engineer who worked on this kind of tunnel and silo construction made his career in the United States postwar: it would be interesting to know where he served his apprenticeship!

## Rocket Silos at Watten and Wizernes (B-21) and the *Regenwurm* installations

In *Hitler's Miracle Weapons Volume 2* the role which the 'special installations' (rocket silos) in France were to have played for the V-1 and V-2 campaigns was reviewed. A comprehensive survey of the gigantic but ultimately vain attempts by the Germans to complete the fixed bases for Hitler's miracle weapons would swell this volum several times over![109, 110] Limiting the considerations to connections between the 'special installations' and the America Rocket programme, we find that there were only two rocket sites in France, at Watten and Wizernes, which could have housed the America Rocket.

The Watten complex was suggested by Oberst Thom on 4 January 1943 following a fact-finding mission the previous month. Work on the bunker in the Eperlecques Wood began in May 1943 and was scheduled to be sufficiently advanced by October 1943 for operations. Watten could easily have housed and fired rockets twice the size of the V-2, so great were its dimensions. After 27 August 1943 and until August 1944, continual heavy air raids checked progress and the silo was still not operational when the Allies overran the area. A great deal concerning the Watten rocket complex remains a mystery, particularly the underground floors inaccessible due to permanent flooding (perhaps for laser or atomic-type experiments?), and the rocket lift system similar to the US *Minuteman* intercontinental rockets.[111] Regarding the peculiarities of structure B-21 at Wizernes mention was made in Volume 2. Construction began in June 1943, a few months after Watten, and terminated in July 1944 when massive air raids turned the access area to the silo into a moonscape. During the war Wizernes was considered a threat to the United States because its openings were oriented exactly along the Great Circle route for New York. Wizernes was the major scheme which Hitler wanted completed at all costs despite the Allied invasion. Even after its capture the Allies were never able to understand completely what exactly had been worked on in the interior of Wizernes.[112]

In Volume 2 it was explained that Organisation Todt was given instructions on 1 June 1944 to build immediately three so-called *Regenwurm* installations. One was to neighbour Wizernes silo, the other two were to be in Normandy at Haut Mesnil (south of Caen) and La Meauffe (north of St Lo.).[90E] Before the invasion the British had identified the latter two as part of the original V-2 organisation, but they were never bombed before the invasion. Afterwards when RAF technical officers looked over the small-scale railway tunnel

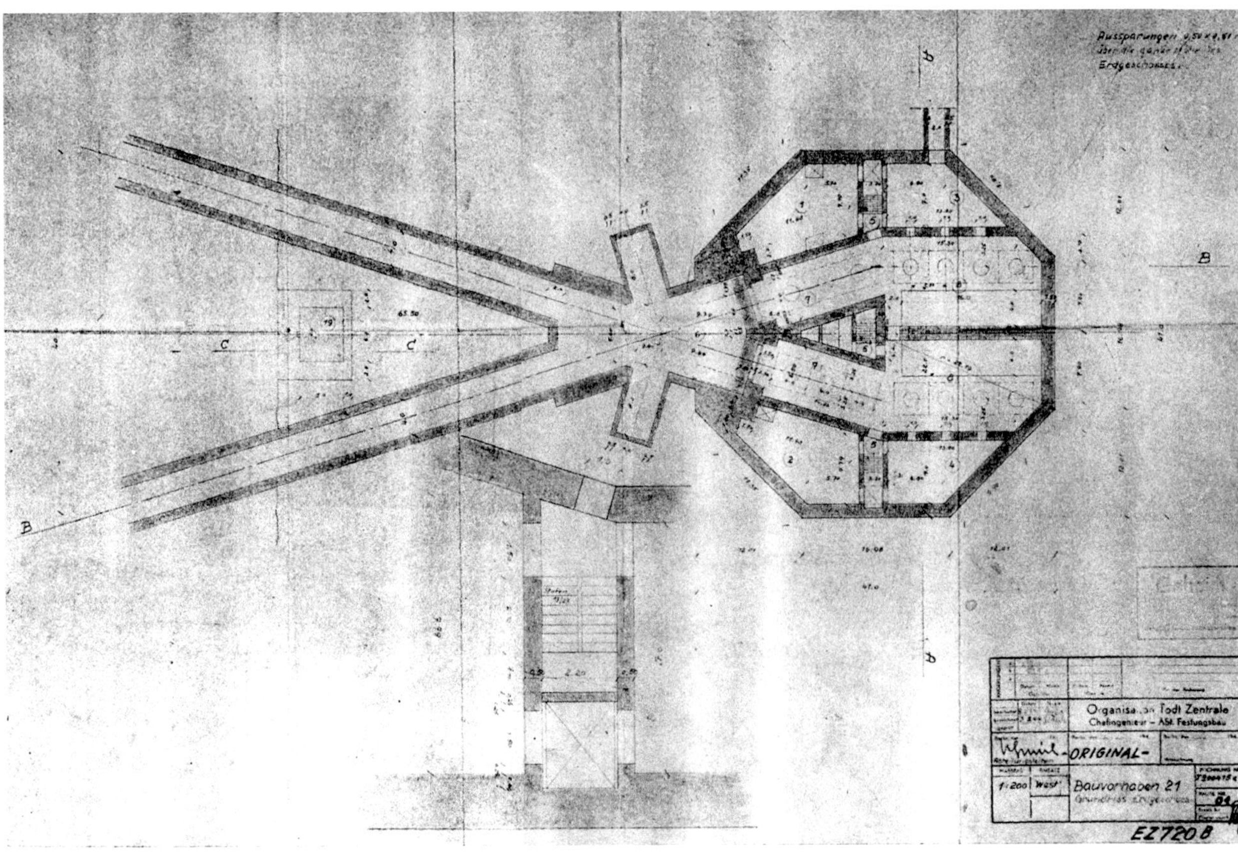


V–2-/A–9-/A-10-rocket silo (B-21) at Wizernes – codename ‚Schotterwerk Nordwest (SNW)'. Although today one of the national monuments of France, its role remains something of a mystery. B-21 was suitable for firing the A-9 and A-10 as well as the V-2. Its orientation is not towards any European target but along the Great Circle route to New York (17° 30'). After the war, former Armaments Minister Albert Speer described this as a "coincidence"!

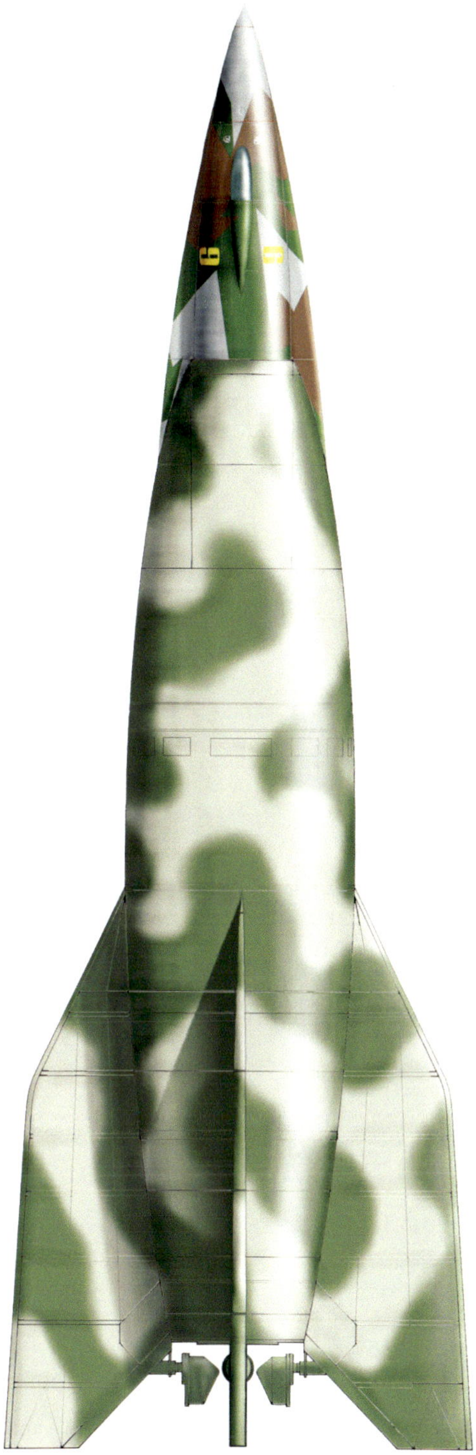

A–9P/A–10 (early manned version, Peenemünde March 1945), colour scheme: A–10: RLM grey/white 1945 on RAL 6003; A–9A: splinter scheme RLM 81/82/74. (Graphics: Igor A. Shestakov)

A–9/A–10B (early version, Peenemünde March 1945). (Graphics: Igor A. Shestakov)

Note: the placing of images alongside each other on the same page does not indicate they are drawn to scale.

Project A–11 (Bad Sachsa, March 1945), colour scheme A–11: RLM 99 on RAL 6003; A–9 nose: cloud scheme RAL 6003/RLM74/RLM 99. (Graphic: Igor A. Shestakov)

Note: the placing of images alongside each other on the same page does not indicate they are drawn to scale.

EMW A–11/II ‚Japan – Rocket' (Project Peenemünde/Bad Sachsa, 1945), colour scheme: RLM 82/84. (Graphics: Igor A. Shestakov)

Note: the placing of images alongside each other on the same page does not indicate they are drawn to scale.

Space–Shuttle forerunner A–13(?)/ Sänger, 3-stage rocket, colour scheme: splinter scheme RLM 82/83, above it wave scheme, RLM grey/white 1945. (Graphics: Igor A. Shestakov)

Note: the placing of images alongside each other on the same page does not indicate they are drawn to scale.

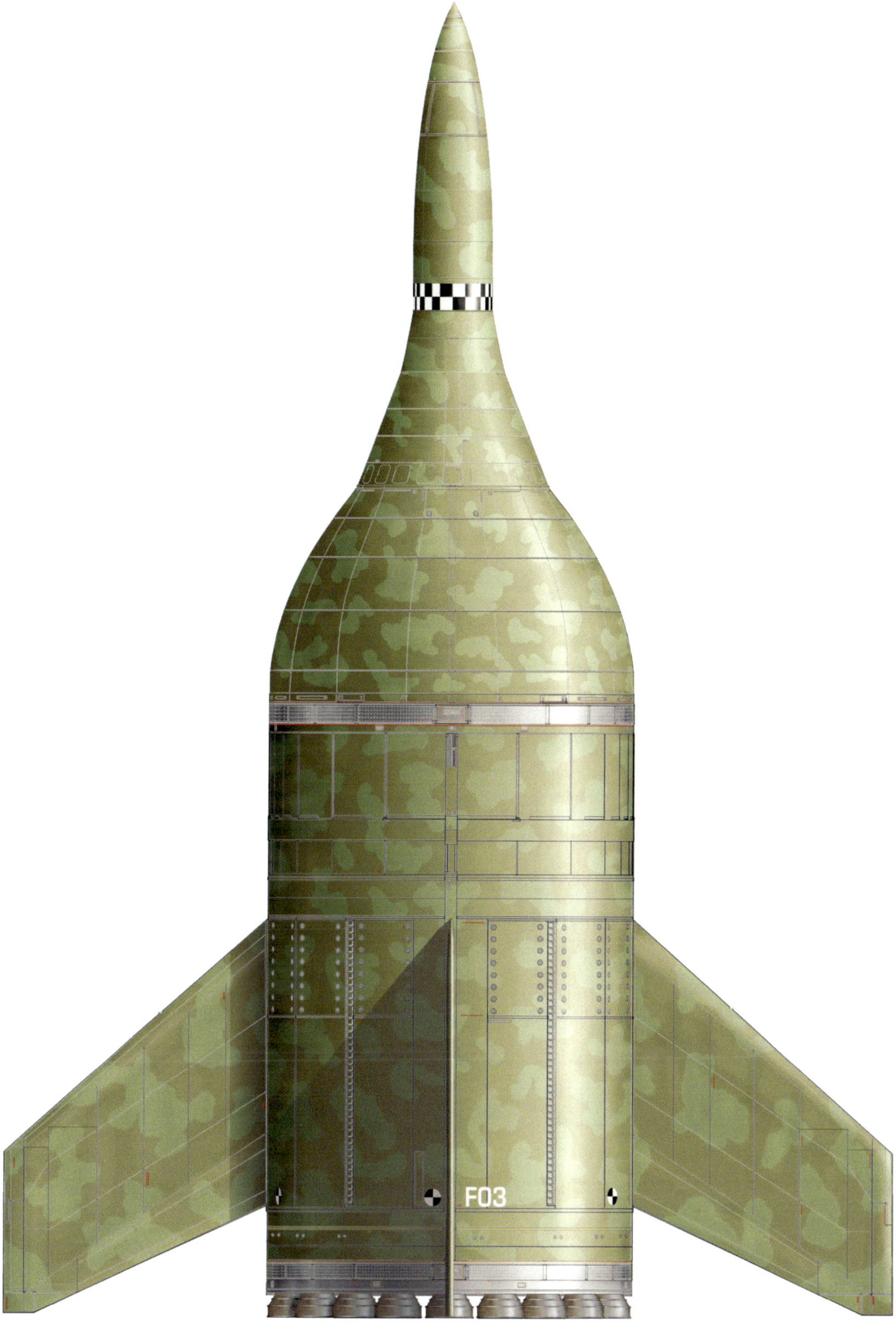


EMW A-12 3-stage rocket for space transport or intercontinental payloads (Project Peenemünde/ Bad Sachsa, 1945). Colour scheme: cloud dazzle RLM 82/83. (Graphics: Igor A. Shestakov)

Note: the placing of images alongside each other on the same page does not indicate they are drawn to scale.

Dornier Do 217K2 ‚America – Bomber' with large Sänger–ramjet, Istres (Southern France), 1944. Colour scheme: upper side: RLM 72/73, lower fuselage: RLM 65. (Graphics: Igor A. Shestakov)

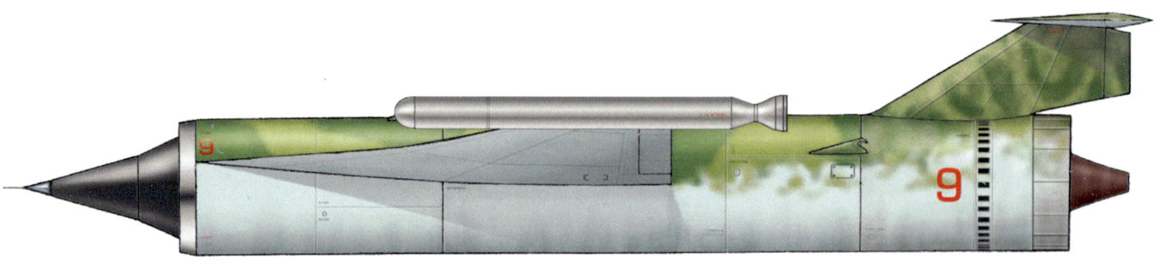


Tromsdorff–D–6000–Ramjet intercontinental missile with rocket-launch boosters at the wing-tips. Colour scheme: upper side: RLM 82/83, lower: RLM 76, solid fuel rockets: RLM 02. (Graphics: Igor A. Shestakov)

Note: the placing of images alongside each other on the same page does not indicate they are drawn to scale.

Space-Island 'EMW Fliegende Artillerie Hitler' (artist's impression). 50 years was needed to realize this space station with which Hitler aimed to control the world after his victory. Pockets of opposition were to be ‚struck by lightning' and wiped out from space. (Graphics: Igor A. Shestakov)

Note: the placing of images alongside each other on the same page does not indicate they are drawn to scale.

Forerunner of the A–10: 'Entwurf 1936'. (Author's model)

A–4B with solid fuel booster rocket (Peenemünde, March 1945). (Author's model)

Note: the placing of images alongside each other on the same page does not indicate they are drawn to scale.

Project 'Horse and Rider': duck-winged manned A–9p with ramjet on the A-10 first stage. (Author's model)

Duck-winged A–9 with elongated fuselage and two ramjets (project). (Author's model)

Note: the placing of images alongside each other on the same page does not indicate they are drawn to scale.

A–4/A –10 with six motor aggregate (early version). (Model: Herminio Pimentel Espinoza, Photo: Aescala models®, www.geocities.com/aescalamodels)

A–4a(tomic)/A–10 with two-phase motor. (Model: Herminio Pimentel Espinoza, Photo: Aescala models®, www.geocities.com/aescalamodels)

Note: the placing of images alongside each other on the same page does not indicate they are drawn to scale.

A–9/A–10 with six-motor starting aggregate (early version). (Model: Herminio Pimentel Espinoza, Photo: Aescala models®, www.geocities.com/aescalamodels)

Manned A–9/A–10 with six-motor starting aggregate (early version). (Model: Herminio Pimentel Espinoza, Photo: Aescala models®, www.geocities.com/aescalamodels)

Note: the placing of images alongside each other on the same page does not indicate they are drawn to scale.

Single motor A–9p/A–10 (later version). (Model: Herminio Pimentel Espinoza, Photo: Aescala models®, www.geocities.com/aescalamodels)

A–4/A–10 late version with two-phase motor, opened state. (A–10 fuselage removed). (Model: Herminio Pimentel Espinoza, Photo: Aescala models®, www.geocities.com/aescalamodels)

Note: the placing of images alongside each other on the same page does not indicate they are drawn to scale.

Late version A-9/A–10 with two-phase motor and long-winged A-9. (Model: Herminio Pimentel Espinoza, Photo: Aescala models®, www.geocities.com/aescalamodels)

'Project Zossen'–Intercontinental Aggregate rocket. (Author's model)

Note: the placing of images alongside each other on the same page does not indicate they are drawn to scale.

Manned V-2 on A-10 with booster rockets to reach orbital flight path. (Peenemünde, April 1945?) (Author's model)

Note: the placing of images alongside each other on the same page does not indicate they are drawn to scale.

EMW ‚Interglobal'–Transport-rocket project. (Author's model)

Note: the placing of images alongside each other on the same page does not indicate they are drawn to scale.

Heinkel He 111H–20 remote control aircraft for the Fi103 (V–1) with ‚Berlin' radar, trailing aerial and radio beam installation (Antwerp, 1944/45). (Author's model)

U–boat Type IXD with with radar-remote *Hörnchen* and light-beam installation (1945). (Author's model)

Note: the placing of images alongside each other on the same page does not indicate they are drawn to scale.

The west side of the northern part of the Watten complex. (Source: IBA/Kurt Grasser)

The huge B–21 (Wizernes) installation with the „cupola", „ventilation block" and the railway entrance – galleries given the name »Ida«. (Source: IBA/Kurt Grasser).

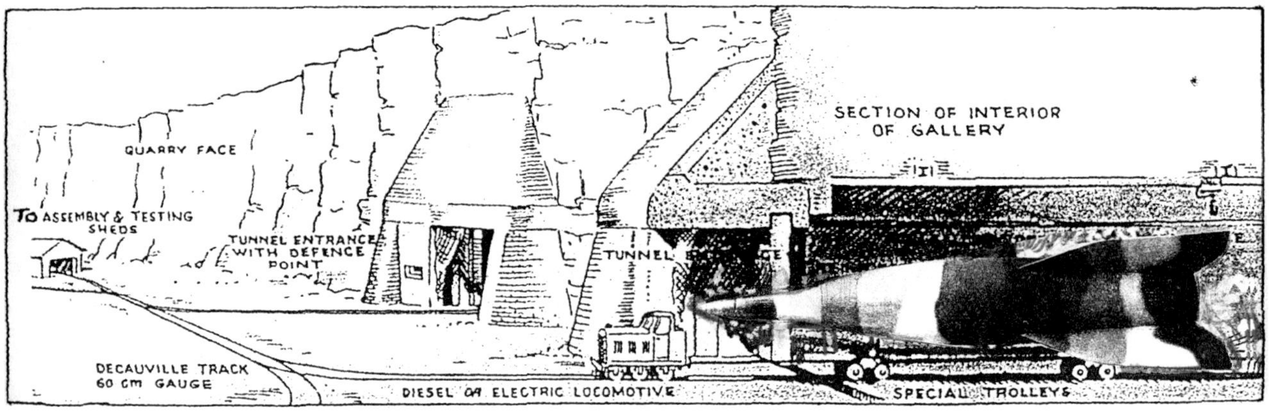


Depiction of an A–10 in the Regenwurm installation at Haut Mesnil (modified to conform with a PRO sketch by scientist Phil Henshall).

hewn into the rocks they found something amazing. There were apparently two kinds of tunnel mouth at Haut Mesnil and La Meauffe. The tracks within the more simple tunnel described a curve of radius 15 metres. This corresponded to the minimum radius for moving a horizontal V-2. The other, better quality tunnel entrances with massive concrete walls and steel beams had a light-gauge railway track with a curve-radius of 30 metres. Captured German documents for the two locations report that in the passages with 30 metres radius more loading and supply installations for rockets were to be fitted than in those of 15 metres radius. Accordingly in the *Regenwurm* passages a rocket could be worked on which was twice the size of the V-2.

The PRO files have a noteworthy 'omission'. Whereas the RAF officers described the smaller passages very precisely, the files are silent as to the purpose of the larger tunnels. This will probably mean that the RAF technical officers understood a different purpose for the 30-metre tunnel systems and this purpose has not been declassified over the last sixty years or so. Moreover the files do not indicate any reaction to the purposes which *were* reported. In all probability it was known that there was a larger German rocket than the V-2 for which concrete firing silos had been built in Normandy. It is not difficult to imagine the apprehension to which this discovery must have given rise at a time when the first V-2s had not yet hit England, and here was an almost complete silo system for a rocket twice the size. For the Americans, who were intended to be on the receiving end of these large rockets, the invasion of France dealt a severe blow to Hitler's V-Weapons plans against the United States. After the loss of France in August 1944, the Germans would have had to search out alternative solutions very quickly if they wanted to hit New York from longer distances.

Sketch of the mysterious rocket bunker at Ebensee. (Source: Deutsches Museum, Munich)

## Project *Salamander Z*

As was mentioned earlier, on the orders of OKH on 20 October 1943 at Gmunden on the Traunsee a gigantic underground factory codenamed *Zement* (Z) was built to produce the America Rocket. Existing structures (water course, railway line) were envisaged for consolidation into an extended test range on a neighbouring valley slope near the Steinkogl. Besides the test sites for engines of up to 200 tonnes thrust, launch platforms were to be installed. The files for Project *Salamander Z* in the German Museum at Munich are incomplete insofar as they omit any description of the launch platform for the America Rocket, the main reason for the planned installations at Gmunden.[114] Nevertheless on the basis of the available data, some important conclusions are possible. The project files for 16 November 1944 show planned permanent launch sites located on the edge of the slope in such a way that the burn-gases could escape below through a concrete pipe. The rockets were to be brought to the firing towers by narrow gauge railway and lowered into the towers by crane.

Since officially the development of the America Rocket was abandoned in 1942, it might have been expected that the declassified project files of *Salamander Z* should show no firing tower for the larger rocket, which is precisely the case: today's Munich project maps show firing towers only for the A-4 and *Wasserfall* rockets. the rest are 'missing'. Even if one suspects their existence, the question of whether the steep firing slope for the America Rocket was proceeded with must be considered uncertain. However, the censors overlooked the sketch of a rocket firing site in one of the plans of the valley slopes and which may have been an A-10 site. Published literature of course will say no more than that only A-4 and A-4B starts went ahead on the Steinkogl. One finds a bunker-silo alongside. This was the Preliminary Design A of 19 December 1944 for a water-cooled silo to take the A-4, A-4B, the 18 metre rocket and A-10 (see Volume 2). Unfortunately here too the German Museum has only incomplete files so that it cannot be determined whether the bunker was intended for tests or operations. With the exception of small structural measurements, such as the completion of the weir for the mountain stream intended for cooling, the *Salamander Z* project itself was never completed.

## Secret events at Peenemünde in 1944 – preparations for the A-10?

The production of the rocket ramps and the A-10 engine tests at Peenemünde would have proceeded without major outward modification to the production halls or engine test stands since the site had been proportioned for giant rockets in 1936. The case is different as regard the launching sites and tank installations. These could only have been set up with the greatest caution. They were obvious from the air to the regular photographic reconnaissance missions flown by RAF Mosquito and Spitfire aircraft over Peenemünde, and the Germans must have been on constant alert for further air raids.After the major air raid in August 1943, the Peenemünde authorities had devised a crafty camouflage system to provide the Allies with the impression of a badly damaged and abandoned base. Since the A-10 did not simply appear from nowhere, there must have been preparations for it contained in Allied aerial photographs from early 1945 which remain classified, and so recourse must be had to RAF photos taken one year earlier. The British writer and rocket scientist Philip Henshall drew the attention of this author to a photograph of 19 February 1944 released by the PRO in which the first modifications at Peenemünde are apparent, this being the so-called Teststand XI.[115] The site, together with two similar structures set apart from the main testing area and its test and firing installations, lay on the north-south axis, had its own railway track and several great tubes within the circular area such that they formed a cross. Outside this circle some extra buildings are to be found.

In April 1944 the British commented officially on these structures, saying that they amounted to a hydrogen peroxide manufacturing plant with an annual output exceeding 2000 tonnes.[116] In July 1944 the Air Ministry, despite an earlier directive of 18 April 1944 that no aircraft were to be detached from scheduled bomber operations to attack the hydrogen peroxide plant, produced a file of fresh targets and specified Peenemünde as important for its hydrogen peroxide production. The British had known for some time that the V-2 rocket fuel was liquid oxygen and alcohol.

Accordingly one is asked to believe that all three of the subsequent heavy bombing raids on Peenemünde were intended to destroy the hydrogen peroxide factory. Afterwards Teststand XI looked like a moonscape. What work was done here to the war's end is unknown, for no further Allied reconnaissance photographs have ever been released even though Peenemünde was photographed regularly from the air until the cessation of hostilities. Simply because no hydrogen peroxide was produced at Peenemünde at any time, the target must have been something.

What mysterious activities were conducted around Teststand XI and the other circular sites with similar surrounding walls of compacted earth? General Dornberger stated postwar that Teststand XI was the 'acceptance test stand' for mass-produced rockets, but failed to explain how these tests were possible when great crossed pipes obstructed the ground. Nor did he refer to the purpose of the incomplete test stands nearby depicted in the 1944 photographs.

Were the pipes camouflage, mock-ups, ramps for test firing rockets or launch towers perhaps? Philip Henshall noticed that a large group of pipes led from the centre of Teststand XI to outside the perimeter and that the bearing of these pipes was identical to the line of fire of other launch sites on the Baltic coast, especially the elliptical Teststand VII, from where most V-2 tests towards the Baltic were made. (From photos, the early launch sites at Cape Canaveral bear a few similarities to Teststand XI at Peenemünde.)

The purpose of the circular teststands at Peenemünde, and the extent to which they were part of the America-Rocket programme, remains unknown. Scientist Philip Henshall, with whom this author transacted much information about

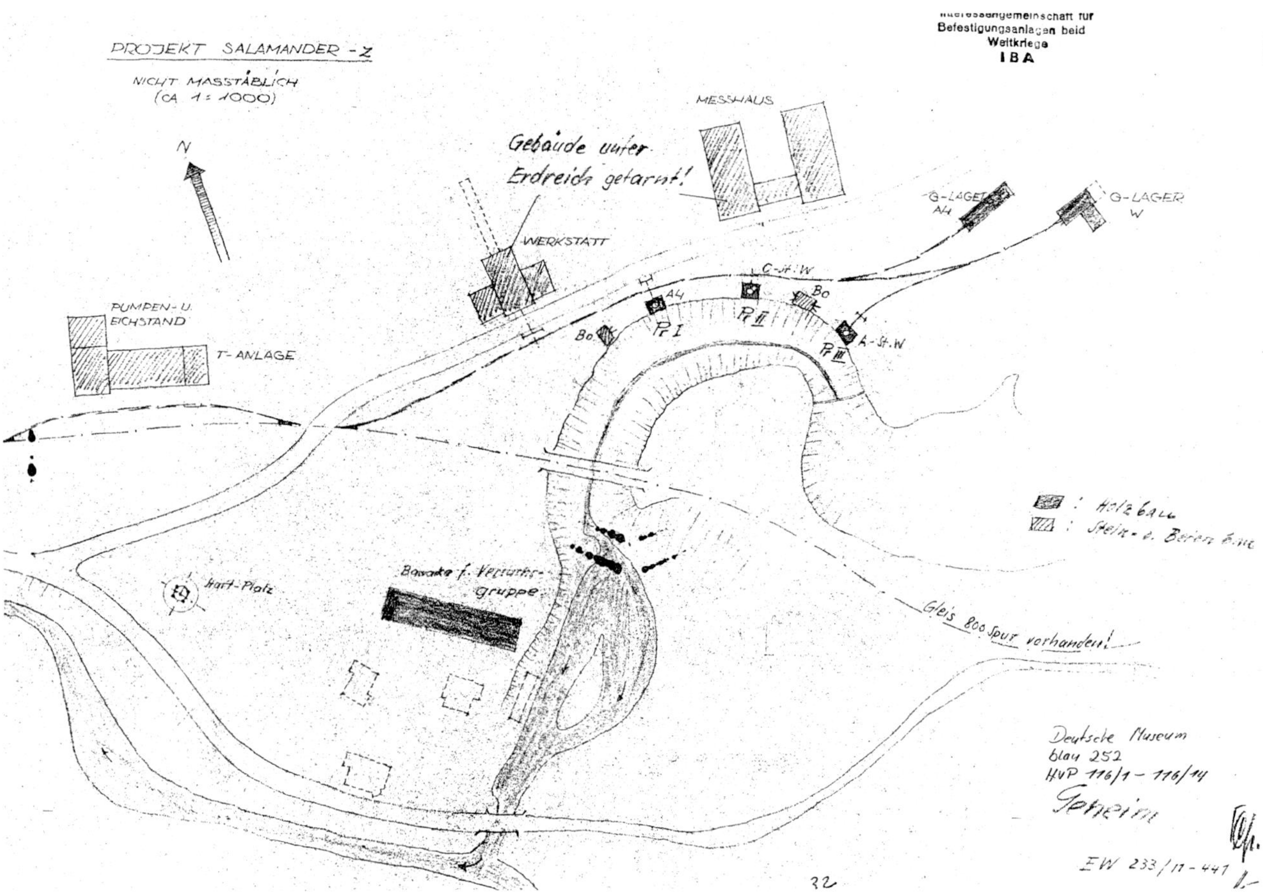


Layout of the open firing base for the A–10 ‚America – Rocket'. (Source: Deutsches Museum, Munich; IBA)

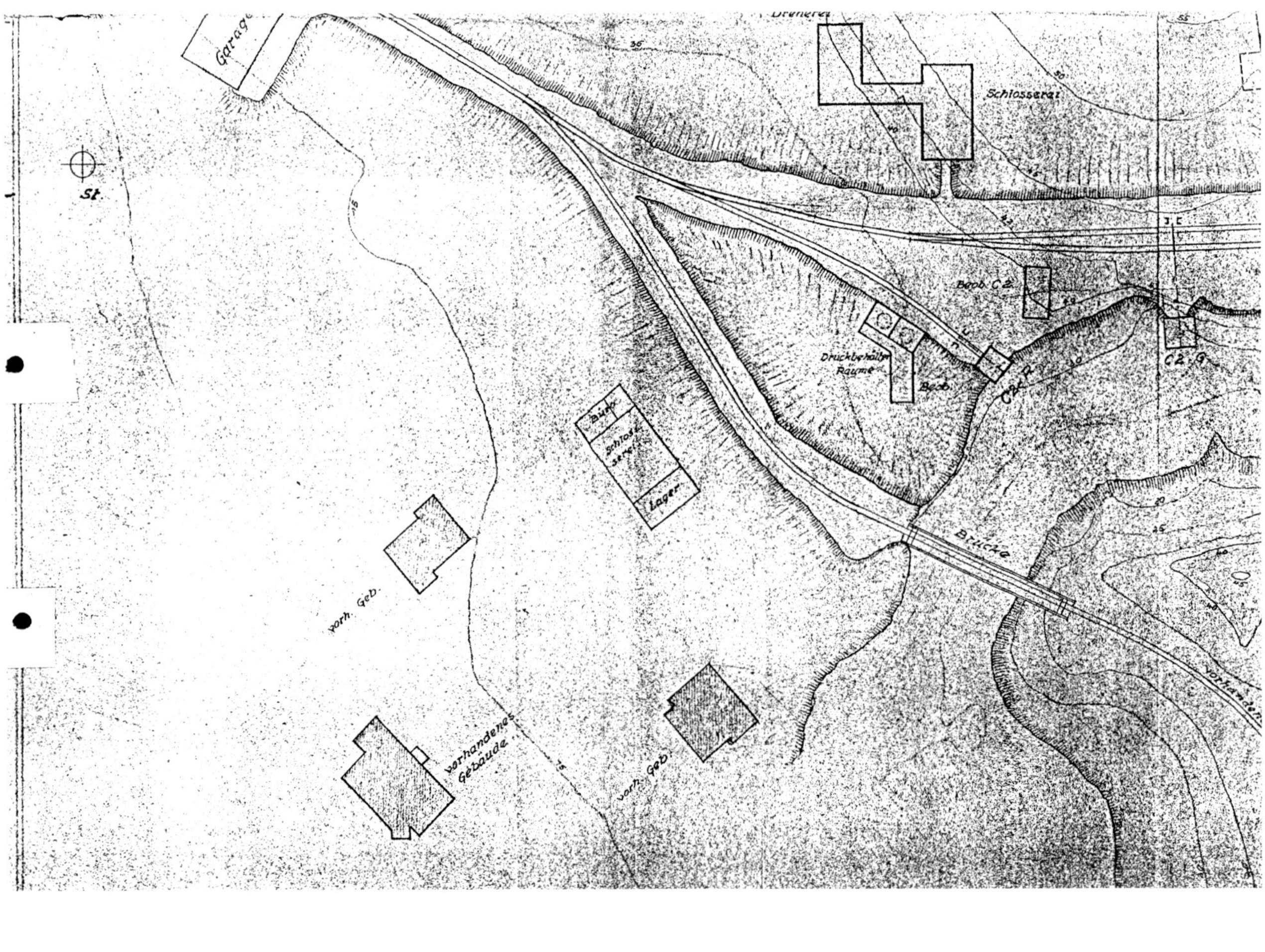

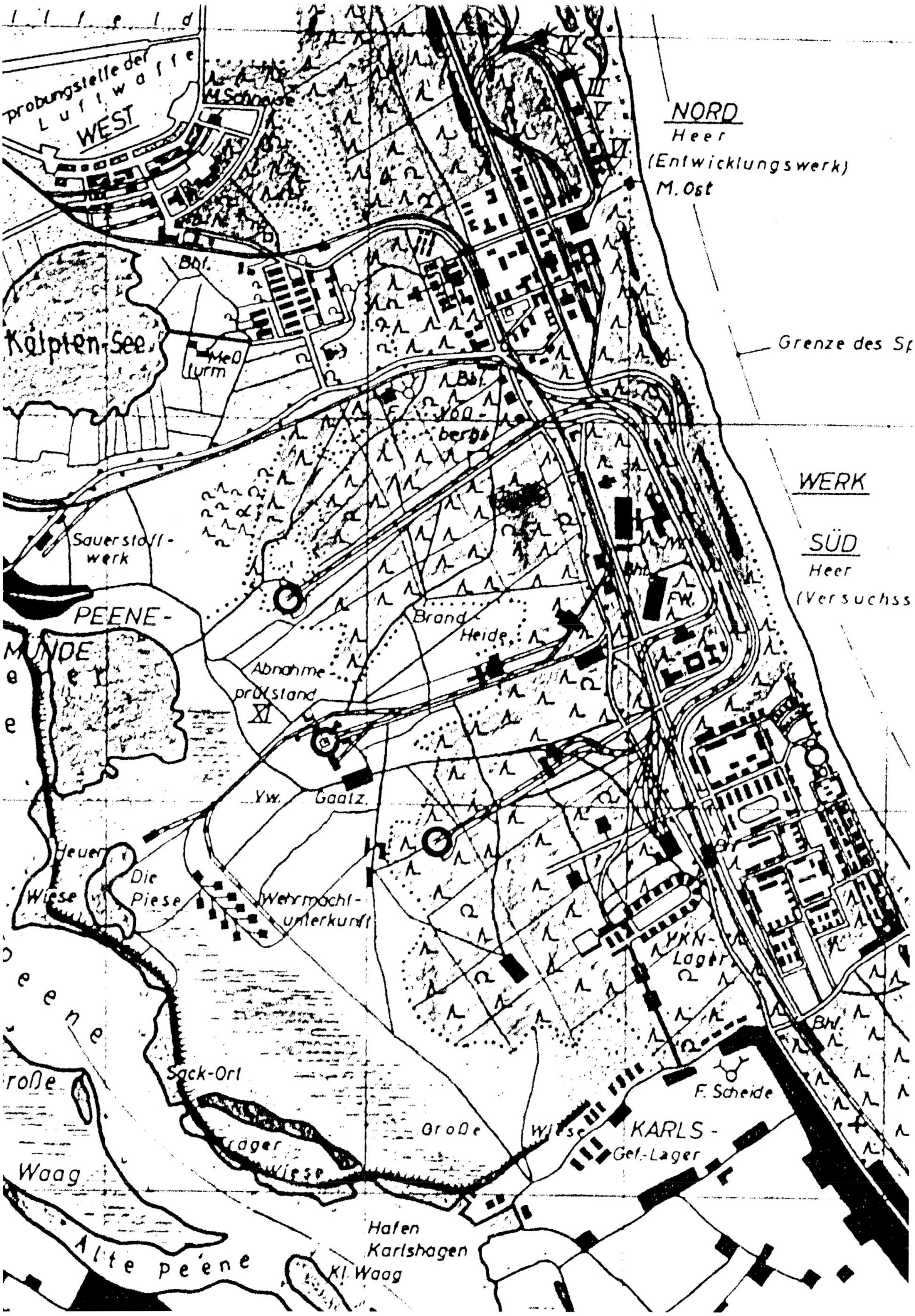


Contemporary drawing of the 'America-Rocket' circular test stand at Peenemünde.

Peenemünde, was certain that the America-Rocket was produced there.[117, 118] Teststand XI was oversize for V-2 rockets but not the A9/10 and many other large developments which released many times the energy of V-2 burn at launch. Access to the terrain surrounding Teststand XI remains prohibited to the present day, and one wonders at such draconian measures being necessary to 'protect the public' against the dangers of 'old ammunition lying around'.

## B. Miracle weapons target – New York

### Hitler's '11 September' was scheduled for 56 years earlier!

In the latter years of the war, New York was more Hitler's preferred hate-target than London. Since the time of Kaiser Wilhelm II, countless ideas and suggestions had been advanced as to how one could hit the city seen simply as the symbol of the United States. Its very 'unreachability' exercised an especial fascination and just some of the bizarre plans to get round the technical and military problems of the New York operation would merit their own book. It is therefore not surprising that in view of the apparant unsurmountability of the enterprise which New York presented from the military point of view, relatively early the German plans encompassed unconventional methods of attack as for example with giant rockets.

In the autumn of 1930 when Lady Drummond-Hay looked over the 'rocket fields' at Berlin Reinickendorf at the instigation of Henry Ford, her journalistic sense and instinct may have told her that behind the spectacle a military objective was concealed which had to be taken seriously. The basis for her correct inference that one day the primary target of German rocket plans would be the United States is not known. In those days a transatlantic rocket belonged in the realms of science fiction. Scarcely a decade later in 1939, while it was still neutral, Dr Dornberger considered that he was already in a position to announce that it was possible for Peenemünde to build rockets with which to attack the United States from Western Europe. On 29 July 1940 when Peenemünde engineer Graupe presented the first concrete suggestion for a 2-stage intercontinental rocket, this was not a sign of German hubris but much more a case that ways and means were being sought to head off the feared intervention of the United States on Britain's side.

Hitler's point of view was that the best way of keeping the United States neutral was to overwhelm Britain. The United Kingdom in German hands would pull the carpet out from under Roosevelt's feet. If this were to be combined with a numerically strong U-boat fleet in the North Atlantic and the ability to hit New York with giant rockets whenever the occasion demanded, Germany's position would probably have been unassailable. Certainly the chances for a peaceful settlement with Britain, on which the Third Reich had set its sights in 1940 after the whirlwind military campaign in Europe, would most probably not have been endangered by the United States. A German deterrent against which there was no defence would obviously have been the best possible advantage to have.

Meanwhile, despite its outward guise of neutrality, the United States had begun to provide massive support to Britain and the USSR with deliveries of materials. From the summer of 1941 a virtual state of war existed in the North Atlantic between the US Navy and German U-boats. A strategy of deterrence was now too late. In consequence on 13 June 1941 Dr Dornberger sent a memorandum to Hitler in which he discussed not only the A-4, but the winged A-4, the A-9 and "a 2-stage rocket to hit the United States". The arguments apparently impressed Hitler deeply for on 21 August 1941 he replied that "this development is of revolutionary significance for the course of war strategies for the whole world". This shows that he had already included the intercontinental rocket in his calculations, and that he was in no way an enemy of rocketry, as has been often stated.

Bormann's stenographer Henry Picker confirmed in his book *Hitlers Tischgespräche* that Hitler regarded the A9/10 as the means to bombard the United States into an attitude in which it was 'ready for peace' after it entered 'direct war' with the Third Reich from 11 December 1941. In his famous meeting with Dr Dornberger on 7 July 1943, Wernher von Braun gave him the official order to build the V-2 and also the A-10. Thus the A-10 project grew from the planned deterrent into the ultimate 'miracle weapon' of the future which would overwhelm Hitler's arch-enemy Roosevelt. In that way Hitler created a direct connection between the Atlantic rocket and its warhead of mass destruction.

The America-Rocket was amongst those weapons on which until the longest preliminary work had been dedicated and which included in great haste from the summer of 1944 the U-boat A-4, U-boat V-1, intercontinental jet bomber, orbital bomber to attack New York. By now it had become a desperate race against time which was running out ever faster for the Third Reich.

### When the American public had to prepare for a V-3 intercontinental rocket attack

In December 1941 the American public – but not the Roosevelt Government – was taken completely by surprise by the Japanese attack on Pearl Harbor. At the end of 1944 it seemed that a similar situation was threatening anew with the difference that its effects were far more threatening for the country and its morale than in the earlier 'day of infamy'. Now the American people, previously overwhelmingly against entry into the war, stepped up alongside their President in their rage and determination to overcome the Axis Powers of Germany and Japan. At the end of 1944 it was hoped for an early peace after the German retreats on nearly all land fronts, and the American public was assured that their own homeland would not be visited by the war even if there were repeated German threats to use new weapons against the United States of which the American man in the street had no concept.

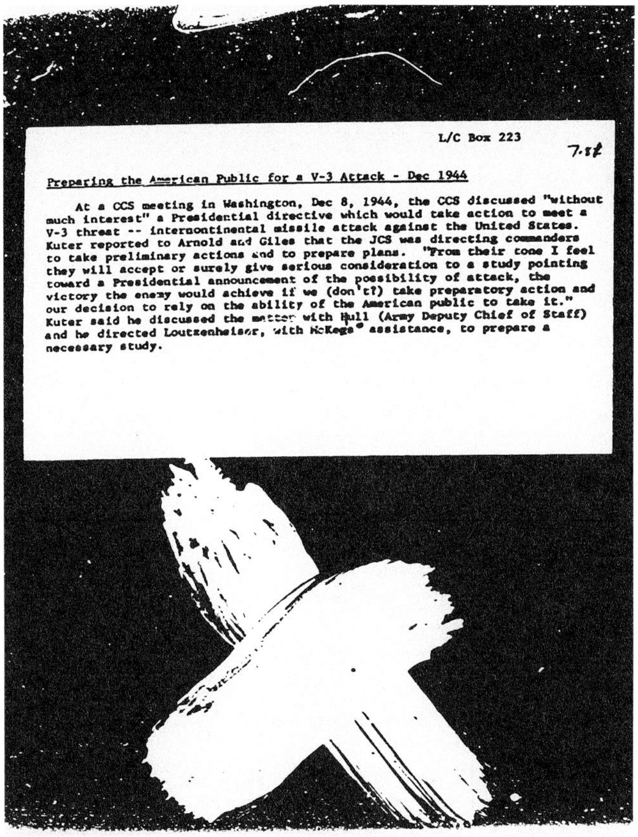

L/C Box 223

7·8f

Preparing the American Public for a V-3 Attack - Dec 1944

At a CCS meeting in Washington, Dec 8, 1944, the CCS discussed "without much interest" a Presidential directive which would take action to meet a V-3 threat -- intercontinental missile attack against the United States. Kuter reported to Arnold and Giles that the JCS was directing commanders to take preliminary actions and to prepare plans. "From their tone I feel they will accept or surely give serious consideration to a study pointing toward a Presidential announcement of the possibility of attack, the victory the enemy would achieve if we (don't?) take preparatory action and our decision to rely on the ability of the American public to take it." Kuter said he discussed the matter with Hull (Army Deputy Chief of Staff) and he directed Loutzenheiser, with McKegs' assistance, to prepare a necessary study.

"... .and the truth has come to light!" US General Arnold reported in a microfilmed USAF document, declassified only in 2001, that American High Command (CCS) had considered on 8 December 1944 how to inform the US public about the imminent danger of attack by German V-3 intercontinental rockets. In the actual words used, no less than "the risk of a German victory" was being run.

Lördag 2 december 1944

**Raketbomben för New York färdig i år?**

Minister Speer meddelade vid ett sammanträde med rustningsrådet för den tyska industrin att Wehrmachts överkommando ansåg de resultat som åstadkommits med V-2 tillfredsställande. Ytterligare förbättringar håller på att vidtagas. V-3, som är avsedd för beskjutning av New York, är så pass färdig att man har beräknat de första provskjutningarna till slutet av denna månad.

samarbete med italienarna och tyskarna måste ha kostat livet eller friheten för tusentals av hans landsmän. I stället för att gå och "pösa" som en [illegible] i en stad som förr försåg honom med ammunition att användas mot de allierade skulle han arresteras och ställas inför en domstol.

A. J. Cummings.

(Copyright AT och News Chronicle.)

The motivation for the CCS meeting of 8 December 1944 was possibly German Armaments Minister Speer's broadcast threat that New York was to be attacked with the V-3. This was reported for example in the Scandinavian newspaper *AT* on 2.12.1944. Subsequently the Mayor of New York, La Guardia, threatened the Germans that New York would sever trade with Germany for 100 years. (*New York Times*, 14.12.1944)

**LA GUARDIA'S ADVICE DRAWS NAZI IRONY**

LONDON, Dec. 13 (AP)—A German spokesman commented with "biting irony" today, the Berlin radio said, on Mayor La Guardia's statement that New Yorkers would not deal with the Germans for 100 years if New York were bombarded with V-3 weapons.

[In a broadcast Sunday Mr. La Guardia said: "To the Nazis: Don't think you will get away with it. If an attempt is made to bomb a defenseless city, the people of New York will have no business relations with Naziland for 100 years to come."]

"Apparently the Americans have gained permission to bomb Turin, Milan, Ravenna, Cologne, Munich or Vienna at discretion, while it is a deadly sin to do harm to New York," the spokesman said. "This American statement is grotesque."

The spokesman, described as 'amused," added:

"This shows that La Guardia reckons with the fact that the National Socialists will rule Germany for the next 100 years at least."

The National Socialist party in Germany will not continue in power another 100 weeks, let alone 100 years, Mayor La Guardia said yesterday, when told of the Nazi interpretation of his broadcast remarks.

"It is up to the German people to put them out of business without further delay," he said. "Naturally, our country is not going to stand by and let the same gang build up another war machine in Germany. With enemy forces on German soil, both on the eastern and western fronts, the German people should act and act quickly.

"I think that the Nazis understood what I said, hence their anxiety."

A USAF microfilmed document (illustrated) from General Arnold proves that in December 1944 the US Government was not only having to reckon with V-1 flying bombs fired from U-boats alone, as is maintained today: at a meeting of the American High Command (CCS) in Washington on 8 December 1944 a directive from President Roosevelt was discussed as to "how one should prepare the American public for the V-3 peril – attacks on the United States by intercontinental rockets." Thus the files of the highest US generals contain information that at the end of 1944 the Americans had finally come to terms with an impending threat from German giant rockets. At the same time the Joint Chiefs of Staff (JCS) ordered the competent commanders to introduce measures to combat the threat by a pre-emptive strike and to draw up the corresponding plans.

Whereas the Americans might still hope to combat rockets and missiles fired from U-boats by sinking the U-boats, there was no defence against German ICBMs (V-3 incoming rockets). It therefore had to be discussed how one's own people should prepare for an almost unstoppable rocket barrage. That the participants at the CCS conference did so without much enthusiasm, as General Arnold reported, may reflect this. A study ordered by the Deputy Chief of the Army Staff, Hull, was to suggest how the President should word his public announcement respecting the possibility of V-3 attack.

In the study consideration was given to the victory which the Germans would win if the United States failed to take pre-emptive action or decided that the American people could 'take it' as the British had done in the Blitz. According to a leading US general it was also feared at the highest level on 8 December 1944 that if New York were attacked by intercontinental rockets, this would lead to a Nazi victory.

From what is known today about this CCS meeting it is clear that the consequences to be expected after a V-3 attack against the United States would have been fearsome. A warhead of one tonne HE would not have caused the American Government too much of a problem, and additionally such pinpricks would only have enraged the US public. Measures such as those discussed on 8 December 1944 for the President's speech to broadcast a general advanced warning would only have been taken if a national catastrophe was imminent. The German V-3 intercontinental rocket represented such a real threat of catastrophe!

## The planned attacks on the United States: the German weather stations in Canada, Greenland and the Polar Sea

In the planning and execution of the German rocket attack on the United States, weather forecasting for the Atlantic and target areas would have been decisive for the success or failure of the operation. Stenographer Henry Picker stated that in 1943 Adolf Hitler had sent U-537 to the northern tip of the eastern Canadian Labrador Peninsula to erect a meteorological station for the A-9 rocket attack planned for 1945.[119] Scientists Dr Kurt Sommermeyer and Dr Walter Hildebrandt assisted by the U-537 crew set up the automatic weather station on a hill 50 metres high no more than 400 metres inland on the coast of St Martin's Bay, Labrador, south of Cape Chidley. The station was operational from 23 October 1943, and for the first time continuous weather data was available to the Germans.

Although Picker's book had appeared in numerous editions from 1951 onwards, the Canadian authorities denied categorically for decades that any such German station could ever have existed anywhere on Canadian territory. It was therefore some time before this weather station (codnemed *Kurt*) was identified, but finally in 1981, after a meeting with U-boat veterans, meteorologist Franz Selinger provided the Canadian authorities with the exact coordinates taken from the U-boat War Diary, and photographs in proof.[120] RCAF reconnaissance flights confirmed that the station existed and was intact, and the Canadian coastguard service mounted an expedition to which Franz Selinger was invited. The large ice-breaker *Louis S. St Laurent* with two helicopters for ferrying purposes was the operational centre. The Canadians dismantled and removed weather station *Kurt*. It has been reassembled for the interest of the public and is on permanent display at the Canadian War Museum, Ottawa.

There is at least one other attempt to locate a site in Canada but which came to grief on 18 September 1944. The German meteorological service had commissioned U-867 to set up a second weather station further south than *Kurt*. Besides the weather specialists the boat appears to have had a German agent aboard destined for Canada. During the voyage there occurred a number of unexplained strange events.

Eight days out from Kiel the commander of U-867, *KptzS* Arved von Mühlendahl, reported a drained battery and diesel defects so serious that he was forced to request the presence of a tug to tow him in to Norway. During the wait he was attacked by Allied aircraft but fought these off successfully. The RAF bombing achieved no hits, but the boat, apparently unable to dive, eventually sank (was scuttled?), the crew taking to the rubber dinghies. The RAF machines circled during this operation contenting themselves with taking photographs of the crew on the life rafts. Although German Naval High Command sent tugs and other U-boats to the rescue, hoping to save U-867 and its valuable cargo, no survivor was ever found. U-867 had not signalled that the boat was being abandoned, and the bodies of the crewmen washed ashore later had wounds suggesting that the life rafts had been machine-gunned by the RAF with the men still aboard. The cause of the original damage, whether sabotage or other circumstances, remains unknown.

The failed salvage attempt also poses questions. The boat was so important that it was one of the first frontline U-boats to be fitted with a snorkel at commissioning. It is therefore incomprehensible why air cover could not be sent only 200 miles from Norway for a special U-boat adrift for many hours. At Stavanger and Opstal BF 110G long range fighters were at readiness and the position of the disabled boat was known. The mysterious loss of U-867 was just a foretaste of the meteorological war developing to full intensity in and around the American continent.

From the end of August 1944, simultaneously with the 'intensivisation' of the America project, an increase in German meteorological activities in the Greenland area was noticed. Meanwhile Allied air superiority and ULTRA decryption was

The German automatic weather station Kurt on Labrador in 1943. It is now on permanent diplay in the Canadian War Museum, Ottawa. (Source: Photos No. 70/71, Jak P. Mallmann Showell Collection)

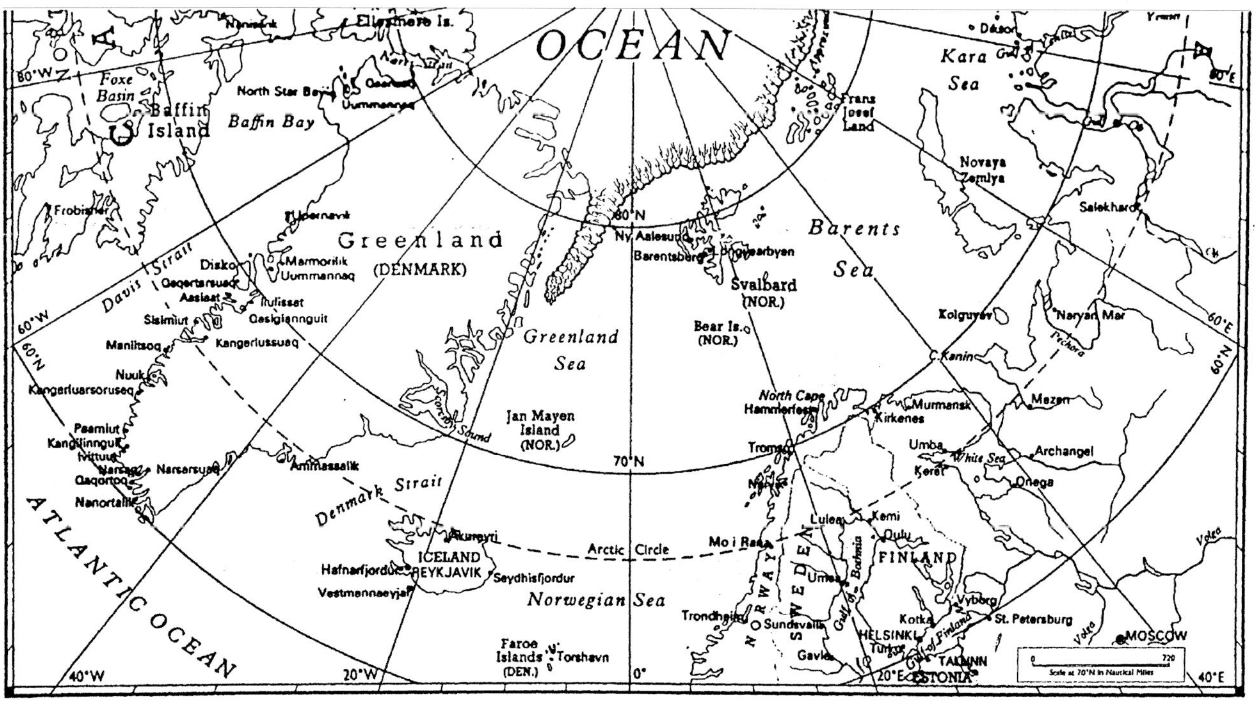


Overview, "weather fighting front" in the Far North, 1944/45. (Map: *Lloyd's Maritime Atlas*)

Seite 2 "Wiener Montag", Montag, den 29. Dez. 1947.

# Deutsche Kampfgruppe noch auf Grönland?

**Von U-Booten an Land gesetzt -- Seit fast sechs Jahren in der Schneewüste**

Wien, 28. Dezember. In mehreren ausländischen Blättern erschienen in den letzten Tagen Berichte, die so phantastisch anmuten, daß man sie mit Vorsicht aufnehmen muß. Jedenfalls wird man ergänzende Meldungen abwarten müssen, um Klarheit darüber zu gewinnen, ob die Meldungen in allem und jedem stichhältig sind. Eskimos haben, so heißt es, dem Kommandanten einer amerikanischen militärischen Station gemeldet, daß sich auf Grönland noch eine etwa 150 Mann starke deutsche Kampfgruppe befindet.

**Die „weiße Todesrotte"**

Im Frühjahr 1942, also vor nahezu sechs Jahren, hatten Unterseeboote deutsche Soldaten in Grönland an Land gesetzt. Anführer der Gruppe war ein Hauptmann namens Hammerlein, der vor dem Krieg mehrmals an Polarexpeditionen teilgenommen hatte. Die deutschen Soldaten, die sich die „weiße Todesrotte" nannten, waren aufs beste ausgerüstet und mit den modernsten Behelfen versehen. Etwa 80 Kilometer von dem Hafen Angmagsalik entfernt, wurde eine Station errichtet, von der aus die Truppe Hammerleins meteorologische Meldungen nach Deutschland funkte. Mit Unterseebooten kamen später Lebensmittel, Arzneien und auch zwei Geologen, so daß man mutmaßte, die Deutschen wollen nach Uran suchen.

Den Berichten der Eskimos zufolge brachte ein deutsches Schiff später auch ein zerlegbares Flugzeug. Im Herbst 1943 erschienen in einer Eskimosiedlung 50 deutsche Soldaten, unter denen eine schwere Schlägerei entstand. Zwei der Soldaten, die durch den jahrelangen Aufenthalt in der Schnee- und Eiswüste Grönlands offenbar schon völlig zermürbt waren, verübten Selbstmord.

In den folgenden Jahren wurden noch mehrmals Lebensmittel, Arzneien und anderes Material von U-Booten aus an Land gebracht. Im Herbst 1944 kam der letzte Transport, mit dem auch 30 Mann an Land gingen.

Sie trugen den Aussagen der Eskimos nach andere Uniformen als jene Soldaten, die sich schon seit 1942 auf Grönland befanden und so vermutet man, daß es sich um SS-Leute handelte.

**Feuergefecht mit Eskimos**

Diese 30 Neuankömmlinge bezogen das gleiche Lager wie die 120 alten, hielten sich jedoch von diesen völlig abgesondert. Im Mai 1945, kurz nach der Kapitulation Deutschlands, verschwanden die 150 Deutschen aus der Umgebung von Angmagsalik. Die Eskimos glaubten, die 150 Mann hätten sich in amerikanische Gefangenschaft begeben, bis nun vor kurzem Eskimos nach der Rückkehr von einem Fang meldeten, daß die Deutschen sich noch immer auf Grönland befänden. Zwei der Grönländer waren, als die Deutschen ihrer ansichtig wurden, erschossen worden, die übrigen drei konnten flüchten und die Nachricht bringen, daß sie 170 Kilometer nördlich von Angmagsalik auf die Deutschen gestoßen seien.

The mysterious German activities in the Far North did not conclude with the capitulation in 1945. The Austrian *Wiener Montag* newspaper's edition of 29 December 1947 and an article in a 1951 edition of the *Ostdeutsche Zeitung* supplies reports of *Wehrmacht* serving units and telegraphists with short wave equipment holding out in Greenland into 1949.

Das abenteuerliche Schicksal deutscher Fernfunker in Grönland

# Die letzte Einheit kapitulierte 1949

Daß in der furchtbaren Chronik des Zweiten Weltkrieges auch Begebenheiten enthalten sind, die Stoff für einen erstklassigen Abenteuerroman liefern würden, zeigt das 1951 von der *Ostdeutschen Zeitung* publizierte, jedoch schon lange wieder in Vergessenheit geratene Schicksal einer kleinen deutschen Wehrmachtseinheit, die Ende Mai 1944 – vor fünfzig Jahren – auf Grönland abgesetzt wurde und sich unangetastet vier Jahre lang durch die Fährnisse der Nachkriegszeit schlug.

Im Frühjahr 1944 ließ das Oberkommando der Wehrmacht 50 km westlich von Lombvik auf Grönland eine deutsche Fernfunkstation errichten, die unter Leitung des Feldwebels Kulik stand. In Lombvik selbst lagen zwei gut ausgerüstete deutsche Kompanien, die erst im Sommer 1947 von einem amerikanischen Kommando gefangengenommen wurden.

*Da sich das bittere Kriegsende auf* Grönland „ohne viel Aufhebens" ereignete, konnte den Amerikanern die Existenz einer weiteren deutschen Gruppe verborgen bleiben. Die Eskimos, die von Amerika nichts Gutes zu erwarten hatten und daher den Deutschen freundlich gesinnt waren, schwiegen eisern, und so blieben die Landser unbehelligt.

Da die mit der Außenwelt lediglich über ihre Empfangseinrichtung in Verbindung stehende Gruppe genau darüber informiert war, welchen Leidensweg Deutschland beschritt, kam man überein, zunächst den Gang der Dinge abzuwarten. Ausschlaggebend hierfür war vor allem, daß alle Angehörigen der Gruppe Kulik aus Ostdeutschland jenseits der Oder und Neiße stammten, also keine Aussicht hatten, in ihre Heimat zurückzukehren. Die Soldaten richteten sich häuslich ein, schlossen mit den Eskimos enge *Freundschaft und* gingen auf die Jagd nach grönländischen Schneehühnern.

1949 nahm der Funkgefreite Harry Gebert erstmals mit Deutschland Funkverbindung auf. Ein Funkamateur in Essen hatte die letzte deutsche Einheit im ewigen Eis aufgespürt. Von nun an erhielten die Männer in der Einöde der kurzen Polartage ständig Nachrichten aus Deutschland, wo gerade drei demokratische Staaten nach Weisung der Alliierten gebildet wurden.

Deutsche Wehrmachtssoldaten am Polarkreis 1941

Da ihnen eine Rückkehr noch nicht tunlich erschien, beließen es die „Nordpoldeutschen" beim Funkverkehr mit Amateuren. Unverschlüsselt und unter dem Rufzeichen des ehemaligen Oberkommandos der Wehrmacht wurde über den Äther gesprochen bzw. gemorst. Ein Zufall wollte es jedoch, daß dieser Funkverkehr in die Empfangsanlage eines bei Spitzbergen stationierten russischen Torpedobootes geriet, dessen Funker seinen Ohren nicht traute, als er das Rufzeichen des OKW in den Hörer bekam. Als man die zwischen Grönland und Essen ausgetauschten Nachrichten abgehört hatte, wurde unverzüglich Meldung nach Moskau erstattet. Daraufhin erteilte die Sowjetzentrale Befehl, die deutsche Fernfunkstation bei Lombvik auszuheben.

So fand sich die Gruppe Kulik eines Tages, vier Jahre nach dem Zusammenbruch, von 150 Sowjetsoldaten eingeschlossen, die auch von ihnen die bedingungslose Kapitulation verlangten. Es blieb nichts übrig, als der Aufforderung Folge zu leisten. Die Gefangenen wurden an Bord russischer Schiffe gebracht und später in Stettin entlassen. Feldwebel Kulik fand Aufnahme bei seinem Funkfreund in Essen.

**Hans-Ulrich Kopp**

making life difficult for the Germans at sea. On 1 September 1944 off eastern Greenland the *Edelweiss I* mission failed when the weather observation ship (WBS 6) *Kehdingen* was sunk by the icebreaker USS *Northland*. On 4 October 1944 the mission of weather ship (WBS 11) *Externstein* was ruined when US troops landed in north-eastern Greenland from the icebreaker USS *Eastwind* and destroyed weather station *Edelweiss II* which had been set up by *Externstein*. The American captured two officers and nine of the weather station's other ranks and seized two years' supply of provisions.

The official version of history states that after the loss of *Edelweiss II* the Germans abandoned their intention to erect new weather stations on Greenland. This claim is tailored to fit the explanation that increased German interest in the weather of Greenland from the summer of 1944 was all to do with the forthcoming Ardennes Offensive in December 1944, because from the summer of 1944 Hitler knew he would be needing a period of bad weather over Belgium six months later.

On 15 December 1944 the Swedish newspaper *Svenska Dagbladet Snällposten* published a Reuters report originating from the US military which stated that over the previous few weeks several attempts by German commandos to set up bases in Greenland had been foiled.[123] This had involved casualties, boats had been sunk and a radio station destroyed. During the mission the American ships had fought off an attack by German twin-engined bombers.[124]

German activities on the weather fronts off Canada, Greenland and in the polar sea region continued into 1945 long after the Ardennes Offensive, and so the purpose was patently something else. On 1 April 1945 for example, weather ship (WBS 10) *Windhuk* ran aground on the Polar coast and sank.[125, 126] Its mission remains as mysterious as the last voyages of the (alleged) whale-catcher WBS *Zenit* and the even more mysterious WBS *Doris*.[127]

Until the war's end the Luftwaffe flew long-range supply flights to Greenland by BV 138 and BV 222 flying boats. Whom they were supplying is unknown, but there must have been recipients! Whether the preventive measures of the US Coast Guard and Navy were successful is doubtful. On 3 February 1945 a memorandum from the Joint Intelligence Staffs entitled *Enemy Activities in Greenland* was produced 'on request'. This means that the highest Allied military circles were concerned to know why the Germans were so keen on having Greenland bases. This interest was so great that German units were still to be found there long after the war. Although this has been considered mere rumour in the past, the sensational circumstances can now be confirmed. In the spring of 1942 U-boats put ashore German soldiers on Greenland.[130] Group leader was *Hauptmann* Hammerlein, before the war a polar explorer. The self-styled 'White Death Unit' was provided with the most modern quality equipment. 80 kilometres from Angmagsalik harbour a station was set up from where they transmitted meteorological reports to Germany by wireless. Later U-boats arrived regularly with food, medical supplies and also two geologists whose purpose there remains unknown (uranium, underground bases?). The unit was observed regularly by pro-American Eskimos who betrayed them later. According to their reports a German ship had also brought a dismantled aircraft. The last transport had arrived in the autumn of 1944 when thirty more men came ashore. These men wore different uniforms to the Germans who had first arrived in 1942. These thirty new arrivals settled in the camp with the 120 men of the 'White Death Unit' but kept themselves separate. In May 1945, shortly after the capitulation, all 150 Germans near Angmaksalig vanished. Two years later Eskimos informed the Americans that there were still German soldiers present in Greenland, some being at a place 170km kilometres north of Angmaksalid, where the Americans captured them.

In the spring of 1944, OKW had set up another long-range radio station about fifty kilometres west of Lombvik under the leadership of an NCO, *Feldwebel* Kulik.[131] In Lombvik itself were two well-equipped German companies who remained at liberty until captured in the summer of 1947. Kulik's group evaded the Americans and was sheltered by friendly Eskimos, their transmitting station surviving into 1949. *Funkgefreiter* Harry Gebert used to exchange uncoded messages with a radio ham in Essen using the OKW call sign. It was only a question of time before this traffic was monitored and triangulated: the Russian got there first and 150 Soviet troops surrounded Kulik's unit, demanding its surrender. The prisoners were shipped out aboard Soviet ships and were later released at Stettin.

Another mysterious German base is said to have existed on the east coast of Greenland. Codenamed *Biberdamm* it was supposed to have been an underground U-boat base.[132] Nothing further is known. From these examples however it is clear that the Third Reich had soldiers and bases on Greenland until the war's end whose purpose may have been to assist in a planned rocket attack on the United States.Together with the secret German weather stations described in Volume 1, the stations on Labrador and Greenland made a line Greenland-Sputzbergen-Franz Josef Land-Iceland, Jan Mayen to Bear Island where the weather for Europe 'brewed up'. Besides the manned stations there were numerous automatic buoys dropped into the sea by U-boats and aircraft and which surfaced briefly every twelve hours to transmit weather data to a German receiving station. These buoys would remain surfaced when the accumulator battery was flat and would be recharged by U-boat.[132]

U-boats were used as 'weather boats', and some had meteorologists aboard. In February 1945, five boats, U-1231, U-1064, U-773, U-1230 and U-870, acted at sea in this role, significantly more boats than in any other month of the war with the exception of October 1944, when four boats were used for the purpose.[133] In the last desperate few months when the Rhine and Oder were the last major natural defences against Allied armour, the Germans were placing great value on collecting perfect data about the weather conditions in the North Atlantic, something which official histories do not find paradoxical. The whole thing only makes sense if one accepts that the leaders of the Third Reich were hoping to launch an unconventional attack against New York. Of the 29 U-boats detached to weather duty in the entire Second World War, there must have been a compelling motive to keep these boats out of the frontline, having regard to the increasingly desperate overall military situation.

It is worth noting that U-1230 and U-1231 intended for the Gulf of St Lawrence in Canada left Norway for Flensburg within four days. To ship special equipment? In March and

April two other boats, U-1009 and U-889 were reassigned to weather duty. All seven boats mentioned survived the war.

German scientists, especially the meteorologists, were in a position to supply Dr Kammler with the required weather details for the transatlantic rocket attack. The connection between Hitler's planned rocket attack against the United States, the German stations on Labrador and Greenland, and the noticeable increase in weather reporting activities from the summer of 1944 lead one to suspect that from then until the present time the material particulars have been suppressed or 'painted over' so that the published versions of history are not vulnerable to challenge.

### Ground Zero 1945: German homing beacons on the Empire State Building

After the US Government had sought advice at the beginning of December 1944 regarding the steps to be taken to protect their homeland against German rockets and missiles armed with weapons of mass destruction, there were occurrences on 26 and 30 December 1944 which apparently reinforced their worst fears: on those two days the FBI arrested the German agents Colepugh and Gimpel respectively in New York. The two men had been put ashore from U-1230 on the night of 29 November 1944 as part of Operation *Elster* which had several aims, two of these being (1) espionage against the Manhattan Project and (2) sabotage to destroy this programme and the American armaments industry. A third aim almost never mentioned in the literature may have been the installation of radio beacons in the centre of New York to guide home German heavy rockets.

SS-RSHA was responsible for the selection of Agent 146 Erich Gimpel, a radio engineer recruited by the *Abwehr* for Peru in 1935. His companion was William Curtis Colepugh (Agent 146/II), an American subject of German stock who had studied at the Massachusetts Institute of Technology and had been one of the best students of Professor Ralf Hudson, an electronics technician.

Before the mission the SS familiarized Gimpel with the V-2 rocket for months at Peenemünde, Nordhausen and The Hague. AEG and Siemens experts, sworn to silence, had shown him new methods of radio remote control. *Obersturmbannführer* Otto Skorzeny was ordered by Hitler to smooth the path for Gimpel. Even Colepugh mastered the technique to become a spy.

As the Germans were still not in a position in 1944/1945 to bombard New York with rockets or missiles in a massed attack, they were forced to modify their design and use single launches. If a lone rocket fell miles from the target, it would obviously not have the desired effect of terrifying the American public, and the hoped-for accuracy to achieve the calculated effect was to be made possible by a homing beacon at the target.

After the war the British writer Newman described his insight into the project thus: "The Germans wanted to predict, for example, that on a certain day and at a particular time the Empire State Building in New York would be hit. The effect on morale would be so much greater than with the hit-or-miss methods of hitherto. It was a convincing argument: a piece of theatre to create panic. It required great precision. However, if the Empire State Building was announced as the target, and the rocket or flying bomb missed, it would be a severe let-down. Skorzeny reported to Himmler that two possibilities had been proven in trials. The first found practical application after the war – radio remote control. The other was more sensational. The Germans were experimenting with a new radio device to guide the rocket not from its base, but from the target. A German agent would place the device in the Empire State Building at the indicated time, or the homing beacon would be installed earlier in the target building and activated later by radio signal. The device would function for only a few minutes and attract the rocket like a magnet. Himmler liked this idea." Operation *Elster* would make the scheme reality.

This all indicates that if the intention was to ship out agents with the transmitter, then rockets existed which would receive the signal and head for the transmitter. Whether the *Elster* beacon was intended to guide home flying bombs or rockets fired from U-boats, or the A9/10 intercontinental rocket, is unkown. All three would have been suitable for the method.[135]

The arrest of the spy Erich Gimpel ended Operation *Elster*. That is not to say that the Germans had no other radio-remote and homing beacons in America until the war's end, for as mentioned in Volume 1, *Elster* was only the last-known U-boat operation against the United States and it cannot be ruled out that there were earlier or later operations of this kind never discovered or revealed subsequently. Jak Mallmann-Showell, author of *Deutsche U-boote an feindlichen Küsten 1939-1945* reported that while researching for his book he found that in at least two cases pages containing details relating to landings on the coast from U-boats subsequently lost had been torn out from the U-boat Command War Diary. Mallmann-Showell formed the opinion that this had been done after the war from which one assumes that the idea was to conceal something important from the public.[136] The well-informed Italian journalist Luigi Romersa reported that a total of twelve agents were sent to the United States to install small ultra-short-wave transmitters in a number of skyscrapers for the purpose of homing in rockets.[137] Indications for such activities are to be found in the annals of the U-boat War from the autumn of 1944 onwards.

Four days after the beginning of Operation *Elster*, on 30 September 1944 U-1226 left Norway for Canadian waters and disappeared. In June 1993 Edward Michaod and Paul Mathias reported that they had "with absolute certainty" found the wreck of U-1226 four miles off Cape Cod and only 12 metres down.[138] The postwar history had always assumed until then that the boat had been lost to accidental causes south of Iceland. The two Americans stated that U-1226 was one of four U-boats on an espionage mission and had been hit and sunk by a single 20 kilo bomb dropped by an aircraft based at Hyannis. The competent US, German and Canadian authorities were swift to reject jointly any possibility of such a 'find' and assured the public that if the men actually *had* found a U-boat, it could not possibly have been U-1226 ...

In this connection one recalls the 'suicide mission' of U-853, lost with all hands between Nantucket Island and New York on 6 May 1945.[139] This boat had been proceeding in what appeared to be an incautious manner towards the US coast (sometimes surfaced) since 23 April 1945 and sank two merchant ships between Portland and Nantucket. Whilst the U-853 mission makes no sense within the known history, rumours were circulating before the boat sailed from its base at Stavanger on 23 February 1945 to the effect that the mission was very special, perhaps a suicide mission.

According to later newspaper reports, a certain Hans Bergerdans called as a witness at the Nuremberg Trials stated there that he had been paid to stow huge quantities of American travellers' cheques in shell cases aboard U-853. Did the boat succeed in landing this valuable cargo on the US coast? For whom was it intended? It predicts that in the spring of 1945 – long after the arrest of Gimpel and Colepugh – German activities were continuing which required a major financial investment. The numerous treasure-hunters who dived the U-853 wreck postwar found no trace of the cheques although they searched the boat meticulously from stem to stern. It is therefore probable that the last freight from U-853 to the addressees (who never existed, say the historians) may have been delivered before the boat met its end.

By 30 December 1944 the American Government and military were certain that a German rocket attack on New York was threatened and imminent, and they knew where the blow would fall. (One wonders if there were any unexpected changes in the tenancies of the Emprire State Building in this period!). Established historians find it incomprehensible that a massive defence programme should have been introduced now as a counter-measure against German rockets following the arrest of Gimpel and Colepugh. Machine-gun positions were erected on the roof of the important New York skyscrapers (defence against sabotage troops?) while a large number of ships and aircraft were mobilized for anti-rocket/missile precautions. A massive naval operation, *Teardrop*, was set up to combat rocket-carrying U-boats. Nowadays historians make light of these apparently pointless manouevres on the US home front when the war's end was in clear sight, but surely this does an injustice to the US military which did everything possible to protect the public and keep the enemy at arm's length.

## Had Operation New York already begun?

Mid-Atlantic, off Rabat, 28 February 1945: U-869 sank with all hands in a barrage of depth charges. The position given in the literature as the boat's last resting place is 34°30'N 08°13'W. The successful Allied vessels were the destroyer USS *Fowler* and the French submarine chaser *L'Indiscret*.[140]

In 1991 a fishing boat trawling about 60 miles off the coast of New Jersey tangled its nets in an underwater obstruction.[141] Later at the location, at a depth of 70 metres, professional divers John Chatterton and Ricky Kohler discovered the wreck of a German U-boat. This came as a surprise, because according to US Navy sources no U-boat was known to have been sunk within 100 sea miles of where the find was made.

The divers established that here was the wreck of U-869. The apparent proximate cause of loss was a giant gash in the 2.5-cm thick pressure hull. The conning tower had detached and lay alongside. These details indicated a massive explosion leading to the submarine sinking – so how could a boat 'proven sunk' off Morocco finish up on the seabed off New Jersey? At that time there were no minefields so close to New York, and neither the US Navy nor air force claimed to have sunk a U-boat in that area in the spring of 1945. Moreover there are nowhere to be found any reports of torpedo attacks or activities by U-boats. Why was U-869 in a position it should not have been?

U-869 had left its base in Norway on 8 December 1944 with orders to patrol directly off the port of New York. The boat was commanded by 27-year old Helmut Neuerburg. Apparently the BdU had cause to believe that U-869 had too little fuel to cross the Atlantic, and so instructed Neuerburg to operate off North Africa. Subsequently U-boat Command had 'lost contact' with U-869 and listed the boat as 'missing off North Africa'. The American and French navies then reported their successful depth-charging of a U-boat off Rabat on 28 February 1945. All this was carefully crafted by historians into the official history of the last voyage of U-869, and if the boat had not snagged the net of a fishing boat off New Jersey it would have remained so in the reference books forever.

Who knows the real story? It seems improbable in the extreme that Neuerburg, who supposedly had no radio, was short of fuel and could not count on contacting anybody to arrange refuelling on the other side of the Atlantic, would have proceeded to the United States coast without authority. The experts have a solution but not a shred of evidence. During an attack on a merchant ship off New Jersey, a rogue torpedo fired by U-869 must have run in a circle and destoyed the boat. There is really no other way it can have happened.

The problem of explaining the voyage of U-869 seems to arise from Neuerburg having had a special mission. Although stating officially that U-869 had been sunk by their naval forces off Morocco, during the latter part of the war they had been so concerned that U-869 was making for New York that they sent two extra anti-submarine groups with the aircraft carriers USS *Core* and USS *Croatan* to intercept the U-boat.[142] This was overkill to prevent the arrival of a single U-boat. The two task forces were unsuccessful in locating U-869, which became the boat off the American coast that never was.

Here we remind ourselves of the numerous warnings made by the highest American military offices respecting the threatened German U-boat rocket attack on New York. There is no evidence that U-869 was fitted as a rocket carrier. Presumably the American divers would have noticed an *Ursel* battery if one had been fitted. The boat was heading in the wrong direction if evacuating leading Nazis or valuables, and as there were no attacks on merchant shipping, all that remains is the 'secret role' which must have been important enough for a smokescreen to be laid over the affair postwar.

This author's theory is that U-869 must have had a part to play in the planned attack on New York. It is known that in an attack with intercontinental rockets against New York, surfaced U-boats could guide the flight in the glide phase by the use of director transmitters. Was U-869 such a boat, surfacing only at night to snorkel depth to recharge the batteries? By means of the new *Kurier* radio transmitting system, U-869 would have been able to receive and send undecipherable messages proof against interception from underwater. The *Kurier* system, which sent high-speed impulses at 250 Hz within an 0.44 second period, was tested at the front at the war's end and could be used for direction finding.[143] U-869 would therefore have been waiting submerged for the decisive order to surface coordinated with teh launch of the A-10 in Germany. U-869 was one of the few German U-boats definitely fitted with the *Kurier* system. A coincidence? Another possibility is that the boat lying off New York had a 'final mission' to land agents bringing ashore homing beacons. If one accepts that U-869 was involved in a miracle weapons plan for an attack on New York, the postwar mythologizing of this boat becomes understandable, for otherwise the victors would have to admit that Operation *New York* had already begun. Since the discovery of U-869 three divers have lost their lives exploring it. How many other German U-boats are still to be found, empty hulls or iron coffins, in positions which historians will argue they cannot be?

## 'Teststand XII Ready!' The threatened orbital launch against New York

In 2000, the former American *Mercury 7* astronaut Gordon Cooper published his book *Leap of Faith* in which he described the early US space programme and new details about its German roots. Referring to the former Peenemünder 'Jack Kentner' alias Dr Joachim Kuettner, who worked for the USA, he stated that at the war's end "a manned V-2" was on the firing platform at Peenemünde.[144] All systems had been tested, the rocket was fuelled and ready to fire eastwards into a low-energy orbit. The plan was to hit New York with an explosive payload. This 1945 manned rocket flight – sixteen years before the first American manned flight – was only a week away, according to Cooper.

US astronaut Gordon Cooper is speaking here, may it be noted, of nothing less than a pure orbital flight in 1945. The rocket would have been fired to the East because this was with the rotation of the Earth. This means that the speed of the Earth's spin and the speed of the rocket would be combined to save fuel in circling the Earth. Coming from an insider such as Cooper the author was taken aback by these revelations, for this would presuppose a rocket *ready to fire* whose capacity was significantly greater than a 'standard' A-10, which could 'only' transport a winged rocket on suborbital glide paths. Moreover an A9/10 flight across the Atlantic was only possible in the shorter westerly direction.Unfortunately Gordon Cooper describes the mysterious orbital rocket only as "a manned V-2". Other American postwar sources stated that the America Rocket was "a V-.2 with 3000 miles range": 3,000 miles would have been too short for the system described by Cooper. The Peenemünde rocket capable of orbital flight either an A-10 of increased range/power (or hybrid), or a new rocket altogether. Von Braun's A-11 design would have had the necessary thrust for low orbital flight.

A planned orbital firing from Peenemünde eastwards is clearly significant in view of the German live-rocket tests against the Urals factories in March 1945 mentioned earlier. These tests were not carried out for the purpose of firing the odd rocket into the Soviet Union, but to prove the low-energy 'long range method' which only worked on the eastwards course. Knowing these details provides a picture which means only one thing: the desperate efforts of the Peenemünders led by *SS-Obergruppenführer* Kammler were on the threshold of their decisive conclusion by the spring of 1945.A reliable source has stated to the author that only a few days before Dr Kammler signed his alleged 'Peenemünde evacuation order' on 31 January 1945, the camouflaged warhead was conveyed there. Now he had to act before the traitors and saboteurs destroyed it. Everybody left on the Usedom Peninsula had now to concentrate exclusively on the goal of getting the America Rocket operational. After all unnecessary witnesses and colleagues had been removed by the February 'evacuation', from March everything was ready to test-fire the intercontinental *Thor's Hammer*.

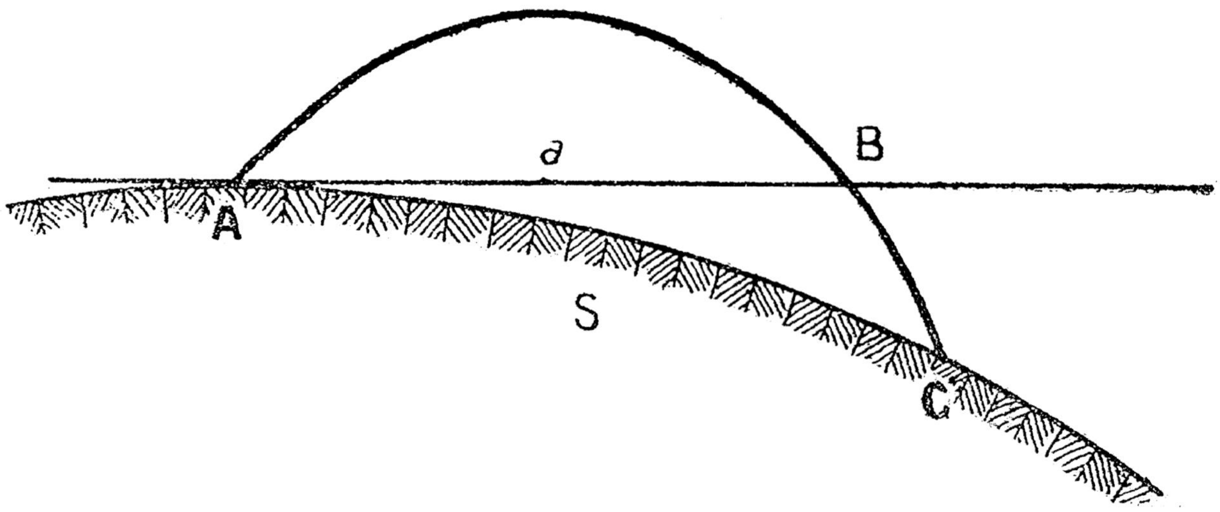


Influence of the curvature of the Earth on the A-9 flight path (Albert Ducrocq, 1947).

This involved Teststand XII.[146] No declassified Peenemünde document mentions a Teststand having a number higher than XI. Where was Teststand XII? No air reconnaissance photographs can be found in the public domain which show Peenemünde between February and April 1945, although we may be certain that they exist. Are they withheld because they show traces of the existenced of Teststand XII or of other installations which 'never were'?

As the reports mention several test starts of large rockets, one would expect to find in these missing photos corresponding signs of a launch or other activities strongly suggesting one. Accordingly there are numerous reasons which can be conceived for keeping these photographs classified. Other points remain to be clarified: when and why was the planned miracle weapon operation abandoned and what happened to the intercontinental rocket at the war's end? Was the manned rocket flight to attack New York abandoned because of the imminent capitulation, for purely technical reasons or did Dr Kammlergive it up as hopeless at the last gasp?Gordon Cooper's statement that the rocket was fuelled up provides a clue. Those who know rocket technology will confirm that tanking up with these dangerous fuels would not have been performed unless the rocket was ready to go. The fuelling-up procedure is today one of the last steps taken before firing the rocket. Were there unclarified (political?) matters which required a further week before the launch? Did these seven days save New York? The implication is that the rocket fuel must have been Visol/Salbei allowing the launch to be held back. The rocket would have had to have been fired more or less immediately had the propellant been liquid oxygen/ alcohol.

Yet even had Peenemünde been in a position to fire the rocket, the risks for a Reich in a state of imminent political and military collapse would have been immense. That a (single) successful rocket armed with a WMD hitting New York in early May 1945 could have achieved any reversal of Germany's fortunes is dubious, for the Allies were bound to have responded by doing everything in their power to overwhelm and punish the few enclaves of resistance still in German hands following the event. The German people, some under a foreign yoke, others still holding out, would have been vulnerable and defenceless in such a case to Allied bacteriological and chemical weapon attack. The consequences of such a final ending to the proceedings defy the imagination.

With regard to other miracle weapons (see Volume 1) there is a greater probability that it was decided not to proceed with the New York orbital flight although technically everything was as good as ready. The fate of the manned rocket with which Hitler was still hoping to change world history at the last gasp is unknown. The Soviets did not find it upon occupying Peenemünde. Theer were hints in the 1990s that at the war's end a 'special V-2' was removed from Peenemünde in all haste by the Germans and sunk.[147] Was this the monster orbital rocket to which Dr Kuettner and astronaut Gordon Cooper alluded?

Insofar as one is prepared to accept the events described here and the interpretation placed upon them, it will be seen why Dr Dornberger swore his colleagues to silence at the end of hostilities. His subordinates were forced to take an oath never to speak postwar of the work on which they had really been engaged, for the development was within a hair's breadth of escalating affairs, so bringing humanity to the edge of the abyss.

## Was Hitler preparing to strike back from the Bavarian Alps?

After the loss of Peenemünde and Thuringia, the leaders of the Third Reich still had the possibility of using their miracle weapons from an alpine fortified retreat. Many consider this to have been speculative – was it true?

It was mentioned in Volume 2 how numerous Allied secret reports refer to German plans of which little knowledge has become available. Besides project *Salamander 2* and the open A-10 rocket site at Ebensee, authorities such as IBA-researcher Kurt Grasser expect that in the area surrounding the Führer-HQ on the Obersalzberg there were other rocket launch sites.

Even if this research is still in its formative stage, nevertheless there is a large body of opinion on the Allied side which believes that the Germans had serious plans to strike decisively with their miracle weapons from the Bavarian Alps.[148] One of the most important witnesses for this was Sir Roy Fedden, then a senior official of the British Ministry of Aircraft production, who made the allegation in a four-part article for the *Daily Telegraph* newspaper.[149] Sir Roy had spent the final two years nine months of the war as Special Technical Adviser to the Ministry, and one of his jobs before vacating this important post was to head a technical mission to Germany. It lasted about one month.

His team, consisting of eight technicians and engineers, left England on 12 June 1945, flying out in two Dakota aircraft with their own jeeps, field kitchens and sleeping necessities. During their stay in the former German Reich they travelled several thousand miles and also visited southern Austria. Sir Roy Fedder wrote of it: "The Nazis record of treachery and deceit sometimes blinds us to the fact that on important issued they occasionally told the truth. When our invasion armies were threatening his Fortress Europe, Hitler promised that if the German people would only hold out and give him time, German scientists would provide them with new weapons which would change the course of the war. Again when the Reich was crumbling under the final onslaughts from West and East, Nazi propaganda laboured to create a vision of the Southern Redoubt, an inner fortress from which in a few months Germany would strike back with terrible weapons which would snatch victory at 'one minute past twelve'. In these respects they were not entirely lying. In the course of two recent visits to Germany, as leader of a technical mission for the Ministry of Aircraft production, I have seen enough of their designs and production plans to realize that if they had managed to prolong the war some months longer, we might have been confronted with a set of entirely new and deadly developments in air warfare."

In this connection Sir Roy Fedden made a few observations about possible German atomic weapons: "There is some reason to believe that Hitler had been promised atomic explosives by October of this year, and if Germany had been first to use them the idea of changing the whole course of the war from a small base in the southern German mountains is by no means so far fetched. A new range of very high-speed fighters and jet bombers was already flying, or within a few weeks of flying, when the war ended. Immense developments were under way with robot rocket weapons, some of which had already started in production. They were simple and cheap to make, and with atomic explosives even a few such devices could have placed air warfare on a new nightmare plane of impersonal long distance annihilation such as we have not so far contemplated."

Until today Sir Roy's hint continues to mystify the experts because he confirmed not only the existence of other secret miracle weapons besides jet aircraft and the V-1 and V-2, with which the Germans would revolutionize air warfare, but he also spoke of "a small base in the southern German mountains" from where victory would be seized from the Allies "at one minute after twelve". It seems certain that by "small base" he did not mean the Austrain Ebensee, but so far nobody has discovered where he did mean!

From a military perspective in the closing phase of the Second World War it would have made little sense to have defended 'Fortress Bavarian Alps' as a place of refuge for the remnants of the German Army and Nazi leadership simply for the sake of doing so. The story remains uninvestigated. This Fortress was dismissed for decades as a phantom whipped up by the Germans to create irrational fears amongst the Allies – yet from their own sources it seems to have been a serious project.

Sir Roy Fedden had travelled the Bavarian Alps during his mission and his observations confirm that the alleged bastion was not only important but had as its purpose stubborn resistance aimed at wearing down the Allies and so gain time for the unbridgeable differences between the USSR and Western Powers to collapse the alliance. It was also from the Southern Redoubt that the tide of the war was to be turned by a last "trump up their sleeve" – the use of the newest miracle weapons.

As with many other German intentions in the last phase of the war, the project offered too little too late and fell prey to the squabbling and games of rank between the various German military and political factions which persisted until the very moment of defeat. Even revolutionary technological ideas had to take a back seat in this environment.

## A bad calculation? The timetable of Hitler's rocket czar

When one judges the chances for the success of Hitler's miracle weapons from today's standpoint, it is important to establish what timetable the Third Reich leadership had set down at the end of 1944, for from that one can calculate if the chance existed to have the miracle weapons operational in due time, or if there was from the outset no way to reconcile the dreams and the real possibilities. Fortunately there are sources to shed some light on this question.

An important witness was General Dornberger, whose work staff met in Berlin for the first time on 27 January 1945 in order to concentrate totally on developments to the exclusion of unnecessary parallel projects. Reflecting on this programme he wrote postwar that he considered it important to know exactly how much time Germany had left.[150] He must therefore have asked his superior office, Dr Kammler, where and how long the Government believed it could continue to hold out while combined Allied forces gradually squeezed the country towards it centre from West and East. Dornberger stated that while Kammler had not glossed over the seriousness of the situation after the failure of the Ardennes campaign and the success of the Soviet major offensive, for some incomprehensible reason he remained optimistic and referred to a period of at least six months remaining during which Germany could introduce the new weapons. This must have been the time frame on which Hitler was relying!

The Chief of the Reich Research Council, Dr Osenberg, told Allied interrogators after the capitulation that Germany might have won the war by the introduction of new weapons if another six months had been available.[151] By then the A-4 with WMD warhead, A9/10 and other super weapons would have become operational. This timetable "ready by the summer of 1945" recurs repeatedly with other important German projects (Ho XVIII, Ju 287). Was this forecast, made at the turn of the year by Third Reich leaders, the result of wishful thinking or was there more behind it?

An Allied secret document of 5 January 1945 comes to an astounding conclusion.[152] Nowadays it is little known that in January 1945 the Western Allies were very concerned at the likely future course of the war. The significant report in this respect was prepared by the Office of the Director of Intelligence, USAAF in Europe HQ, for Brigadier-General George C McDonald. Mention is made immediately of the notorious wrong prediction by Allied Combined HQ SHAEF after D-Day to the effect that Germany would surrender by the end of 1944. The document stated that this SHAEF forecast had exercised a strong influence on planning in Washington and in the European theatre of war. All questions regarding equipment, fighting tactics and USAF training and supply were tailored to fit this date. Almost ironically the document then goes on to say that Hitler's Germany was ignoring this date and working with great resolve to keep the war going for a long indeterminate period into the future and that Germany thought it possible to achieve superiority in weaponry and military leadership(!)

From the standpoint which we are invited to adopt today, this high-level Allied assessment of the German leadership in 1944/1945 is little short of astounding. Why were the Allies so concerned that they might be manoeuvred into a corner? The paper is at least a dig at errors in Allied thinking rarely stated so baldly in the present. The report continues by saying that the USAAF, with the exception of a few modifications and improvements, was fighting in the European theatre with the same weapons as it had had in 1942. The equipment and aircraft of the USAAF between 1942 and 1944 had been superior in practically every respect to those of the enemy. According to the document, this period ended on 31 December 1944 not only with Germany still fighting, but still fighting with weapons it had not had in 1942. Germany now led the world in proven jet aircraft, long range rockets, new kinds of U-boat, and had the best tanks in certain classes. A great part of German manufacturing capacity had been transferred underground and the Third Reich was now straining every muscle and nerve for the final battles along its borders. Despite their considerable superiority in numbers and equipment, Allied ground troops were presently more engaged on the defensive than in attack. If this situation did not change soon, or if the Russians failed to reach Berlin, the Allies would have to live in the grim expectation that they would have to face a Germany with new military capabilities for at least the greater part of 1945. (A handwritten note in the margin of the document, unfortunately not signed, even mentions that certain Allied military men were already thinking of a 10-year war!)

Does all this signify that at the end of 1944 the Americans, for all their admitted enormous productive capacity, found themselves in serious difficulty and that the Western Allies saw no possibility to increase their arms potential in the short term? Possibly one could draw here the historical parallel with the German *Wehrmacht* in the autumn of 1941 when it lost the race against time. Was there a chance that history might have repeated itself in reverse, and would that also mean that after December 1944 time was running against the Allies?

The real difference from the German situation in 1941 was that the Allies were never in danger from Germany quantatively, i.e they would never be inferior numerically in troops and machines, and so their fear must have lain in the weapons sphere and the armaments policy of the Third Reich.

This development was perhaps a forerunner of similar tendencies postwar. From 1945 armed conflicts quickly shifted into wars of pure technology in which superior Powers aimed to swiftly overwhelm potential enemies with only conventional weapons at their disposal and with minimum casualties to themselves. Would this danger have emerged in 1945 had the war rumbled on?

On 27 December 1944 US Chief of the General Staff General George Marshall told the US Minister for War Henry Stimson: "... more battles like that for Aachen and the other in the Hürtgen Forest are not up for ANY discussion. We cannot do THAT any more, moreover we should ask the American people to decide if they are prepared to keep fightıng and to form the divisions necessary for the purpose or not."

A few days later George Patton, the most successful US general of the Second World War, then C-in-C, US 3rd Army, noted in his diary on 4 January 1945: "We could still lose this war. This entry is all the more remarkable because I have never written anything like that at ANY OTHER point in the war."The apparently over-optimistic estimate of the situtation by *SS-Obergruppenführer* Dr Kammler must have been based, as the foregoing examples show, on existing probabilities. But everything turned out quite differently to what the Allies feared and the Germans hoped for. The reserves of raw materials held by the Third Reich at the end of 1944 were sufficient to allow a further full year of hostilities.[153] Ultimately the depleted and exhausted German armies could hold out only four months, a third of the time required by Kammler. Especially in the West from the end of March 1945 there were distinct signs that resistance was beginning to break down amongst German troops. No more time remained to build the Last Redoubt in the mountains of southern Germany, and it is unknown if the *Wehrmacht* leaders were resolved to deploy their miracle weapons against the Western Allies even so late as 'one minute to twelve'. Most probably the weapons were held back deliberately, as indications suggest. Thus in January 1945, Allied C-in-C General Eisenhower and Field Marshal Montgomery received a telegram from *Feldmarschall* Keitel suggesting a kind of temporary truce on the Western Front for 100 days to give the *Wehrmacht* the chance to concentrate the maximum weight of its forces against the Red Army and to inflict on them "a devastating defeat between the Vistula and Oder rivers".[145] The reply from the Allies, one may be surprised to learn, was not one of outright rejection, as might have been expected. Instead, Keitel, Eisenhower and Montgomery subsequently exchanged seven telegrams. Montgomery was inclined to allow the Germans to withdraw their troops from West to East insofar as the 'democracies' were occupying France, Belgium the Netherlands and Luxemburg and could establish a 'security line' on the western German border. OKW responded with a counter-proposal that the *status quo* be maintained in the West. If the *Wehrmacht* failed to obtain success against the USSR within a set time frame, German and Allied forces might have the opportunity to march across Germany eastwards as far as they wanted ... Apparently the exchange of telegrams was halted when it became known to the Soviets. This may well explain certain events difficult of comprehension.

When in mid-January 1945 the Germans saw the scale of the Soviet winter offensive on the Eastern Front, they instigated regular troop transfers from the Western Front in order to stave off the catastrophe developing in the East. Thus the entire 6. SS *Panzerkorps*, ten panzer divisions, 6 infantry divisions, 10 artillery corps, 8 rocket brigades and large sections of the Luftwaffe were moved from the Western Front to the East with a month's grace. The weak and depleted divisions which remained behind in the West 'held out' against a totally superior western Allied combined Power until March 1945. After the successful crossing of the Rhine at Remagen by US forces, and the British airborne landings at Wesel, German fighting units fell apart almost indecently quickly, while in the East, German resistance for every square metre of ground was remorseless to the last day.

Had the German forces on the Western Front simply had enough – understandable after such a long resistance – or was there more behind this 'falling apart' than the simple soldier at the Front could imagine? If one compares the course of events on the Western Front and their timely conclusion, one might gain the impression that this followed exactly the scenario – reported by Russian sources – contained in the exchange of telegrams between OKH and the Western Allies.

It should not be forgotten that during the Ardennes Offensive an Allied secret document from British 21st Army Group HQ fell into German hands. The memorandum described how under Operation 'Eclipse' Germany was to be divided into Allied zones of occupation administered by the Americans, British and Russians after their victory. Hitler received this document at the end of January 1945, and although it is not known how large was the circle of Party, business and *Wehrmacht* people who knew of 'Eclipse', it seems certain that important levels of the German leadership were precisely informed as to the ultimate war aims of the Allied coalition.

SECRET

HEADQUARTERS
UNITED STATES STRATEGIC AIR FORCES IN EUROPE (REAR)
Office of the Director of Intelligence

AAF Sta 390
APO 633, U.S.Army
5 January 1945

MEMORANDUM:

TO: Brigadier General George C. McDonald, D. of I., Hq. USSTAF.

1. You will recollect that the SHAEF forecast, arrived at after D-day in 1944, placed the capitulation of Germany at the end of December of that year. It is believed that this SHAEF forecast strongly influenced the planning in Washington and in this theater. Predicated upon this date, questions of type U.S. Air Force equipment, weapons, tactics, training and supplies were decided.

2. Hitler's Germany did not place the termination date of this war at the end of 1944. Hitler's Germany had indicated with determination and virility that it expects this war to continue for a long and indefinite period of time, and that it is struggling to gain supremacy in weapons as well as generalship.

3. With the exception of a few modifications and improvements the U.S. Air Forces in this theater are fighting with substantially the same weapons as they used in 1942. From 1942 through 1944 the aircraft and equipment of the U.S. Army Air Forces were superior in practically every detail to anything the enemy had in this theater. Indeed, weapons and equipment in general, whether belonging to the Ground Troops or to the Air, enjoyed for the U.S. superiority during this first period. This period ended December 31, 1944 with Germany still fighting, but Germany is not fighting with the weapons of 1942. She is leading the world in tested jet propelled airplanes, long range missiles, new type submarines and, in certain classes, better tanks. A large part of her manufacturing facilities have gone underground and she is bending every sinew for the last stand on the Vaterland frontiers.

4. Our Ground Armies, despite superiority in manpower and quantity of equipment, are presently engaged more in defensive than offensive fighting and, unless this state of affairs is quickly changed or the Russians actually drive through to Berlin and victory, we must face the grim expectation of fighting Germany and her new capabilities through greater 1945.

5. The new submarine threat is mounting and we may expect that the Admiralty and our Navy will soon bring pressure to bear on the United States Strategic Air Forces to go after submarine yards, pens and components manufacture. The tank and armored vehicle industry is proving a fresh and considerable menace in the present Western campaigns, so pressure might be expected from the Ground Armies to devote a part of our bombardment weight to these production centers. A special report has been prepared by Lt. Col. Haines dealing with the growing menace of jet aircraft. Oil, viewed from the standpoint of your Directorate of Intelligence, is still the

SECRET

6. CONCLUSION:

a. The war has not terminated in accordance with SHAEF Plans.

b. SHAEF timing has dominated the development of equipment, training programs and establishment of manpower and supply for this theater.

c. The first cycle and period of the war has ended without the capitulation of Germany and with Germany leading in the development of principal new weapons and methods, which will be included in her capabilities during 1945.

7. RECOMMENDATION:

That this Directorate of Intelligence prepare a careful analysis of over-all German capabilities for 1945 as they may effect our flying formations and our target systems; that this analysis be submitted to the Deputy Commanding General for Operations with a request that it be forwarded to the proper authorities, including the Assistant Chief of the Air Staff, Intelligence, Washington, D.C., along with appropriate requests prepared by the Director of Operations for equipment and training methods capable of equaling and surpassing the enemy's offensive and defensive capabilities.

LOWELL P. WEICKER
Colonel, A.C.
Deputy Director of Intelligence.

SECRET

Not only Dr. Kammler erred in his calculations. This US document of 5 January 1945 predicts a longer war than anticipated on the grounds of poor forward planning and inferiority in the technical field – despite Allied superiority in men and materials!

Accordingly, one is surprised that OKH was disposed to allow the Western Allies to march across the Reich despite the agreement of the Allies amongst themselves that the Western Allies' zones of occupation would end no further east than the Elbe river. After the discovery of 'Eclipse', all German illusions about negotiations with the West should have been dispelled and, as this appears not to have been the case, one assumed that possibly there were plans on the part of the Western Allies (hidden today) to fight side by side with Hitler's forces against Soviet Russia. A number of remarks and dealings by Field-Marshall Montgomery and General Patton after the war point to such a possibility. The Soviets themselves gave voice to their outrage in April 1945 with their famous and mysterious allegation of "the greatest betrayal in world history" and took defensive measures (see Volume 1). What actually transpired in these last months of the war may never be revealed, but one suspects that Dr Kammler must have had firm grounds on which to base his optimistic timetable of six months until the German miracle weapons could be brought into operation.

## America's Battle against the 'V-3 Peril'

How did the United States react to the threat against their nation? In 2001, after one of his lectures on the subject of 'The German atom bomb', publisher Thomas Mehner was approached by a lady who told him that in the 'bad times' just after the war she ran a dance hall frequented by GIs.[155] In time she built a long-term relationship with two officers. One day she asked them why the US air force had reduced so many small and medium sized German towns (Würzburg, for example) to rubble and ashes in apparently senseless raids. One of the US officers replied that from a particular point in time the Americans knew for certain that Hitler had atom bombs and was going to use them against the United States. It was even known which skyscraper in Manhattan was to be the target. In the desperate attempts to defend the USA against this terrible danger, the Americans had set out to destroy every place which might harbour the manufacturing and assembly plants for the German atom bomb or which might have the remotest connection to it. These targets included small towns spared until then.

All pure hearsay and gossip of course, and there is no evidence that the US officers had knowledge of any such policy or precautions, yet one must ask, did the Americans know *as a fact* the threat to their cities of the eastern seaboard?

On 30 October 1944, Allied HQ in Europe SHAEF was warned of the danger that German U-boats carrying V-1 flying bombs would leave European ports within a few days to attack New York. By 18 November 1944 SHAEF had sent at least seven more warning telegrams on this subject signed by General Eisenhower. In one of these the flying bomb was designated 'V-13' which may have been a typographical error for 'V-1/3' or 'V-3'.[156] The character '3' in the SHAEF telegram is not unimportant. In Part Four of a secret document respecting the CCS-Conference of the Stockholm-Tokyo series of 9 December 1944, it was mentioned that the American authorities – as previously the British – were having concerns about a German nuclear weapons attack. Confirmation came from other high-ranking US officers. On the basis of information received from extremely reliable German moles in Turkey, George Earle informed Presiden Roosevelt on 5 December 1944 that the Germans were about to deploy a new secret weapon, the V-3, against the US East Coast.[158] The following night Roosevelt told a female cousin that the Germans had a weapon called the V-3 which would destroy everything within a kilometre of the impact point. The Germans were planning to fire this weapon at New York. Roosevelt feared that the side which used the new explosive first would undoubtedly win the war.

On 16 November 1944 the President had learned from FBI-chief Hoover that a turned agent (Alfred Meiler?), working under FBI control in the USA, had received instructions from Berlin to research how the American people would react if the Germans used "an explosive based on disintegrating uranium" against the United States. The American preoccupation was not solely with V-1 flying bombs fired from U-boats 300 kilometres offshore, for on 9 December 1944 they were seeking advice on what could be done in the case of German attacks with "V-3 intercontinental rockets". Leading US military officers seemed to be well informed about what Wernher von Braun's team had hidden up their sleeves for use against America.

For the Americans, the U-boat fired V-1 and intercontinental rockets were merely the vehicle to bring the feared 'V-3' into the United States. If they did not wish to run the risk of being forced to capitulate to Germany and Japan at the last moment, they could not stand idly by as events unfolded. Informed of the impending danger – the Allied and neutral Press organs had published vital information over the last few days – the mayor of New Yor, La Guardia, stated in a radio broadcast on 10 December 1944 that if the Germans attacked an undefended city, the citizens of New York would refuse to do business with Naziland for the next 100 years.[159] In order to avoid creating panic in the United States, the same day La Guardia brought American rocket expert Alfred Africano, President of the American Rocket Society, to the microphones to reassure the public that it was technically impossible "to buid rockets with such an enormous range".

On 13 December 1944 Radio Berlin reacted – as reported in a *New York Times* article – "with biting irony" at La Guardia's threat that in the case of a V-3 attack there would be no more trade with Germany. The German broadcaster pointed out that it was perfectly all right for the Americans to bomb Turin, Milan, Ravenna, Cologne, Vienna or Munich without the least compunction but it appeared to be a criminal felony to do the same to New York. The American statement was grotesque, he went on, and closed with the sardonic observation that La Guardia at least had confidence that the National Socialists would be running Germany for at least the next 100 years … .

In his response of 14 December 1944, La Guardia said that the NSDAP would not rule Germany for more than another hundred weeks, and that it was the business of the German people to rid themselves of it before even worse happened. He added significantly: "I believe that the Nazis understand what I said, therefore their outrage at it."

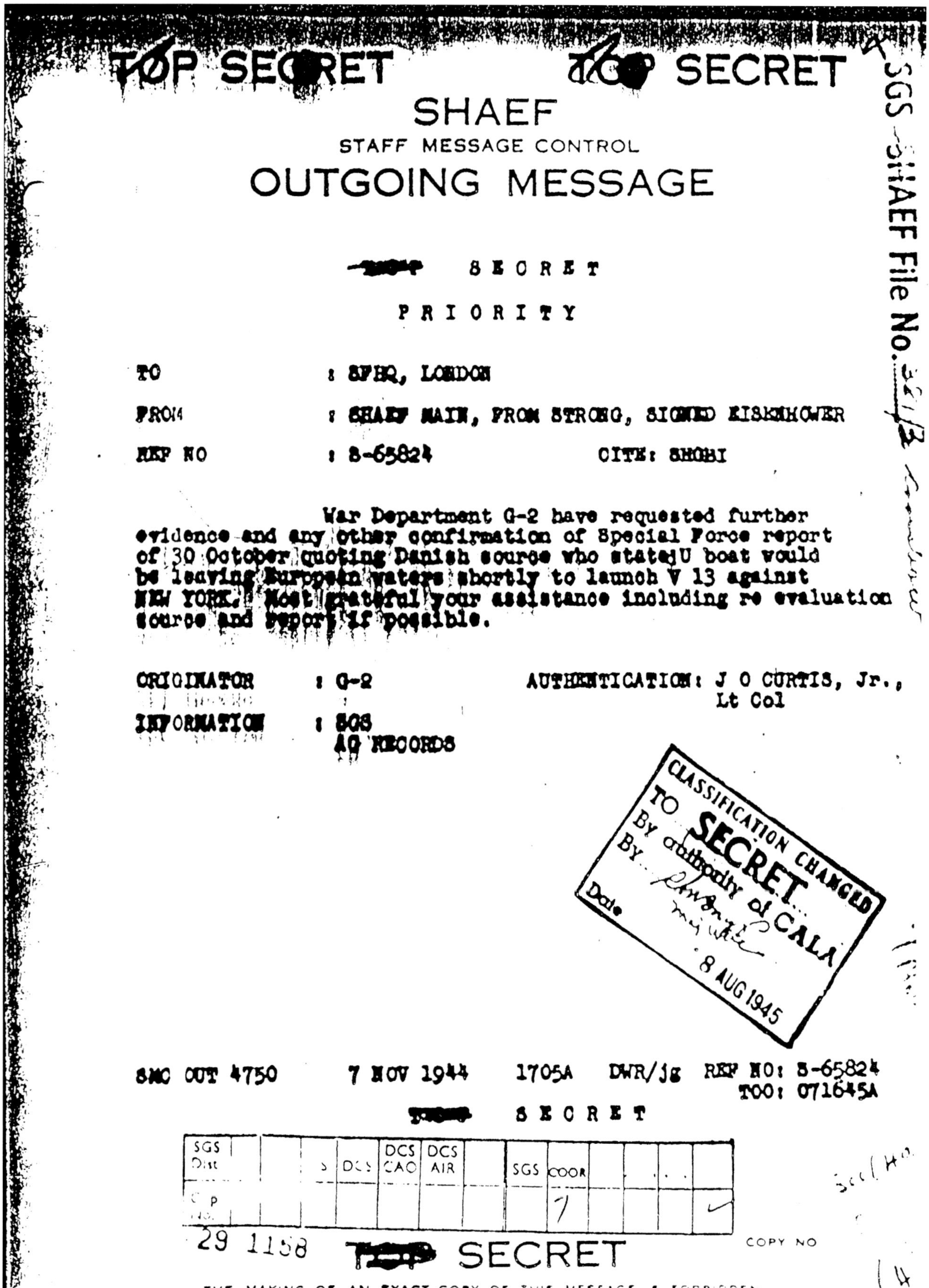

TOP SECRET TOP SECRET

SHAEF

STAFF MESSAGE CONTROL

OUTGOING MESSAGE

~~TOP~~ SECRET

PRIORITY

TO : SFHQ, LONDON

FROM : SHAEF MAIN, FROM STRONG, SIGNED EISENHOWER

REF NO : S-65824 CITE: SHGBI

War Department G-2 have requested further evidence and any other confirmation of Special Force report of 30 October quoting Danish source who stated U boat would be leaving European waters shortly to launch V 13 against NEW YORK. Most grateful your assistance including re evaluation source and report if possible.

ORIGINATOR : G-2 AUTHENTICATION: J O CURTIS, Jr., Lt Col

INFORMATION : SGS
AG RECORDS

CLASSIFICATION CHANGED TO SECRET By authority of CALA By ... Date 8 AUG 1945

SMC OUT 4750 7 NOV 1944 1705A DWR/js REF NO: S-65824
TOO: 071645A

~~TOP~~ SECRET

| SGS Dist | | | DCS | DCS CAO | DCS AIR | | SGS | COOR | | | | |
|---|---|---|---|---|---|---|---|---|---|---|---|---|
| P | | | | | | | | | | | | |

29 1158 ~~TOP~~ SECRET COPY NO

THE MAKING OF AN EXACT COPY OF THIS MESSAGE IS FORBIDDEN

SGS – SHAEF File No. 381/13

SHAEF document of 7 November 1944 regarding the threat to New York by „V-13"s launched from U-boats. Was this a typographical error for the V-1 or V-3, or did it relate to something even more sinister?

L/C Box 54

7.37

Countermeasures Against V-2 Installations

Arnold had some discussions with Vannevar Bush in July 1944, about the best way to burn out the heavy concrete V-2 launching installations. Bush apparently suggested that a fire be started around one of the two openings that would create such a draft from within that a fire started around the other opening would be drawn within the cavity. Arnold sent this information to Gardner, July 24, 1944, suggesting that a technique be used of dropping belly tanks of gasoline around one opening to start the draft. Then after an interval of about 1 minute, a load of belly tanks be dropped near the other opening.

Gardner replied July 28, saying that it did appear that fire might offer the best immediate possibilities of destroying the V-2 bunkers since explosives did not seem to work. Gardner said Arnold's suggestion of using two fires at either end of the concrete structure was tried out and tested at Eglin Field. He mentioned that in tests, this technique had proved very effective, although he did not know how to get the pilots in Europe to come down long enough to get the gasoline in the right place. In any event, he was going to conduct additional tests, as soon as he got the right specifications for simulating the German structures. Arnold thought this interesting enough to send to Marshall for his attention. Marshall's initials are recorded on it.

2

Actually, the V-2 replica construction because not enough information about the internal structure of the V-2 launching site was received. Gardner wrote Arnold, Sept 23, 1944, saying they had gone ahead to pour about 100,000 cubic yards of concrete, "about the size of Boulder Dam" but he didn't think that was right. He said they were copying a structure captured on the Normandy Peninsula, but had never been able to determine what the interior arrangement would have been. Since then, Gardner said they had information that convinced him the building that was captured in Normandy was nothing more than a bombproof machine shop and that the Germans were actually launching the V-2 from a plain horizontal block of concrete, very much like the 4th of July fireworks rocket launch.

In any event, he said the building that was going up, could be used for bomb testing. He said he was not hurrying this project as they did the CROSSBOW project, but was hoping to get sufficient information to complete it. Moreover, he doubted that the Germans would ever duplicate this particular installation that was captured.

Arnold read this letter and sent it to Giles in apparent agreement that nothing should be done at that time.

US General Arnold's document on the failed attempts by the United States to replicate the German rocket silos in Normandy.

It is clear from the foregoing that the US authorities believed they might be facing a German WMD attack against their easternmost cities and whilst wishing to put the populations on alert were anxious to pressurize the German leaders into not embarking on such an escalation of the war if possible.

The Americans thought at first, so it is alleged, that the attacks might come from nuclear-tipped V-1s, and in the spring of 1945 they had further fears that U-boats might fire V-2 rockets from Lafferenz barges from positions well offshore in the Atlantic. The danger of attack by long-range bombers was apparently no longer taken seriously after the Germans lost their Biscay aerodromes (or reports on the matter remain secret), while at the latest from December 1944 they did expect attacks from intercontinental rockets. The Americans had been alarmed to discover in 1943 that the rocket silo at Wizernes in France was very probably built to fire at New York. After the war, Generals Arnold and Spaatz reported that even after capturing the silo in the summer of 1944, the Allies had not been able to establish the exact purpose of Wizernes and Watten.[160] It was a disappointment, for no effort had been spared to determine what ominous threat these V-Weapons bunkers represented to the United States.

In order to find the best way of destroying these monster bunkers they were copied at great expense at an unknown site in the United States, and on 23 December 1944 General Arnold received a report informing him that until then 100,000 cubic yards of concrete had been invested in the project – a quantity equal to the Boulder Dam – but despite everything the copy was not right, and work was now proceeding in Normandy to copy another captured bunker. This also failed to yield the secrets of its internal structure. General Arnold was then informed that this project, in contrast to Operation 'Crossbow', should not be suspended as it was still hoped to obtain sufficient information regarding the original purpose. It was doubted, however, that the Germans would reproduce in the same form the installations captured by the Allies. General Arnold was persuaded, on the basis of the assessment in the report, of the futility of pursuing the idea, and it was therefore decided to use the failed bunker copies for bombing tests: another way had to be sought if the German intercontinental rocket menace was to be overcome.The Americans seemed to know that the bombing of Peenemünde in the summer of 1944 had not really set the project back by very much and therefore other methods were necessary. It may be no coincidence that from the autumn of 1944 the Americans began to flood Germany with spies whereas their ally Great Britain, which had much more experience in operating agents on the European continent, were rather pessimistic regarding the planned espionage operation.[161] The British made clear their reservations regarding the survival prospects of the American agents. It is noteworthy that this great operation started just at the moment when Hitler's military defeat was supposed to have been clearly in sight to American eyes. Was there some special urgency for these suicide missions in Germany?

Another fact of interest is that during the last months of the war a number of black-painted Douglas A-26 Invaders were stationed in England and parachuted OSS agents into Germany in large numbers by night. Strangely there is a general silence about the details of these nocturnal flights, not even a photo of the aircraft can be found.[162]

At the war's end there were US agents in nearly all towns of military interest to the Americans.[161] The loss rate of spies originally viewed as 'disposable agents', mostly turned German PoWs, Jews and Communists was, as expected, high. The few whose missions in the last months of the war are known operated primarily against the German oil industry, V-Weapons and jet fighters. Joseph E Persico wrote in his assessment of the American use of spies in the Third Reich that American bomber raids, artillery bombardments and troop advances were often made against target areas reconnoitred and reported on by American agents. Decisive attacks were said to have been made possible against V-Weapons installations but unfortunately no indication is provided as to location. It is known that until the February 1945 evacuation (and later) Peenemünde was under intensive Allied espionage scrutiny and that even the close circle *of SS-Obergruppenführer* Kammler and American mole was suspected, as to whose identity Kammler's men remained puzzled long after the war.

There seem to have been direct Allied sabotage operations against the V-3. Colonel Keck claimed at his famed press conference in the summer of 1945 that in the previous two years in German occupied areas almost fantastic sabotage missions were carried out by Allied secret commandos, which bettered any spy novel. These actions had succeeded in identifying Third Reich secret laboratories between Strasbourg and Hillersleben which were working on the new apocalyptic explosive. These laboratories and other testing sites discovered by agents were then razed to the ground by the US 8th Air Force and the RAF – "Thus the atomic work of the Germans were finally destroyed".

In the former DDR Dieter Wolf reported in 1966 a possibly coincidental case. According to Wolf an American agent parachuted over the Lehnitzsee shortly before the American blanket bombing raid on 15 March 1945 on the Auer uranium and thorium factory at Oranienburg. His mission was to reconnoitre the Auer works but he was caught by the SS. Shortly afterwards the Auer works were destroyed with 1700 tonnes of bombs dropped by the Americans. Delay fuzes resulted in bomb explosions years later which caused problems to clearance work. Was the US aiming to prevent the Soviets rebuilding the works postwar?

The American aggression against the Auer Company and many other interesting locations is incomprehensible if one doubts that there was an apocalyptic explosive project after June 1942 and that the Americans were aware of it at the latest by the recapture of Strasbourg in November 1944.

Colonel Keck spoke in his report of commandos entering the Third Reich over land, from the coast or infiltrated through the frontlines, but almost no details of these possibly decisive secret missions have been made known. Over the further official reactions of leading US politicians and military men with regard to the threat to New York after 14 December 1944, few public statements have been made, and so far as is known they relate mainly to the threat from German U-boats. Thus on 8 Janaury 1945 US Admiral Jonas Ingram, C-in-C US Atlantic Fleet, warned that within the next 30 to 60 days the Germans would attempt 'buzz bomb' attacks against New York and Washington.[164] The V-1s could be launched at New

York from aircraft, U-boats or surface ships from about 200 miles offshore and would have the 100-floor Empire State Building as the target ... Ingram was probably thinking here of the failed missions of the German agents Gimpel and Colepugh who were to have installed homing beacons in the building. He went on to say that the US Navy and USAAF would be well prepared with secret plans (Operations 'Bumblebee', later 'Teardrop') to ward off any German U-boat rocket attack against the coast of the United States. Massive air and naval forces would be mobilized for this purpose.[163, 165, 166]

When Reich Armaments Minister Albert Speer made the surprising announcement over radio Berlin that V-1 flying bombs and V-2 rockets would hit New York on 1 February 1945, this caused renewed panic amongst the highest military circles in the United States, already pumped up after an earlier similar threat against New York in December 1944 by Speer shortly before the arrest of the two German agents, who were to place homing beacons on the Empire State Building.

While it was hoped privately that '*Teardrop*' and '*Bumblebee*' would protect the US coast against attacks by German U-boats (and aircraft?), the danger of intercontinental rocket attack was immeasurably more difficult to protect against. Here one is reminded of the statement by an American officer to a German female witness recounted earlier. Possibly it was known on the basis of espionage reports that an enormous threat was developing in the heart of Germany. Hitler's America Rocket was near completion!

If the Americans were to prevent the attack by German intercontinental rockets they had three courses of action open to them: to end the war by defeating Germany: to destroy the rocket silos by bomber attacks or commando missions or to 'trade' the non-use of the weapons by negotiation. As it appears, all three methods were tried. Despite the absence of official documents to that effect, it is noteworthy that in the last seven months of the war, the Allies dropped 75% of their total wartime bomb tonnage on Germany territory, and it cannot be denied that in this period a series of small and medium sized towns, spared the full fury of the Allied tactical bombardment until then, became the targets. Did the US authorities believe that in all these places the laboratories of the German atom bomb and rocket scientists were to be found?

In ignorance of the exact circumstances of the plans to destroy Hitler' miracle weapons in the last months of the war, the United States wanted to run the minimum risk. This led to the grotesque overkill of 1945, an example being the deployment of whole anti-submarine carriers groups to hunt down lone Atlantic U-boats. What remains uncertain is what Allied measures against the 'V-3 peril' finally achieved.

In November 1945 General H H Arnold, Supreme Commander USAAF, submitted to the US Minister for War his third formal report.[167] This was not only an account of air force activities at the end of the Second World War, but also a warning with regard to future wars. He predicted a "36-hour war" which would begin with an atomic-rocket strike against key cities of the United States. "With the available weaponry in the future an enemy air power could, at any time and without the possibility of early warning, launch devastating air strikes against our centres of population and our industrial, economic and administrative heart ... radar of enormous range might give the United States a reaction time of 30 minutes ... low flying cruise missiles like the German V-1 might reduce this short span further and radar would be no kind of protection against atomic missiles possibly imported by agents (by submarine? See Volume 1) ... Although the difficulties of the future seem impossible to resolve, we should intensify our efforts to discover an effective defence against attacks in the future by missiles similar to German V-2s armed with an atomic warhead ... ."

The November 1945 report recommended as a suitable means for defence against possible future perils the construction of protected underground rocket silos with their own production installations for atomic warheads. These subterranean bases would be served by underground railway connections. The author believes that General Arnold's report was based on earlier German war plans form March/April 1945 for the launching of atomic A9/10s (and other large rockets?). In his report, General Arnold spoke unequivocally of atomic long-range rockets as 'present equipment'. How is that possible? The corresponding American and Russian rockets were apparently still on the drawing board at that time.

## Summary: Miracle Weapons Target New York

Chief of the US General Staff George C Marshall wrote in his report of 10 October 1945 to the War Minister that at the end of the German War in Europe the United States had been at the outer periphery of the enemy rocket range.[168] After his capture, Göring had stated, so it is reported, that "it is certain that the cities on the US East Coast would have been taken under rocket bombardment if Germany could have held out for two more years. The first attacks might have begun much earlier." What he meant by that is clear today: in 1947 the new 'pure' intercontinental A-11 rocket would have been in mass production bringing all US cities into range. At the war's end the first pre-series A-10 could have just reached the easternmost cities of the American seaboard (such as New York). There would have been the rocket attacks "which might have begun much earlier" according to Göring, and were either fired during the period at the end of March/beginning of April 1945 in desperate 'test-attacks' or mass-produced from November 1945 when the A-10 entered commission.

Senior US civil servant Leo T Crowley stated therefore in the postwar period that from this point in time New York might have been reduced to rubble by "improved V-2s".[169] The US military *Intelligence Bulletin* was less pessimistic in its April 1946 edition and put the beginning of regular operations of the 'New York rocket' at February 1946. This discovery came as a shock.[170] Whether the attacks would have begun with a WMD, or radioactive isotopes or initially with conventional explosives (as a warning?) is unknown, but all indications point to the use ultimately of a WMD against Manhattan. Whilst the great rocket fired from Rudisleben on 16 March 1945 headed north, there were three firings from Peenemünde towards the Atlantic which remain a mystery. When these occurred has not been disclosed. Perhaps one of them might even have been a 'trial shot' towards the United States: the British newspaper *Daily Mail* reported from New York on 5 May 1945 a noteworthy occurrence over the Atlantic coast of the United States the previous morning involving a so-called 'V-bomb scare'.[171] A great band of blue light lit up amongst the clouds and a dull explosion rattled beds and shook buildings. Army, Navy, police and G-men spent hours going over all the reports from as far inland as Chicago. Meteorologists suggested that the lightning could have been a 'bolide', a large kind of meteor. It would have been several miles in diameter and been travelling at a speed of 20 miles per second. The question which occupied scientists in this connection was where this cosmic body had landed. Since no reports of a terrestrial impact had been forthcoming, they thought it must have come down in the sea(!) or burnt up in the atmosphere.

So, did civilisation escape a tremendous cataclysm by a hair's breadth on 4 May 1945 when a colossal meteor entered the atmosphere over the Atlantic coast of the United States and vanished without trace? Or was this an event which had its origins in the Third Reich? The latter cannot be ruled out, for despite the negotiations in train that day for the capitulation of the German Reich, Peenemünde was still in German hands … even a V-2 fired from a Lafferenz barge towed by a U-boat was postulated. If the event described was a (failed?) V-attempt against the United States, it was well after the usual hour when the Germans fired off their V-weapons. If one follows the theory of the man-made demonstration, the question must be posed as to how one tonne of explosive and a few kilos of remaining rocket fuel could have caused such a grandiose manifestation of light and such a massive explosion as to make scientists think it might have been a 'bolide'?

U.S. COAST HAS A V-SCARE

Huge flash and bang

From Daily Mail Correspondent

NEW YORK, Friday.—A V-bomb scare swept America's Atlantic coastline early to-day when a great band of blue light flashed across the overcast sky, beds rocked and buildings trembled in a muffled explosion.

Army, Navy, police, and G-men were kept busy for hours checking reports, which flowed in from as far inland as Chicago. Meteorologists suggest the flash was a bolide—the biggest variety of meteor which may be thousands of miles in diameter and travel at 20 miles a second.

The question that is puzzling them is where did it fall. They believe it may have dropped in the sea or disintegrated in the atmosphere because there are no reports of its landing.

What was the real cause? *The Daily Mail* report of 5 May 1945 on the early-morning ,V-Bomb Scare' along the American Atlantic coast

# PART III

# *The Music of the Future – the Conquest of Space*

## Section 1: Later further developments of the A-10. reaching for the stars – or world domination?

### Peenemünde's Space Rockets: EMW A-12 to A-15

Nearly all authors in the past have mentioned that after the A-10 other rockets were to follow designated A-11 and A-12, but nothing further is revealed. There are indications stronger than rumour whereby the EMW series extended beyond project A-12. What revolutionary plans for rockets, rocket aircraft, space transporters and orbital stations were to be found in the EMW armoured safes?

The British PRO has declassified CIOS Report XXXII-125 *German Guided Missile Research*. This states: "A-11, A-12, A-13 A-14 further development models of the A9/10 with 3500 miles range. Long-range rockets for attacks on the United States. A-15: This project probably never left the drawing board".

In Appendix 1 of the CIOS Report the following is confirmed in tabulated form. Here it states: "Only the A-15 was never constructed." Therefore the other rockets, according to this official report, had proceeded beyond the planning and drawing board stage.

CONFIDENTIAL / SECRET

GERMAN GUIDED MISSILE RESEARCH

Reported by

Mr. N. COLES. MAP
Mr. R.J. LEES. MAP
Mr.P.R. OWEN MAP
Mr. J.H. WHITAKER MAP
Mr. E.H.COOKE-YARBOROUGH MAP
Maj.. R.A. FELL MAP
Lt. (JG) ROBERTS USNR.
Lt. KOHLENBERG Sig.C.,Paris
Capt. J.W. GILES. A-2,HQ,USAFE

CIOS Target Numbers 4/288 & 6/144
Rockets & Rocket Fuels.
Jet Propulsion.

COMBINED INTELLIGENCE OBJECTIVES SUB-COMMITTEE
G-2 Division, SHAEF (Rear) APO 413.

CONFIDENTIAL / SECRET

- when the fuel was completely burned the unit was released, at the same time starting the normal thrust unit in the A4 (V-2) or A9.

A-11,A12, A13 & A14 – Were development models of the A9 - A10 series attempt to produce a long range rocket projectile for attacks on the North American continent. The range strived for in these and the A15 model was 3500 miles.

A15 – Was to have been a 3500 mile range projectile using the A9 and A10 developments. This project probably never progressed beyond the drawing board stage.

B. V-Series of Missiles.

The V-series of missiles, four known types, two being used by the end of the war in Europe, have been covered by large numbers of technical investigation teams whose reports are available; therefore, it was decided that CIOS Team 367 would not make a complete Technical Investigation of them. However, all guided missile work in Germany was related to the developments of these and the A-Series weapons since they were projects which required much research work, the results, in many cases, being applicable to all jet and rocket propulsion problems. Further, the testing of most Guided-missiles was the responsibility of the scientific group at Peenemünde, and their evaluation and ideas were circulated through most of the scientific and development personnel of Germany.

V1 – Was a jet propelled-ground-to-ground missile which was aerodynamically stabilized. It flew at sub-sonic speeds and could be overtaken by an airscrew propelled aircraft. It was launched either from the ground, or from a "mother-plane." Its maximum range was about 350 km, although this depended on wind. The warhead was 830 kg for a range of 250 km but was later reduced to 500 kg for longer ranges up to 350 km. Maximum fuel load was 1000 liters. Speed between 620 and 650 km/hour. Maximum altitude 2500 meters but normal operating altitude was 1000 meters or lower, depending on cloud cover and wind conditions. Overall length 25-ft 4½-ins, wing span 15-ft. The V-1 was gyro-stabalized and compass guided. Except in experimental launchings, no radio or other external control was used. The cut-off time was regulated by the turning of a small airscrew on the nose of the missile.

V2 – Was a rocket-propelled ground-to-ground missile which

- 6 -

CIOS-Report-XXXII-125 reveals the progress of German rocket technology. Only the A-15 failed to leave the drawing board …

At the war's end did wind tunnel models and the first test parts for the A-10 successors exist or was work already been conducted on building the motors? Russian postwar reports speak of motor test stands for the A-9, A-10, A-11 and A-12 intercontinental rocket/satellite carrier.[173] According to *Encyclopaedia Astronautica* these testing sites were located near Teststand XI.[172] All will be revealed if and when the unretouched British aerial photographs of Peenemünde dating from the year 1945 are released to the public.

### Wernher von Braun's troop-transport rocket (EMW A-?)

Amongst the secret weapons of which almost nothing is known today is the so-called V-Weapon Troop-Transport Rocket mentioned for the first time in the well-known article in *American Magazine* of April 1946 which stated: "More than a dozen other V-Weapons were still in development, amongst them some which were to transport troops in pressurized cabins".[174]

In 1949 the Sino-American Dr Tsien Hsue-Shen proposed a winged single-stage transport rocket on the basis of the German preliminary design. At 24.1 metres in length, 4.9 meteres in diameter and having a mass of 44 tonnes it would have been only a little smaller than the A-10. Dr Tsien's *Spaceplane 1949* looked like an enlarged combination of the A-6 and A-9, and was to transport ten passengers 5000 kilometres in 45 minutes – the same flight factors as the EMW A-10. Dr Tsien visited Germany as a leading American aerodynamicist on technology exchange missions and we have him to thank for an impression of how the German V-Weapon transport rocket would have looked.[175] At the end of the 1950s a similar idea surfaced as a suggestion by Wernher von Braun for the US Army but nothing came of this or Dr Tsien's *Spaceplane 1949* copy.[176] It is not clear at present why the troop-transport rocket should have been classified as a V-Weapon. Was the idea to transport sabotage troops, commando units or agents unnoticed and swiftly over thousands of kilometres, or did the Third Reich planners have some other project in mind for the system?

### EMW A-12

The A-11 was given a final stage on the stacking principle to make the 3-stage A-12 with a gigantic thrust of 12,800 tonnes. It was the counterpart to the *Sänger* bomber of the Luftwaffe. Two versions are known. In Allied postwar reports mention is made of test stands at Peenemünde for the motors to this giant rocket, but the project would certainly have needed a few more years' development before it was realized.

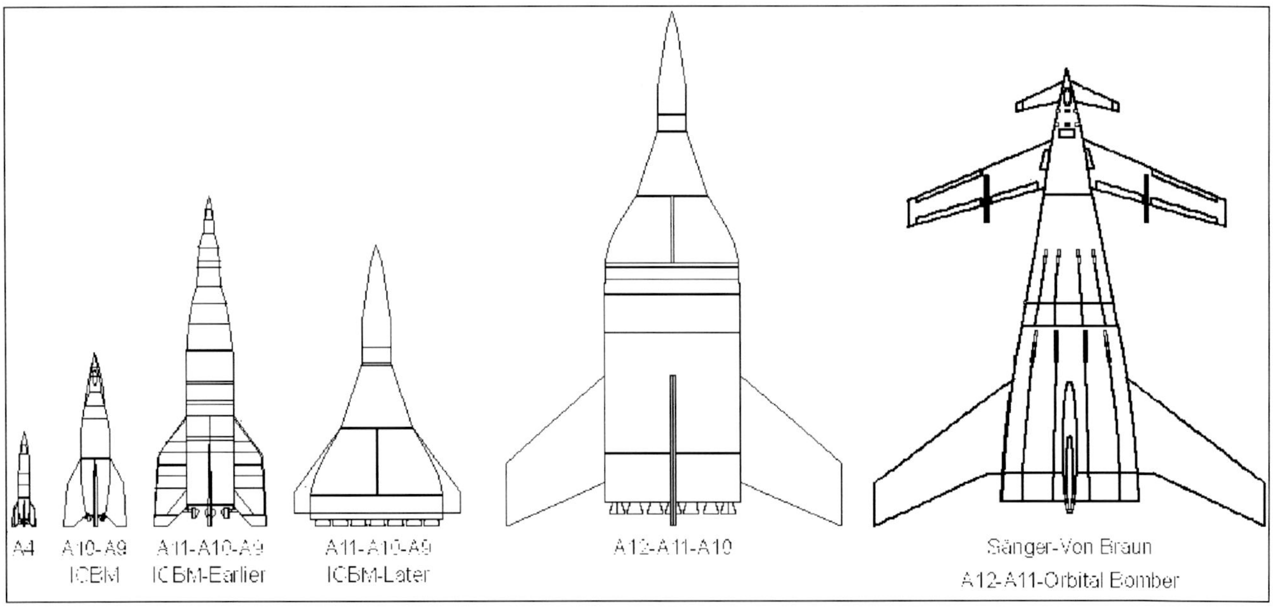


The further developments of the A-4 series with size comparison. (Source: Herminio Pimentel)

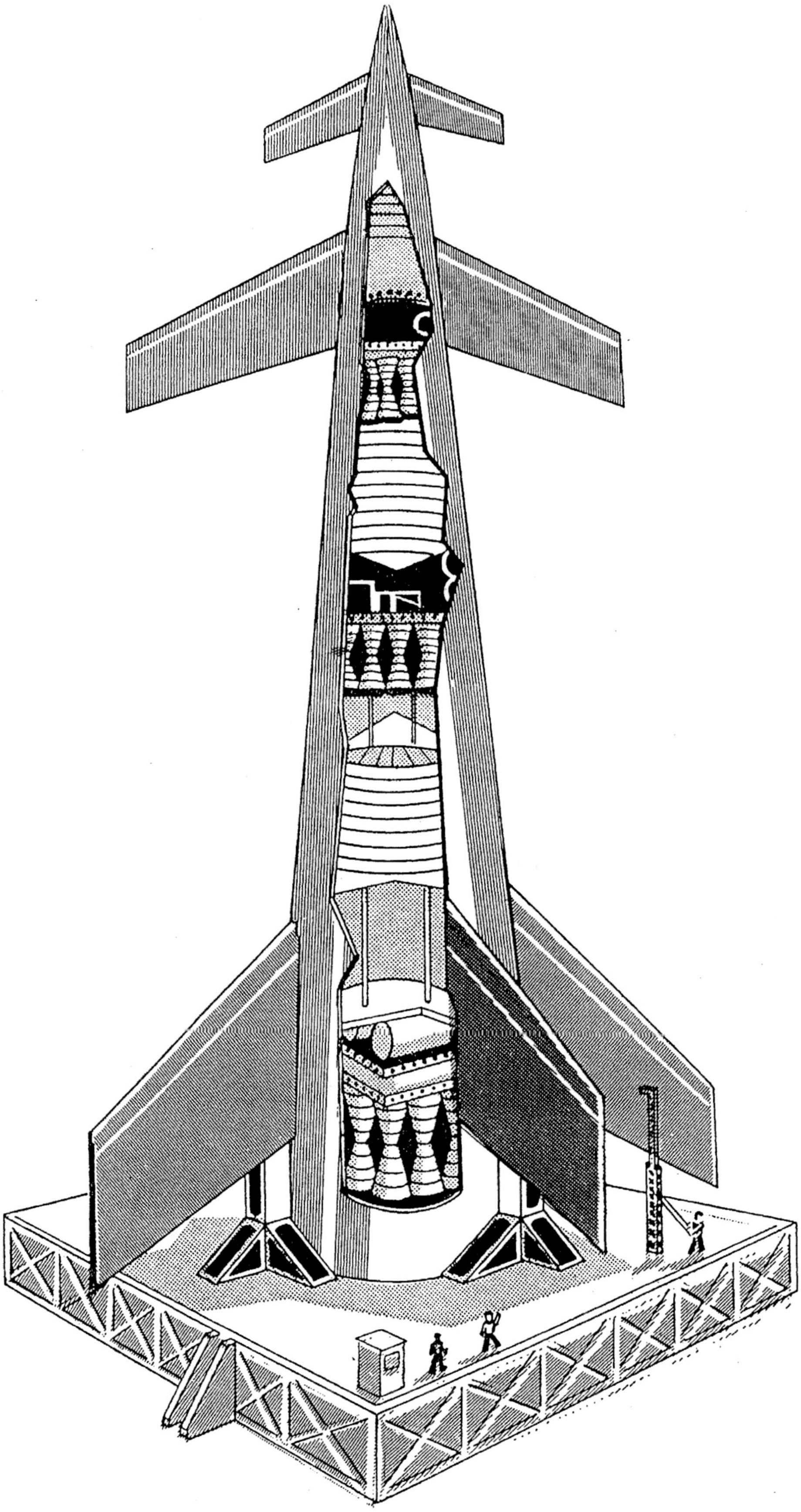

Soviet 3-stage moon rocket as represented in a book published in Moscow in 1957.
Its godfather appears to have been the German EMW A-12/II.

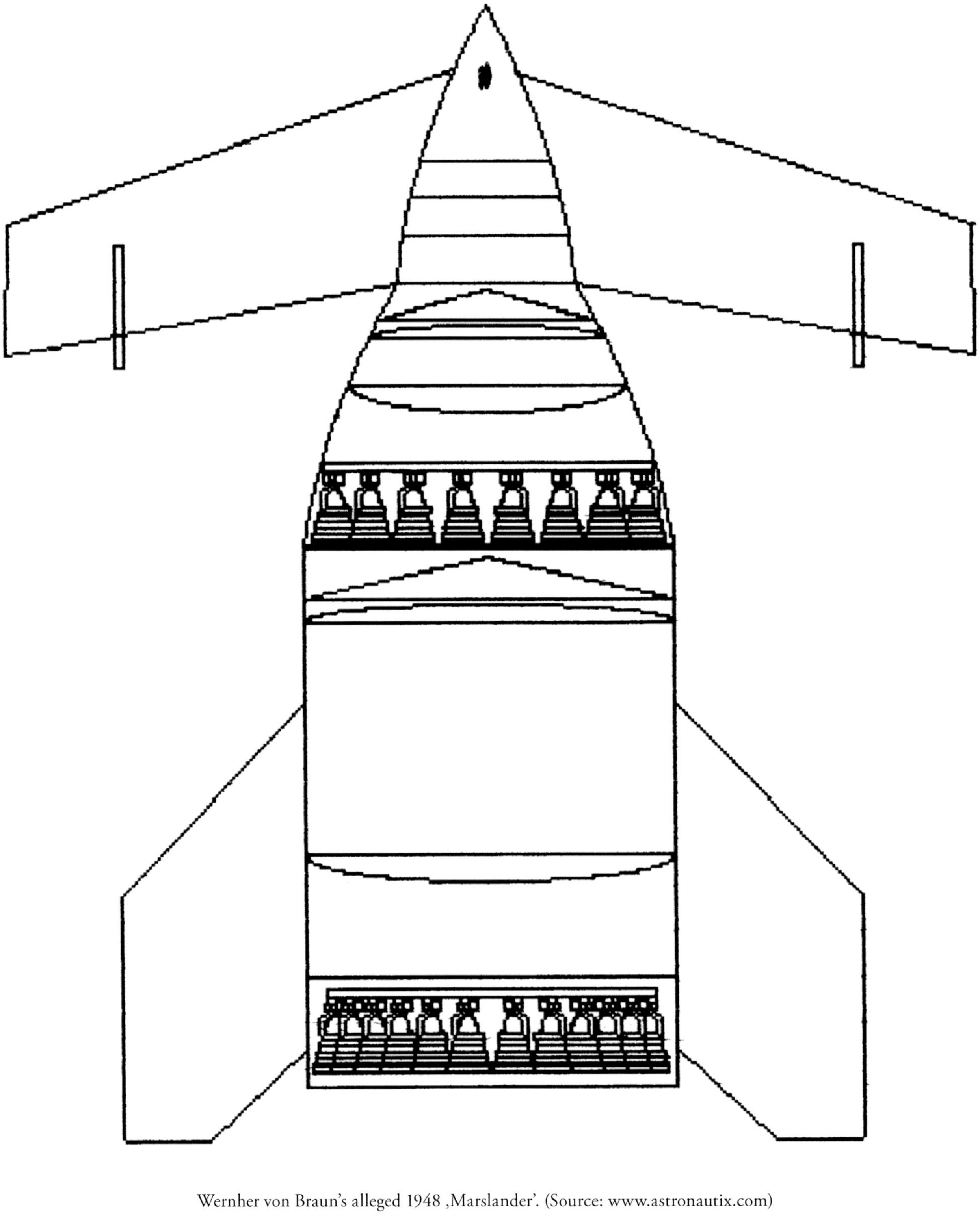

Wernher von Braun's alleged 1948 ‚Marslander'. (Source: www.astronautix.com)

## EMW A-12/I

Work was proceeding on rockets at Peenemünde and Bad Sachsa which dwarfed even the A-11. According to Erich Bergaust, Wernher von Braun informed his investigators of the planned A-12 project. The two parts are described herein as A-12/I and A-12/II. The former was the second stage of a 3-stage space rocket of which the initial stage had 12,800 tonnes thrust.[177] According to other reports the rocket was capable of transporting a payload of 30 tonnes. With this rocket the Third Reich would have been close to orbital flight, not to mention the military possibilities of the system. An alternative payload to military explosives and satellites was a manned re-usable winged version to carry an astronaut. This differed from the later *Vostok* and *Mercury* space capsules only in shape and the manual operation of the Geman project.[178] The status of the A-12 development at the war's end is unknown, but according to CIOS reports it had left the drawing board. The only vestige of the project remaining is a sketch.

## EMW A-12/II Sänger Space Bomber/Reconnaissance Aircraft

The available details of this manned 3-stage rocket project lead us to conclude that it was a departure having little in common with the A-12/I except for the 12,800 tonnes starting thrust and final stage payload of 30 tonnes. The aggregate overall stood 80 metres tall with a girth of 20 metres. Outwardly the rocket resembled no earlier designs. All three stages had glide wings to enable retrieval and re-use. The purpose was to fire the final stage, a manned rocket-aircraft with wings and stabilizers, into Earth-orbit. Once there the astronaut would pilot the craft to perform strategic orbital reconnaissance of whole continents or the transport of miracle weapons to any point required on the Earth's surface. At the conclusion of the mission the end-stage would glide back to its departure point. To this extent the A-12/II was a kind of vertical take-off *Sänger* orbital bomber. Probably suspended during the war, this German project surfaced in almost unchanged forms in postwar USA and USSR. In 1952 in *Collier's Magazine*, Wernher von Braun suggested a slightly modified version of the German system as a 3-stage winged carrier combination for use as a space station, while Soviet publications in 1957 for a planned 3-stage rocket looks suspiciously close to the Peenemünde project even if not all features are identical.

## EMW A-13

This large 4-stage rocket was composed of the EMW A-10(A-11/A-12 with a new A-13 initial stage. Payload was to have been 30 tonnes, its principal task being the setting up and supply of a permanent orbital station.[181] No other details are known.

## EMW A-14

Wernher von Braun's last project to proceed beyond the drawing board before the capitulation was a 5-stage rocket A-10 to A-14 inclusive. Its misison was to circle the moon with three astronauts before making a gliding return to base using the Sänger principle.[179] The existence of the A-14 was confirmed in August 1946 by a British official at the War Office who remarked of it ironically: "Hitler wanted the moon!"[180]

## EMW A-15

This rocket, gigantic even for the 21st century, had six stages, (A-10 to A-15 inclusive) and was intended to land on the moon.[182] According to Allied postwar reports, it was the only rocket in the series still on the drawing board in May 1945. Drawings and plans have not yet been declassified.

## How would the A-13 to A-15 have looked?

Although no plans have yet become available, one can make a shrewd guess as to the direction Peenemünde designs were taking had the Germans had the time to realize their ideas. When in 1953 Wernher von Braun published in the space periodical *Weltraumfahrt* his studies for a Mars project, he produced the design for a space-ferry, but he had already drawn up his alleged *Marslander* at Fort Blioss and White Sands in 1948, based on his last wartime designs.[184, 185]

## EMW A-10 'World' Transport Version

A further development of the EMW A-12 to A-15 orbital rockets was to have been a single-stage EMW A-10 variant for the transport of heavy loads. The removal of the EMW A-9 made possible an A-10 transport rocket capable of taking 30 tonnes of materials (e.g. space vehicles, satellites, space station components, supplies) into orbit. Another version had an A-10 with wings for gliding to enable the re-use of the rocket.[183]

# Section 2: Did 'Star Wars' planning begin for the next war in 1945? Hitler's flying artillery: Germany's space island – the sun cannon to control the world.

*For reasons unknown, this space mirror was portrayed in some quarters as the ultimate goal of the men in Peenemunde*
Ernst Stuhlinger, Frederick I Ordway III – *Wernher von Braun – Crusader for Space* (Krieger, 1994, p.34)

Was an orbital station being planned, probably under the designation 'Hitler's Flying Artillery'? German scientists informed US Colonel Keck that in addition to its 10-point programme the Third Reich was working on many more terrible projects and schemes, e.g. the setting up of a so-called 'space island' on which a giant mirror would be installed to gather and reflect to Earth the sun's rays. The scientists were theorizing that with this method it would be possible to reduce an enemy city to ashes within seconds, and to bring parts of the seas to the boil. The idea originated with Hermann Oberth's article first published in the Weimar Republic in 1929.[186, 187] The inventor had conceived a light-metal device of numerous reflective facets which could be erected in space. He thought it would require fifteen years' development and cost in the region of 15 billion Reichsmarks. He was hoping for all kinds of benefits from the sun mirror. The Earth would receive more of the sun's rays and influence favourably the world's weather and climate. He also foresaw other possibilities, such as the concentration of the sun's rays on narrowly defined areas.

Relatively soon after the outbreak of war the Peenemünde planning office took up this old idea. They worked out that the sun mirror would need a surface of three square kilometres. The space island project resulted from calculations that gravity diminshed to zero at 5100 miles up making it possible to build a permanently orbiting base in space. Although at that stage of technological development such a futuristic project was not feasible, German scientists were convinced that method work over the decades would eventually yield a successful plan. A set programme already existed for the subsequent years. This long term planning continued until the time when Germany began to crumble.

The primary aim was to build a reflector on Earth – possibly of metallic natrium in an environment free of air and other corrosives materials – to gather the sun's rays and reflect them to a receptor station from where small 'sun cannons' would be tested out on mountain tops in the region of the southern German Redoubt, of which more will be described at a later time. Later a larger land version would follow sited perhaps along a coastal stretch for the production of steam and electrical energy. According to the mathematics, the concentration of heat from such an installation would be sufficient to bring seas to the boil or bring about lightning strikes at ground level to raze areas of territory.

After the successful realization of the plan the next aim would be the 'lightning cannon' in space from where countries could be annihilated and the world dominated from orbit. From the space island 'projectile craft' (today's space vehicles) would later be sent into the Cosmos. At Peenemünde concrete thought had even been given to how the station could be put into orbit.

The great mirror weapon would be constructed by sending up prefabricated sections individually by multi-stage EMW A-13 rockets for erection in space. The circular natrium mirror would have 30-feet long apertures for the incoming rockets to dock, and there would be air-locks for men and provisions. Gourd cultures would be grown under flourescent lights to supply oxygen for the space station. Electrical power would come from dynamos driven by solar-produced mercury steam. The exact placing of the mirror would be coordinated by small remote-controlled rockets. The station was to orbit at 5100 miles altitude. By the war's end 'Hitler's Flying Artillery' orbital station project was still on the drawing board.[188, 189] Was this space station one the ultimate goals of the Peenemünders? Probably yes, even if in indignation Wernher von Braun's biographers rejected the idea as a fantasy after the war.

In a report for the Americans on 15 May 1945, Wernher von Braun himself described an allegedly civilian version of this orbital station. It would be a variant of Professor Oberth's proposal for an orbital 'observation station' which just by chance would also have been fitted with a gigantic mirror. This one was of metal foil stretched over a huge framework of metal bars. Von Braun said that its purpose was to supply cities with sunlight and energy even at night.

US scientists mocked the idea when they first heard about it after the war. B.J.Spence, Professor of Physics at North Western University called the idea 'a Jules Verne dream'. Another physicist, Professor Bergen Davis of Columbia University, said that in his opinion there was 'nowhere' far above where the force of gravity was 'neutralized' and a faculty colleague agreed that the whole hypothesis of a 'neutralization of gravity' was nonsense. The American experts were at least unanimous that at 5100 miles altitude there was no air. These learned opinions prove beyond doubt that in 1945 worlds lay between the levels of perception of both nations in the field of space travel.

Fortunately for the Allies the German plans were decades short of realization. What German scientists and engineers had been planning may have seemed to the world's public postwar like some crazy fantasy, but amongst those plans was the notorious 'sun cannon' with which Hitler believed he could become Lord of the World. This shows that Nazi Germany was already thinking of the next war. Fifty years were projected by German scientists for the orbital station, an estimate which coincides with the realization of the modern international space station 'IISS'. At the end of the war incomplete project files for Hitler's 'super weapon' were seized by the Americans in western Austria.

In 1966 during the Vietnam War a modification to the German project was proposed and Professor Edgar Everheart of the University of Connecticut developed the simplified

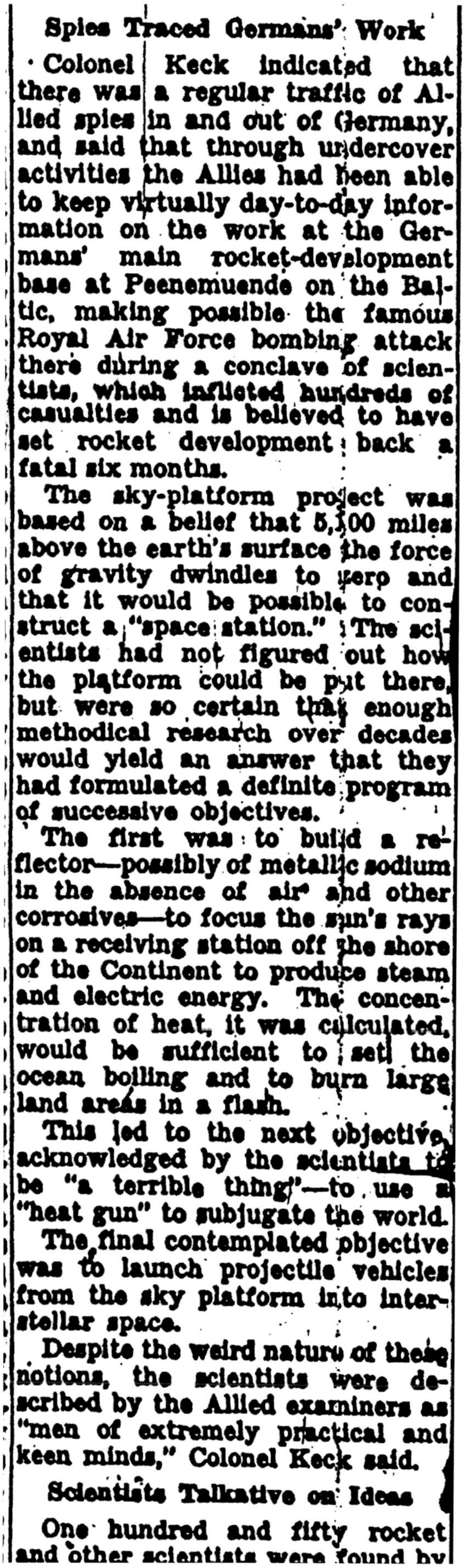

**Spies Traced Germans' Work**

Colonel Keck indicated that there was a regular traffic of Allied spies in and out of Germany, and said that through undercover activities the Allies had been able to keep virtually day-to-day information on the work at the Germans' main rocket-development base at Peenemuende on the Baltic, making possible the famous Royal Air Force bombing attack there during a conclave of scientists, which inflicted hundreds of casualties and is believed to have set rocket development back a fatal six months.

The sky-platform project was based on a belief that 5,100 miles above the earth's surface the force of gravity dwindles to zero and that it would be possible to construct a "space station." The scientists had not figured out how the platform could be put there, but were so certain that enough methodical research over decades would yield an answer that they had formulated a definite program of successive objectives.

The first was to build a reflector—possibly of metallic sodium in the absence of air and other corrosives—to focus the sun's rays on a receiving station off the shore of the Continent to produce steam and electric energy. The concentration of heat, it was calculated, would be sufficient to set the ocean boiling and to burn large land areas in a flash.

This led to the next objective, acknowledged by the scientists to be "a terrible thing"—to use a "heat gun" to subjugate the world.

The final contemplated objective was to launch projectile vehicles from the sky platform into interstellar space.

Despite the weird nature of these notions, the scientists were described by the Allied examiners as "men of extremely practical and keen minds," Colonel Keck said.

**Scientists Talkative on Ideas**

One hundred and fifty rocket and other scientists were found by

Extract from a newspaper report on Colonel Keck's famous press conference of 28 June 1945 giving details of Hitler's project for an orbital station, at the time considered incredible

project *Able* in which a gigantic plastic balloon would be rocketed into orbit carrying a 600-metre diameter lens. The planners calculated that this lens would illuminate a region 350 kilometres wide at night with twice the strength of moonlight. The idea was to limit freedom of movement at night by the Vietcong. The difficulties became apparent quite soon. The necessary precision for working the gigantic piece of equipment could not be effected by radio control from Earth, and the project was shelved.

The idea of the sun mirror was revived in February 1999 when Russian cosmonauts from the space station *Mir* built a reflector mirror, SNAMJA, mounted previously on the *Progress* space ferry M-40. The experiment was to investigate if a sun mirror in space could serve as a light source for whole regions with long winters, for large construction projects and areas of natural catastrophe. The mirror surface was to be from five to eight square kilometres and project to Earth an equivalent of the light of five to ten full moons. Unfortunately the mirror on the probe failed to unfold thus foiling the experiment.

**The space mirror,** revolving around the earth 22,800 miles above the equator, might be a slightly concave disk one mile in diameter. The Germans apparently thought they could focus the rays of the sun (*far left*) to a hot point on a city such as Pittsburgh. At 22,300 miles the speed necessary to keep mirror in motion like a satellite would be enough to carry it around the earth once in 24 hours, *i.e.*, it would stay above the same place as the earth turned. The Germans, complicating the problem, planned to build their mirror at 5,100 miles.

# THE GERMAN SPACE MIRROR

## NAZI MEN OF SCIENCE SERIOUSLY PLANNED TO USE A MAN-MADE SATELLITE AS A WEAPON FOR CONQUEST

In Germany last month U. S. Army technical experts came up with the astonishing fact that German scientists had seriously planned to build a "sun gun," a big mirror in space which would focus the sun's rays to a scorching point at the earth's surface. The Germans, the Army reported, hoped to use such a mirror to burn an enemy city to ashes or to boil part of an ocean. Many U. S. newspaper readers, remembering the eerie success of V-1 and V-2, swallowed nervously.

Plausible schemes to build a station in space were engineered on paper long before the war. European rocket enthusiasts, including Dr. Hermann Oberth, who may have been the designer of V-2, had planned to use the space station not as a weapon but as a refueling point for rockets starting off on journeys into space. The station would revolve around the earth like a tiny man-made moon, obeying the gravitational laws of all heavenly bodies. The centrifugal force of its motion would exactly balance the earth's gravitational pull. Men would live inside the station, breathing an artificial atmosphere. The only major obstacle: constructing a rocket powerful enough to reach a point where a space station could be built. If the modern German scientists had been able to make such a rocket, they might have been able to set up their sun gun. Whether the sun gun would have accomplished what they expected, however, is another matter (*see page 80*).

78

Shortly after Colonel Keck's revelation, in its edition of 23 July 1945 the US magazine *Life* gave further details of the German orbital project. The matter then appears to have been suppressed.

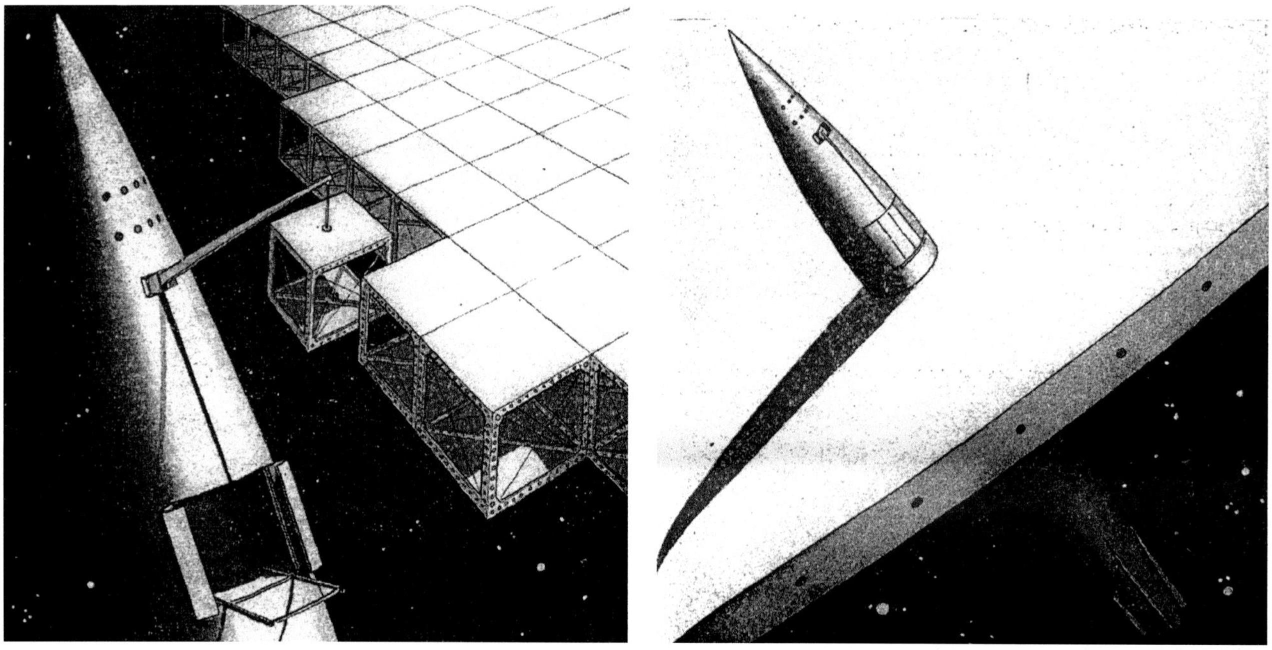

To provide the US public with an impression of the German plan for an orbital sun-mirror, details were supplied in pictorial form. Two examples similar to those appearing in the *Life* article of 23 July 1945 are the building technique for the complex in segments (left) and the docking of a supply rocket (right).

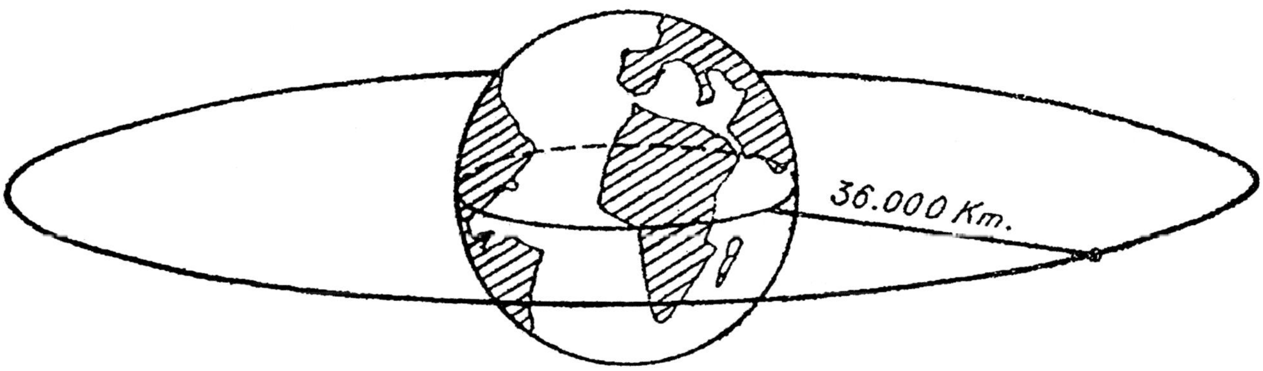


Planned orbital flight path of the German space station above the Equator (per Albert Ducrocq, 1947).

# Panne bei Experiment mit Sonnenspiegel

## Dauerhafte Beleuchtung von Städten wäre ohnehin nicht möglich

**Moskau** – Beim russischen Weltraumexperiment zur Erhellung der Erde gab es Probleme, da der Spiegel sich nicht entfaltete. Das teilte am Donnerstag das „Mir"-Kontrollzentrum mit. Der am Vortag von den Kosmonauten der Raumstation zusammengebaute Rundspiegel war zuvor auf eine Progreß-Raumfähre montiert worden. Um 12.34 Uhr MEZ sollte der Spiegel mit dem Namen „Snamja" (Banner), der einen Durchmesser von 25 Metern hat, entfaltet werden.

Das Experiment soll zeigen, ob ein Sonnenspiegel im All in Zukunft als Lichtquelle für ganze Regionen – Länder mit langem Winter, große Baustellen oder Katastrophengebiete – dienen könnte. Britische Astronomen haben das Sonnenspiegelexperiment ihrer russischen Kollegen jedoch kritisiert. Es sei „eine alptraumhafte Vorstellung", daß die Werbeindustrie die künstlichen Monde für sich entdecken könnte.

Als einen riesigen Werbegag bezeichnete hingegen Andrew Coates vom Mullard Raumfahrtlaboratorium den gesamten Versuch. Die Astronomen sollten sich nicht zu sehr aufregen, forderte er. Sonnenspiegel seien eine ziemlich verrückte Idee, um Städte zu beleuchten. Das Vielversprechende an dem Versuch seien vielmehr die neuen Erkenntnisse für einen Solarantrieb von Weltraumfahrzeugen.

Schon andere Wissenschaftler hatten das Experiment im voraus kritisiert. Aufgrund der hohen Umlaufgeschwindigkeit des Satelliten um die Erde kann ein solcher Satellit nur für kurze Zeit Licht spenden. In einer geostationären Umlaufbahn ... Abstand dann aber so ... benüt- ...

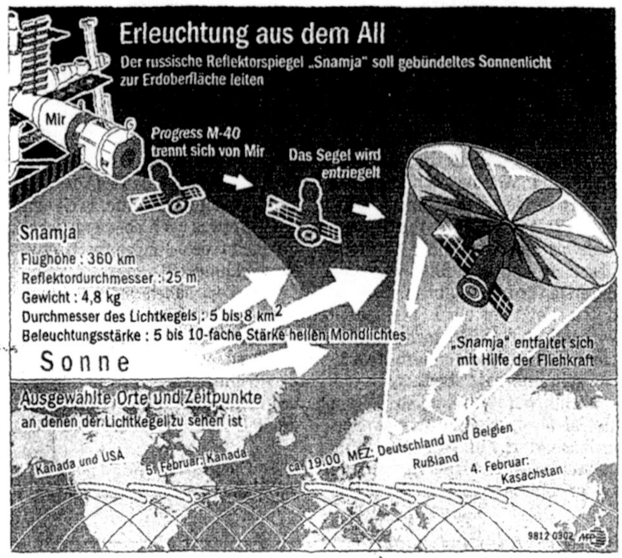


# Neuer Spiegelmond soll Licht nach Sibirien bringen

**Der neue Mond am Himmel – ein sensationelles Experiment russischer Weltraum-Wissenschaftler.**

**So soll es sein:**

9. November 1998: Auf einer Abschußrampe in der russischen Steppe steht eine Rakete, die Außenhaut glitzert in der Sonne. Stickstoff tritt durch Düsen nach außen, bildet kräuselnde Wölkchen. **Knopfdruck – und START!**

Minuten später. Die Trägerrakete wird abgesprengt. Der Kopf des Projektils fliegt weiter, erreicht die vorberechnete Umlaufbahn.

Das Projektil schwebt **außerhalb des Erdschattens** lautlos im All. Das Projektil öffnet sich. Ein Metallstück gleitet in den leeren Raum. Es entfaltet sich.

**Ein Spiegel erscheint!**

Der Spiegel gleißt im Licht der Sonne. Die Menschen auf der Erde sehen den Spiegel wie einen Dauerblitz. **Er ist hundertmal heller als der Mond.**

Der Widerschein des Spiegelmonds trifft unten auf den Nachtschatten unseres Planeten. Langsam wandert er mit der Erddrehung **von Osten nach Westen** – wie Sonne und Mond. Erst über sibirische Einöden, dann über Irkutsk, Kiew, der Hauptstadt der Ukraine.

**Dann geht der Spiegelmond über Frankfurt auf, wandert weiter nach Brüssel, London, verschwindet über dem Atlantik, Richtung Nordamerika.**

Die Menschen, die in den Himmel starren, müssen vor Schmerz die Augen schließen, der kleine Fleck am Firmament flackert wie ein Höllenfeuer.

Der erste künstliche Mond wird wieder in der Atmosphäre verglühen. Danach werden dutzende solcher Spiegelmonde hochgeschossen und im All zusammengekoppelt (Durchmesser: mindestens 200 Meter).

**Was soll das Experiment?**

Die Russen wollen mit dem Riesenmond ihre Städte in Sibirien auch nachts **taghell** anstrahlen. Das spart Strom. Auftraggeber ist der russiche Konzern **Energia**, die Zentrale für Energieverwaltung. Sie sitzt in der Stadt Korolew nahe Moskau. Das Raumschiff heißt „Znamya" (Banner).

Wissenschaftler in aller Welt sind von dem Experiment fasziniert, aber auch viele kritische Stimmen.

**Dr. David Thomas** im Londoner TV-Sender BBC: „Das ganze Ökosystem der Erde ist in Gefahr. **Sex, Schlaf, Essen – alles wird von der Lichtdauer des Tages gesteuert.** Wir dürfen es nicht stören."

**Daniel Green** vom Harvard-Smithonian Center: „Hirnlose Versuche!"

Der Moskauer BILD-Korrespondent: „Die Energia hat im Augenblick Geldprobleme. Sie behauptet, der Versuch werde vertagt." Aber die Planungen sind abgeschlossen.

**Dr. John Morris,** Berater der US-Raumfahrtbehörde NASA: „Keine Nation der Welt hat das Recht, **der Natur so dramatisch ins Handwerk zu pfuschen.** Ich fordere alle Regierungen der Welt auf, gegen den Versuch zur protestieren."

***Am 9. November werden alle Weltraumforscher in den Himmel starren...***

**Die Sonne bestrahlt immer nur eine Hälfte der Erde. Der kleine Satellit wirft mit seinem Spiegel das Licht auf die Nachtseite – ein zweiter Mond!**

On 23 July 1998, *Bild* magazine reported on the Russian ‚space mirror' project which was a small-scale version of the earlier Hitler project. The project, codenamed SNAMJA came to grief in 1999. (Source: *Die Welt* newspaper, 5 February 1999)

# *Conclusion*

*Given a little more time....*

**Summary of German rockets and missiles as miracle weapons beyond the enemy's gaze**

Scarcely ten years after Wernher von Braun discussed with the Chief of the German Army Weapons Bureau the possibility of space travel, Germany succeeded in preparing the technical and organisational means to attack the United States with intercontinental rockets. What did the USA actually believe of this immediately after the threat vanished?

A report by Chief of the General Staff George Marshall published in the *New York Times* on 10 October 1945 stated: "American factories lay at the extreme outer range of rockets fired from Europe". This assertion is nonsense in the face of recorded history which maintains that V-2 rockets were the final word in German engineering genius. Yet Marshall was sure that America had been lucky.[190] At the end of 'the German War' American military and civilian rocket experts were astonished at German progress in the manufacture and remote-control of V-Weapons.

US Colonel Holgar Toftoy was nominated commander of the new Rocket Division at the end of the war, and the USA became indebted to him for the almost perfect transfer of the German rocket and missile programme. For his services in obtaining German rocket specialists, many tonnes of files and at least one hundred ready-to-fire V-2s he was promoted shortly afterwards to Major-General. Toftoy declared later: "We were bloody beginners when my staff brought over the V-2 rockets from Germany. From these we obtained the basic knowledge that saved us more than five billion dollars and ten years research and development".[191]

Major Robert B. Staver was equally candid after discovering Hitler's space programme: "If a reasonable programme is developed to make use of the German scientists, this country (i.e. the USA) will lead the rest of the world by about 25 years. In the next 100 years the programme which will soon be laid down will lead to one of the most exciting scientific enterprises in history."[192]

Besides the scientific and economic significance of capturing German rockets and missiles there came clear statements from the Americans on the military aspect. Thus in the US periodical *American Magazine* there appeared in 1946 a critical article mentioning certain facts still open to debate sixty years later:

"VICTORY IN THE AIR OVER THE GERMANS. We won in the air against the Germans by might, not with foresight: the High Command of our air force clung firmly to yesterday's ideas and weapons. The Germans however developed the weapons of today and tomorrow and used them. After our victory, Allied scientists and engineers visited German Luftwaffe laboratories and testing stations. They could see not only the superiority of new German weapons at a glance, but also found plans for the future which needed years for fruition. That is a sign of the vision of the Germans and their motivation to try out all ideas. How could we have triumphed against these new weapons? Over a dozen other V-Weapons were under development, amongst them rockets for transporting troops in pressurized cabins, or which could be fired from a U-boat submerged at 90 metres. Another could fly at 27,750 kms/hr and cross the Atlantic at an altitude of 800 kilometres."

"Attacks were planned on New York. That was no Utopian thinking. In a year at the latest they would have done it. If out invasion had been delayed by so little as six months, the Germans would have had complete air supremacy, not only on the continent, but over the Channel and southern England. We would have been able to carry out only the less effective night attacks while they could have bombarded England continuously."

"Their bombs would have fallen on airfields, on troop assemblies, have destroyed ports and sunk shipping. The losses would have been enormous, the invasion perhaps impossible. Their better aircraft would have destroyed ours on the ground, just as we did to theirs. Meanwhile V-Weapons would have landed in salvoes. They wanted to fire one thousand V1s at England daily. More effective rockets than the V-2 would have hit all important cities. England would have been completely blockaded. Even if the Germans had not landed in England, in order to avoid total annihilation the British would have had to sue for peace."

"After the conquest of Germany I visited V-Weapons launch sites. I can only say, and repeat over and over: We were just in time! They were not quite ready, and for that reason alone we were not defeated."

His was not a lone voice crying in the wilderness. Other American authorities confirm that Germany's superiority in the field of rocket and missile technologies would have guaranteed victory if more time had been allowed them to deploy the new weapons systems then under development and test.

In view of such bland admissions by informed US sources one is perplexed that modern historians prefer to take none of this into their reasonings. They have been harmonious in maintaining over the decades that after the defeat at Stalingrad, the Germans went on to the defensive militarily and their V-Weapons played no further role in subsequent events to the end of the war.

In the October 1946 edition of *Harper's Magazine*, C – Lester Walker wrote: "All such revelations naturally raise the question: Was Germany so far advanced in air, rocket and missile research that given a little more time she might have won the war? Her secrets, as now disclosed, would seem to indicate that possibility." C. Lester Walker was a journalist of standing with the American military. He had had long interviews with senior officers of the Technical Industrial Intelligence Committee. Assuredly there would have been much which they withheld from him, but what he wrote in his enormous article is easily confirmed from BIOS, CIOS and FIAT reports.

In all probability it will never be certain how close the Germans actually came to destroying New York in rocket attacks, or whether at least they were preparing to do so in a desperate last throw. In the *New York Times* edition of 27 June 1945, senior US official Leo T Crowley wrote that the Germans were only six months short of eradicating New York with 'improved V-2s', while US astronaut Gordon Cooper must have had good reason for stating that at the war's end "only a week separated New York from a possible 'Ground Zero' over a large area". Did the United States escape catastrophe by a hair's breadth?

# *Epilogue*

During the war crimes trials at Nuremberg, Hermann Goering and Albert Speer were in agreement that the danger which humanity would have faced had all the secret weapons under development in the Third Reich come to maturity "defied belief". With the exception of Dr Kammler, these two men were the best placed of the former leaders of the Third Reich to know about weapons "which could never possibly have been".

In his last notes before his suicide on 16 October 1946, Goering drew attention to future 'Star Wars'. His concluding paperwork was confiscated by the Nuremberg prison governor, Col. Burton C Andrus, and has been released only in segments to the present day. The contents of a warning message from Goering to Churchill, then British Prime Minister, written on a label he had peeled away from a jar or tin, have meanwhile become known.

In common with certain experts of the Third Reich in the 1940s, today's military strategists look to space as being 'the uplands' of decisive importance. Long-range ballistic rockets, manned rocket craft and space stations exist in the arsenals of the World Powers as do laser and particle-beam weapons with which the Germans were experimenting in the Second World War. Nevertheless, a 'War in Space' still sounds to us like science fiction even at the beginning of the 21st century, and until now (so we are assured) there have been no bellicose encounters beyond the Earth's atmosphere.

US sources report, however, that during the Cold War the Soviets attempted to 'blind' American spy satellites, and in 2001 the German-born engineer Günter Wendt revealed that the KGB planned to cause the destruction of the moon rockets Saturn V and Apollo 11 by the use of rogue radio signals. Wendt, NASA director responsible for security at the Cape Canaveral firing ramp, worked for the American space agency from 1967-1989. He stated in his book *The Unbroken Chain* that on 16 July 1969 harmless-looking KGB trawlers fishing off the coast of Florida intended to interfere with the Apollo electronics by the use of radio signals and so cause a disaster. The Russian scheme failed when the CIA discovered the plan and installed equipment to jam the frequencies involved. According to Wendt, the KGB also planned to capture the Apollo capsule and crew when it ditched in the Pacific on its return, but were beaten to the retrieval spot by the Americans.

Whether the Americans resorted to like measures against the Soviet space programme is unknown, but it would not be surprising having regard to what is known about how the Cold War was fought. Even after the demise of the Soviet Union, it can be seen that the leading World Powers are arming for war in the Space Dimension. By 'World Powers' one does not mean only the United States and Russia: China has a 'Star Wars' programme with regard to which military experts, such as the former US Defence Minister Rumsfeld, have stressed the dangers of a "Space Pearl Harbour", the threat of a sneak attack from Space.

Who can still doubt that the layers above the Earth's atmosphere and Space itself could be the theatre of war in which an armed conflict of the future is decided? It is in our hands whether Hermann Goering's prophecy of doom will one day become reality, or we ensure that it remains merely a grim reminder to our descendants of how close we came.

# *Notes*

## Notes from Part 1

1 From *Harper's Magazine*, October 1946, p.329.

2, 3 In BIOS Final Report 142(g), British Intelligence mentioned certain tests conducted by the Waffen-SS at Berlin Döberitz in late 1944. When an 'additive' was added to a 50 kg conventional explosive, the devastating effect of the explosion resulted in the extinction of all life within 3 kilometres of the impact point. The suspicion that this was Hitler's apocalyptic explosive is strengthened by two reports from published Allied sources. In a radio broadcast in July 1945 before the US atom bomb attacks on Japan, Wing-Cdr A G Pither, RAAF, stated: *Had they been given the extra period in which to perfect it, the Germans would have used a 'uranium disintegrating bomb'.* He added that pound for pound the weapon had a destructive force one hundred times greater than the V-2 warhead, and could be mass produced. (From: *Flight and Aircraft Engineering* (the official organ of the Royal Aero Club), 26 July 1945, p.87 (Section *Here and There*). In the *New York Times* edition of 22 October 1944 at page E5, an article on the German miracle weapon stated: ...*Neutral sources describe the U-bomb as resembling an aircraft in shape which can be manufactured in different sizes....A radio signal detonates the explosive and the additive simultaneously: the expansion of the explosion when it becomes a gas is greatly increased by the force of the disintegrating uranium atoms....there is no doubt that the Germans are straining every nerve to complete it and put it to use before the forthcoming onslaught by the Allied armies.* The principle on which this additive was built remains a closely guarded secret. (Tr.)

## Notes from Part II

1 In 1962 a DDR quasi-judicial tribunal took depositions from local residents for an enquiry entitled *Befragung von Bürgern zu Ereignissen zur örtlichen Geschichte,* the purpose of which was to enquire into Nazi wartime activities in the Ohrdruf region. The hearing was at Arnstadt Town Hall where the papers were declassified after the reunification of Germany in 1989. The four depositions of interest were: (1) a former Buchenwald inmate gave evidence that he helped erect the staging for an enormously long rocket at MUNA Rudisleben close to Ichtershausen: (2) and (3) a former technician and a former fuel engineer stated that they had actually worked on the construction of the huge rocket over 30 metres long which was allegedly fired on the night of 16 March 1945 from Polte II underground facility one kilometre from Rudisleben. The fourth deponent, Frau Claere Werner, was throughout the war the custodian of the Wachsenburg watchtower near Ohrdruf. She stated that at about 2300 hrs on 16 March 1945 in company with a group of *Reichspost* and *Wehrmacht* plain-clothed officials she was on the tower looking towards Ichtershausen (which is behind Rudisleben from the Wachsenburg Tower) when the area suddenly became bright and something rose towards the heavens trailing a great tail fire. It grew ever smaller heading northwards. Afterwards everybody celebrated until daybreak. (Tr.)

2 This material was added with the collaboration of the author. (Tr.)

## General


(1) Olaf Przybinski, *Spurensuche, Band 10 – Das Geheimnis der deutschen raketengetriebenen Fluggeräte*, p.7, Podzun-Pallas, 2002

(2) Peter P.Wegener, *The Peenemünde Wind Tunnels*, p.31–33, 67/68, 77, 89, 177, Yale University, 1996

(3) Leslie E. Simon, *Secret Weapons of the Third Reich – German Research in World War II*, p.11, 13, 76, 84, 85, 130, 132–133, 140–154, WE, 1971

(4) Friedrich Georg, *Hitlers Siegeswaffen*, Vol 1, p.22–26, Amun, 2000

(5) Ernst Stuhlinger, Frederick I. Ordway III., *Wernher von Braun – Crusader for Space*, p.33, Krieger, 1996

(6) Michael J. Neufeld, *The Rocket and the Reich*, p.283, The Free Press, 1995

(7) Dieter Hölsken, *V-Missiles of the Third Reich*, p.265, Monogram, 1994

(8) Julius Mader, *Geheimnis von Huntsville*, p.330–331, Deutscher Militär-Verlag, 1963

(9) Dr. Walter Dornberger, *V2 – Der Schuß ins Weltall*, p.155–156, Bechtle, 1952

(10) Michael Neufeld, ibid, p.283, The Free Press, 1995

(11) Kammler's Telegram to Dr. Brandt for Himmler's information, 20. October 1943, 20:15 hr, C BA NS 10/ Old 273

(12) Albert Speer, *Infiltration – How Heinrich Himmler Schemed to build an SS-Industrial Empire*, p.354, Macmillan 1981

(13) Henry Picker, *Hitlers Tischgespräche im Führerhauptquartier*, p.683, 2. Ed., Propyläen TB, 1997

(14) Heinz J. Nowarra, *Die Deutsche Luftrüstung 1933–1945*, Vol. 4, p.63–64, Bernard & Graefe, 1968

(15) J. R. Smith, Antony Kay, *German Aircraft of the second World War*, p.654, Patnam, 1978

(16) J. Miranda, P.Mercado, *Die geheimen Wunderwaffen des III. Reiches*, p.75–77, Flugzeuge, 1995

(17) Heinz Magenheimer, *Die Militärstrategie Deutschlands*, p.33–36, 136, 2. Ed., Herbig, 1997

(18) PMP AESCALA, Cat. No. 5073, ENW A-10/A-4, p.3

(19) Franz Kurowski, *Raketenpionier Arthur Rudolph. Geehrt – verfehmt – rehabilitiert*, p.59, Vohwinckel, 2001

(20) Ibid, p.61
(21) Brett Davis, 'V-2 plant survivors publicize their story', via David Monaghan
(22) Dieter Hölsken, *V-Missiles of the Third Reich*, p.265, Monogram
(23) Kurt Grasser, 'Projekt Zement', in: *IBA-Informationen*, p.39–52, Issue 19, 1991
(24) Kurt Grasser, 'Projekt Zement', in: *IBA-Informationen*, S. 37–42, Issue 20, July 1992
(25) OSS-b-1626. F-0.8.2.45
(26) Manuel Castillo, Luis de Caralt, *Himmler et son Empire*, p.345, Graficas Diamante, 1969
(27) Unpublished document, Dr. X, 8. July 2001, author's archive.
(28) Dr.-X files – communication of 22. November 2001
(29) Henry Stevens, *Hitlers Flying Saucers, A Guide to German Flying Discs of the Second World War*, p.91/92, Manuscript, 2002
(30) Ralf Blank, 'Energie für die ›Vergeltung‹ – Akkumulatoren-Fabrik A6 Hagen und das Deutsche Raketenprogramm 1942–1945', in: *Hagener Jahrbuch* 3 (1997), p.141–151, Lesezeichen-Verlag, 1997
(31) Jay Miller, *The X-Planes, X-1 to X-45*, p 136–141, 3.Ed., Midland, 2001
(32) Mark Wade, NAVAHO/X-15, www.astronautix.com (Internet)
(33) Bill Gunston, *Die illustrierte Enzyklopädie der Raketen-Lenkwaffen*, Buch und Zeit, 1981
(34) In *Air force in the Atomic Age* by Dexter Masters and Katherine Wax, published by McGraw-Hill in 1946 (p.26-32). General Arnold mentioned German piggy-back rocket research. These experiments must therefore have involved at least the V-2.
(35) Walter Dornberger, *V2 – Der Schuß ins Weltall*, p.155, Bechtle, 1952
(36) G. Ward Price, 'Fly-Bombs were meant for US-Huge Ramp found', *The Daily Mail*, 30 October 1944, in: Edgar Mayer und Thomas Mehner, *Hitler und die 'Bombe'*, p.181, Kopp, 2002
(37) Jay Miller, *The X-Planes: X-1 to X-45*, p.137, 3. Ed, Midland, 2001
(38) David Myrha, *Sänger – Germany's Orbital Rocket bomber in World War II*, p.49, Schiffer, 2002
(39) Horst Lommel, *Vom Höhenaufklärer bis zum Raumgleiter*, p.219–229, Motorbuch, 2000
(40) Kurt W. Streit/John W. R. Taylor, *Geschichte der Luftfahrt*, p.428–431, Faunas, 1976
(41) Patrick Flannery, letter to the author, 1. June 2001
(42) Scott Lowther, 'Manned A-9, Description', Part Time Models, Lakewood
(43) Fritz Hahn, *Waffen und Geheimwaffen des deutschen Heeres 1933–1945*, Vol. 2, p.137–141, Bernard & Graefe, 1987
(44) Antony L. Kay, *German Jet Energy and Gas Turbine Development, 1930–1945*, p.273–275, Airlife, 2002
(45) Matthias Uhl, *Stalins V-2*, p.95, Bernard & Graefe, 2001
(46) Jaen Cuny, *Les Avions de Combat Français, 1944–1960*, Vol. II, p.116–118, Docavia No. 30, Lariviere
(47) Bill Gunston, *Die illustrierte Enzyklopädie der Raketen und Lenkwaffen*, p.42/51, Buch und Zeit, 2001
(48) Mark Wade G-5 – Groettrup –, www.astronautics.com, 2001
(49) Werner Buedeler, *Geschichte der Raumfahrt*, p.326, Sigloch Edition
(50) Antonio Chover, letter to the author, 2. August 2002
(51) Mark Wade's 'Internet-Space Encyclopaedia' is a unique source of knowledge on all aspects of space travel. www.astronautics.com, 2001
(52) Edgar Mayer und Thomas Mehner, *Das Geheimnis der deutschen Atom-*
*bombe – Gewannen Hitlers Wissenschaftler den nuklearen Wettlauf doch?*, p.54, Kopp, 2001
(53) Julius Mader, *Geheimnis von Huntsville*, p.331–333, 338, Deutscher Militär-Vrlag, 1963
(54) Walter Dornberger, *V2 – Der Schuß ins Weltall*, p.263, Bechtle, 1952
(55) Otto Skorzeny, *Meine Kommando-Unternehmen*, p.156, Universitas, 1993
(56) Dr. X, unpublished document, 24 January 2001, Dornberger, 7 A-10 and Schier
(57) Howard A. Buechner, Wilhelm Bernhart, *Hitler's Ashes*, p.163, Thunderbird, 1989
(58) 'V-2's with a range of 3000 miles would have been ready by VE-Day' *The Daily Mail*, Thursday, June 14th, 1945, p.1
(59) Antonio Chover, letter to the author, 2. November 2002
(60) Albert Speer, *Infiltration – How Heinrich Himmler Schemed to build an SS-Industrial Empire*, p.210/354, MacMillan, 1981
(61) Kammler's telegram to Dr. Brandt for information of Himmler, October 1945, 8:15 p.m., BA NS 19/old 273
(62) Botho Stüwe, *Peenemünde West*, p.783–785, Bechtle, 1995
(63) Michael J. Neufeld, *The Rocket and the Reich*, p.257, The Free Press, 1995
(64) Michael J. Neufeld, ibid.
(65) Jürgen Michels, *Peenemünde und seine Erben in Ost und West – Entwicklung und Weg deutscher Geheimwaffen*, p.114, Bernard & Graefe, 1997
(66) John Foreman, S. E. Harry, *The Messerschmitt Me 262 Combat diary*, p.170, Air Research, 1995
(67) Volkhardt Bode, Gerhard Kaiser, *Raketenspuren – Peenemünde 1936/1996*, p.127–128, Bechtermünz, 1997
(68) Dr.-X-files, letters of 20. November 2000, 21. January 2001, 24. January 2001 und 4. February 2001.
(69) Howard A. Büchner, Wilhelm Bernhardt, *Hitler's Akte*, p.162–163, Thunderbird, 1989
(70) Witness accounts of the 'noteworthy' German terror attacks on weapons factories in the Urals from March 1945 are to be found in the Spanish language edition of the Soviet digest *Sputnik*. A search through all German language editions of *Sputnik* in the German Library at Leipzig failed to identify the item. Therefore the particular edition was missing from the library collection or the item was omitted by the publishers from the German language version.
(71) Dr.-X-files, information, 4. November 2002
(72) Werner Büdeler, *Geschichte der Raumfahrt*, Sigloch Edition

(73) Mark Wade, 'Encyclopedia Astronautica', www.astronautics.com, 2002
(74) Renato Vesco, *Operazione Plenilunio*, p.171, Murcia, 1971
(75) Flaggalleer i Osls pa de allierades day', in: *Dagens Nyteter*, Stockholm,1. July 1945, p.ID
(76) 'V2's with a range of 3000 miles would have been ready by VE-Day', in: *The Daily Mail*, Thursday, June 14th, 1945, p.1
(77) Gordon Cooper, *Leap of faith – an Astronaut's journey into the unknown*, p.154, Harper Collins, 2000
(78) Luigi Romersa, 'Wernher von Braun y la America del Futuro, parte II: Las V2 y la base secreta alemania de Peenemünde', in: *Las Provincias*, p.18, 10. March 1959
(79) Antonio Chover, letter to the author, 2. August 2002
(80) J. Richard Smith, Eddie J. Creek, *Arado 234 Blitz*, p.165, Monogram, 1992
(81) Wilhelm Helmold, *Die V1*, p.153, 154, 221–227, Bechtle, 1988
(82) Myrone N. Cuich, *Armes secrets et ouverages mysterioux de Dunkerque a Cherbourg*, p.134, Jean-Bernard, 1996
(83) Fritz Trenkle, *Die deutschen Funkmeßverfahren bis 1945*, p.86, 98–102, Hüthig, 1986
(84) David Pritchard, *The Radar War*, p.120–122, Patrick Stephens, 1989
(85) Davis Hobbs, *Die Waffen im Weltraum*, p.20–21, Podzum Pallas, 1988
(86) Karsten Porezag, *Geheime Kommandosache*, p.155, Wetzlardruck, 1996
(87) Roland Hautefenille, *Constructions speciales*, p.301, Jean-Bernard, 1995
(88) Benjamin King, Timothy Kutta, *Impact – the history of Germany's V-weapons in World War II*, p.272 (HE III), Sarpedon, 1998
(89) Fritz Trenkle, ibid, p.98/99, Hüthig, 1986
(90) Manfred Griehl, *Heinkel He 111*, p.272, Motorbuch, 1997
(91) Botho Stüwe, *Peenemünde West – die Erprobungsstelle der Luftwaffe für geheime Fernlenkwaffen und deren Entwicklungsgeschichte*, p.679–681, Bechtle, 1995
(92) Renato Vesco, David Hatcher Childres, *Man-made UFO's 1944–1994*, p.146–147, Adventures Unlimited, 1994
(93) David Irving, *Die Geheimwaffen des Dritten Reiches*, S. 337–338, Reinhard Mohn, 1967
(94) Fritz Trenkle, ibid, p.117/118, 2. Ed., Hüthig, 1982
(95) Roland Hautenfenille, *Constructions Speciales*, p.297, Jean-Bernard, 1995
(96) Roland Hautenfenille, ibid.
(97) William R. Lyne, *Space Aliens from the Pentagon*, S. 72–78, Ereatopia, 1993
(98) Bill Gunston, *Die Illustrierte Enzyklopädie der Raketen und Lenkwaffen*, p.17, 58, Buch und Zeit, 1981
(99) Renato Vesco, David Hatcher Childres, ibid, p.148–149.
(100) John Gimbel, *Science, Technology, Reparations, Exploitation and Plunder in Postwar Germany*, p.54, Stanford University, 1990
(101) 'Arnold urges single defense department', in: *Washington Post*, 20. October 1945: p.1–2
(102) Fritz Trenkle, ibid, p.22–23, 145–153.
(103) Renato Vesco, *Operazione Plenilunio*, p.82, Murcia, 1972
(104) Herr Frode Silent was one of these exceptions as he wrote to Spanish scientist Norberto Lahuerta on 12. November 1997.
(105) J. Miranda and P.Merkado, *Die geheimen Wunderwaffen des Dritten Reiches*, p.83, Dörfler, 2002
(106) This information, received by the author from Kammler-researcher Tom Agoston, corresponds from the technical point of view to solutions employed postwar by the Americans
(107) *Der Spiegel*, No. 42, 13. October 1949, '3. russischer Atomversuch', http://www.spiegel.de/spiegel/vor50
(108) The author is grateful to Antonio Chover for his contribution to this chapter.
(109) Phil Henshall, *Hitler's V-weapons sites*, p.38, 122, 150, 166–169, Sutton, 2002
(110) Roland Hautefenilles, ibid.
(111) Phil Henshall, *Vengeance*, p.105–106 (Sutton, 1995) quotes additionally the former curator of the Watten Museum from the 1950s. With the advent of new curators everything relating to this subject vanished. .
(112) Roland Hautefenilles, ibid, p.280-285.
(113) Phil Henshall, *Hitler's V-weapons sites*, p.125–133, 132–141, Sutton, 2002
(114) GD-639.2.8 FE. 1741, Permanent launching sites, Projekt Z Salamander HVP, 1944, Deutsches Museum, Munich.
(115) Phil Henshall, letter to the author, 7. May 2002
(116) David Irving, *Die Geheimwaffen des Dritten Reiches*, p.308–309, Mohn, 1967
(117) Phil Henshall, letter to the author, 20. March 2002
(118) Phil Henshall, letter to the author, 28. March 2002
(119) Henry Picker, *Hitlers Tischgespräche im Führerhauptquartier*, p.683, Propyläen Taschenbuch, Ullstein, 1997
(120) Jak P.Mallman-Showell, *Deutsche U-Boote an feindlichen Küsten*, p.57–64, Motorbuch 2002
(121) Günther W. Gellermann, *Geheime Reichssache – geheime Kommandosache – rätselhafte Fälle aus der Zeit des 2. Weltkriegs*, p.18–24, E. S. Mittler, 2002
(122) Clay Blair, *Der U-Boot-Krieg 1942–1945 – die Gejagten*, p.919–920, Bechtermünz, 1998
(123) Edgar Mayer, Thomas Mehner, *Das Geheimnis der deutschen Atombombe*,
p.118, Kopp, 2001
(124) *ABC* (Madrid, 15. December 1944, p.14)
(125) Erich Kröner, *Die deutschen Kriegsschiffe 1815–1945*, Vol. 5, p.207, Bernard und Graefe, 1988
(126) According to Joachim H. Rudek, *U-Boote an der Wetterfront des 2. Weltkrieges*, Schiffahrtsgeschichtliche Gesellschaft Ostsee e.V. (1999), p.40,WBS 1 sank on 6 January 1945. Were two ships of this designation lost on the polar coast?
(127) Joachim H. Rudeck, ibid, p.34/35, 42/43,
(128) Adam R. A. Claasen, *Hitler's Northern War – The Luftwaffe's Ill-fated Campaign 1949–45*, p.226, University Press of Kansas, 2001
(129) Joint Intelligence Staff, Memorandum of Request Enemy Activity in Greenland, US National Archives RG 457/622
(130) 'Deutsche Kampfgruppe noch auf Grönland?' In: *Wiener Montag*, 29.12.1947, p.2

(131) German Research Projekt (GRP), letter to the author, 2. May 2002
(132) Rudolf Lusar, *Die deutschen Waffen und Geheimwaffen des 2.Weltkrieges und ihre Weiterentwicklung*, p.417, 6. Ed., J. K. Lebermann, 1997
(133) Joachim H. Rudeck, ibid, p.19.
(134) Julius Mader, *Geheimnis von Huntsville*, p.326–337, Deutscher Militär-Verlag, 1963
(135) Friedrich Georg, *Hitlers Siegeswaffen*, Vol. 1, p.198–199, Amun, 2000
(136) Jak P.Mallmann-Showell, ibid, p.15.
(137) Luigi Romersa, 'Wernher von Braun y la América del Futuro, Part II: Las V2 y la base secreta alemán del Peenemünde', in *Las Provincias*, 10. March 1959, p.18
(138) Clay Blair, *Der U-Boot-Krieg 1942–1945 – die Gejagten*, p.924, Weltbild 2001
(139) Albert Baime, 'How close did the Nazis come to attacking the East Coast?', in: *Maxim*, May 2002, p.140–148
(140) Erich Gröner, Dieter Jung, Martin Maas, *Die deutschen Kriegsschiffe 1815– 1945*, Vol. 3, p.110, Bernard und Graefe, 1985
(141) 'Des Rätsels Lösung als Lohn – Die Entdeckung von U-869', p.1–3, *Spiegel* Online, 24. May 2001
(142) Clay Blair, *Der U-Boot-Krieg 1942–1945 – die Gejagten*, p.932–933, Bechtermünz, 1999
(143) Joseph Mark Scabia, *Germany's Last Mission to Japan*, p.148, Jetham, 2000
(144) Gordan Cooper, Bruce Henderson, *Leap of Faith*, p.154, Harper Collins, 2000
(145) Antonio Chover, letter of 23 November 2002
(146) Hans-Joachim Polte, *Militärgeschichtlicher Reiseführer Peenemünde*, p.64, Mittler, 1995
(147) The author begs the indulgence of the readership that no further details can be supplied at present having regard to protecting the source.
(148) Kurt Grasser, letter to the author, 11 August 2002
(149) Sir Roy Fedden, 'German plans to revolutionise air warfare', in: *The Daily Telegraph*, Part 1: 1. October 1945, p.4: Part 2, 2 October 1945, p.4: Part 3, 5 Ocotber 1945, Part 4, 9 Octobner 1945, p.4.
(150) Dr. Walter Dornberger, ibid, p.282–286
(151) Karl-Heinz Zunneck, *Geheimtechnologien* 2, p.36–37, CTT, 1999
(152) Headquarters United States Strategic Air Forces in Europe (REAR), Office of the Director of Intelligence AAF 390, 5. January 1945 – Memorandum to General George C. McDonald
(153) For this assessment account was taken of Germany's requirements of chrome ore. Because of the adverse war situation all sources of the raw material had been closed to Germany – but chrome was not essential to prosecuting the war further. For more on this subject see Werner Maser, Adolf Hitler. *Legende – Mythos – Wirklichkeit*, 16. Ed., p.518, Heyne, 1997
(154) Valentin Falin *Die zweite Front – Die Interessenkonflikte der Anti-Hitler-Koalition*, p.459/460, Knaur, 1997
(155) Archive Thomas Mehner, witness statement, 4. October 2001
(156) SHAEF-Telegrams, 1. November 1944, 3. November 1944, 5. November 1944, 7. November 1944, 11. November 1944, 13. November 1944, 14. November 1944, 18. November 1944, Stockholm to Tokyo, Nr. 232, 9. December 1944, NSA, NA, RG 457, SRA 14630
(157) Preparing the American Public for a V-3 attack – Dec. 1944, L/C Box 223, USAF Microfilm reel 43811
(158) Joseph A. Persico, *Roosevelt's Secret War. FDR and World War II Espionage*, p.382/383, 411, Random House Trade, Paperback Edition, New York 2001
(159) Edgar Mayer, Thomas Mehner, *Das Geheimnis der deutschen Atombombe*, p.54–56, Kopp, 2001
(160) General Arnold: Countermeasures against V-2 Installations, L/C Box 54 1,81, USAF Microfilm reel 43811
(161) Joseph E. Persico, *Piercing the Reich*, p.12–14, 333–334, Barnes & Noble, 1997
(162) Dan Hagedorn, Leif Hellstrom, *Foreign Invaders*, p.169, Midland, 1994
(163) Letter from Kristian Knaack to the author. Knaack's book with many previously unknown revelations about the powerful SS Czar of Technology is expected in publication soon.
(164) Dieter Wolf, 'Neues Deutschland', twelve-part factual report beginning 28. June 1966, quoted in: Günter Nagel, *Atomversuche in Deutschland*, p.284, Heinrich-Jung-Verlagsgesellschaft, 2002 (The USAAF raid on the Auer-Uranium/Thorium factory at Oranienburg is considered by some experts to have marked the opening phase of the Cold War).
(165) Clay Blair, *Der U-Boot-Krieg 1942–1945 – die Gejagten*, p.972–973, Weltbild, 1998
(166) David Monaghan: *V-bombs on New York inside 60 days* – Ingram and Dewey, E-Mail to the author, 21. January 2002
(167) David Monaghan, E-Mail to the author, 19 May 2003 regarding an article in *Life* (November 1945 edition).
(168) George C. Marshall, Biennial Report of the Chief of Staff of the United States Army, July 1, 1943 to June 30, 1945, to the Secretary of War, p.118, Reprint HMS Stationery Office 1945.
(169) These statements, which appeared in numerous US newspapers, were made by Leo Crowley, then Foreign Economic Administrator. He was quoting to a Senate Committee from 29 studies on postwar (Chicago Daily Tribune, 27 June 1945, p.4)
(170) 'Guided Missiles – The Weapon of the Future' in: *Intelligence Bulletin*, April 1946, p.2, 18, War Department, Washington D.C.
(171) *The Daily Mail*, 5. May 1945, p.1, 'U.S. Coast has a V-Scare'
(172) Mark Wade, Peenemünde in: Encyclopedia astronautica, www.astronautix.com (Internet)
(173) Wilhelm Hellmold, *Die V-1 – eine Dokumentation*, p.300, Bechtle, 1988
(174) Mark Wade, Tsien, Spaceplane 1949, in: Encyclopedia astronautica, www.austronautix.com (Internet)
(175) Scott Lowther, *Aerospace Projects Review*, 4. February 2001
(176) Reinhard Hauschild, Hellmut H. Führing, *Raketen – Die erregende Geschichte einer Erfindung*, p.177, Athenäum, 1958

(177) Renato Vesco, *Operazione Plenilunio*, p.171, Murcia, 1972
(178) Mark Wade, A-12 in: Encyclopedia astronautica, www.astronautix.com (Internet)
(179) Renato Vesco, ibid p.172
(180) 'Extra-Atmospheric war', in *Time*, No. 10, S. 30, September 1946
(181) Renato Vesco, ibid.p.171
(182) Ibid, p.172
(183) Ibid, p.171
(184) Ron Miller, *The Dream Machines – A Pictorial History of the Spaceship in Art, Science and Literature*, p.327, Krieger, 1993. Other designs and sketches for spacecraft of the immediate postwar period, as those by Kenneth Gotland and the British Interplanetary Society from 1946, bear amazing similarities to original Peenemünde designs!
(185) Mark Wade, Marslander, in: Encyclopedia astronautica, www.astronautix.com (Internet)
(186) Ron Miller, ibid, p.272
(187) James McGovern, *Operazione Crossbow e Overcast*, p.171, Murcia, 1970
(188) Renato Vesco, *Operazione Plenilunio*, p.70, Murcia, 1974
(189) Edgar Mayer, Thomas Mehner, *Das Geheimnis der deutschen Atombombe*, p.39, 42, 45, Kopp, 2001
(190) Biennial Report of the Chief of Staff of the United States Army, July, 1 1943 to June 30 1945 to the Secretary of War in: The New York Times, 10. October 1945, p.11
(191) Johannes von Buttlar, *Projekt Aurora – Geheime Technologien des 3. Jahrtausends*, p.116/117, VGS, 1999
(192) Wilhelm Helmold, *Die V-1 – Eine Dokumentation*, p.298–301, Bechtle, 1998